CENTRAL ASIA AND THE WORLD

CENTRAL ASIA AND THE WORLD

Kazakhstan, Uzbekistan, Tajikistan, Kyrgyzstan, and Turkmenistan

Edited by

Michael Mandelbaum

COUNCIL ON FOREIGN RELATIONS PRESS

NEW YORK

4/9/95

14.50

COUNCIL ON FOREIGN RELATIONS BOOKS

The Council on Foreign Relations, Inc., is a nonprofit and nonpartisan organization devoted to promoting improved understanding of international affairs through the free exchange of ideas. The Council does not take any position on questions of foreign policy and has no affiliation with, and receives no funding from, the United States government.

From time to time, books and monographs written by members of the Council's research staff or visiting fellows, or commissioned by the Council, or written by an independent author with critical review contributed by a Council study or working group are published with the designation "Council on Foreign Relations Book." Any book or monograph bearing that designation is, in the judgment of the Committee on Studies of the Council's Board of Directors, a responsible treatment of a significant international topic worthy of presentation to the public. All statements of fact and expressions of opinion contained in Council books are, however, the sole responsibility of the author.

If you would like more information on Council publications, please write the Council on Foreign Relations, 58 East 68th Street, New York, NY 10021, or call the Publications Office at (212) 734-0400.

Library of Congress Cataloging-in-Publication Data

Central Asia and the world : Kazakhstan, Kyrgyzstan, Tajikistan,
Turkmenistan, and Uzbekistan / edited by Michael Mandelbaum.
    p.   cm.
    Includes bibliographical references and index.
    ISBN 0-87609-167-2 : $16.95
    1. Asia, Central—Foreign relations—1991– 2. Asia, Central—Politics and government—1991– I. Mandelbaum, Michael.
DK859.5.C456 1994
958'4086—dc20
                                                94-7846
                                               CIP

94   95   96   97   EB   10   9   8   7   6   5   4   3   2   1

Cover Design: Kuan Chang

Contents

List of Maps

ACKNOWLEDGMENTS

This volume is part of the Council on Foreign Relations Project on East-West Relations, which is supported by the Carnegie Corporation. The views expressed in this book are those of the authors alone.

The chapters were first presented as papers at a symposium on "The International Relations of Central Asia," held in Washington, D.C., on June 17 and 18, 1993. The participants in the symposium are listed in the appendix.

The editor is grateful to all those involved in the production of the volume, particularly to Seth Singleton and Daniel Pipes for their suggestions on how to organize it. Special thanks are due to Audrey McInerney for organizing the symposium and supervising the publication of the book.

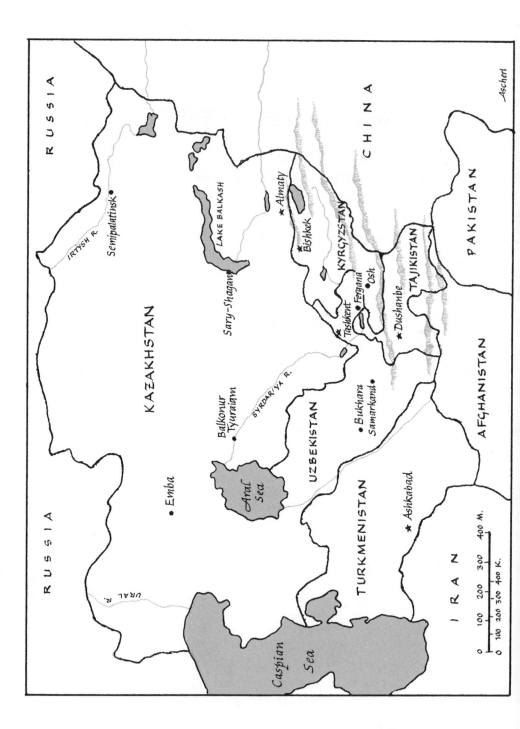

Introduction

Michael Mandelbaum

O NCE UPON A TIME, IN WHAT ALREADY SEEMS A DISTANT AGE AND was certainly a different world, there was a huge, diverse, powerful country known as the Soviet Union. Its rulers believed, or at least asserted, that theirs was the world's first socialist state. It turned out, in the end, to be the last great multinational empire on the planet. Its end came in 1991. In December of that year, like the empires of the British, the French, the Habsburgs, the Ottomans, and the Romanovs before it, the empire that the Bolsheviks had created in the second and third decades of this century collapsed in ruins.

Where once a mighty political monolith had stood there were suddenly fifteen countries. The fifteen constituent republics of the Soviet Union found themselves sovereign states. Russia, the largest, is a vast multinational state, a somewhat reduced and more heavily Slavic version of the old Soviet Union. It was joined by two other predominantly Slavic countries, Ukraine and Belarus. The three Baltic republics—Estonia, Latvia, and Lithuania—became independent, as did Moldova, the Soviet foothold in the Balkans. In the Caucasus, Armenia, Georgia, and Azerbaijan were transformed from imperial provinces to sovereign political communities. So, too, finally, were the five successor states of the Soviet Union that constitute the region to the south of the great Russian heartland known as Central Asia: Kazakhstan, Uzbekistan, Kyrgyzstan, Tajikistan, and Turkmenistan.

1

These last five had independence thrust upon them. In none had there been popular agitation for secession. None of their leaders sided, during the abortive coup of August 1991, with the forces of Boris Yeltsin, whose victory in the confrontation with the coup's perpetrators was the deathblow of the Soviet Union. Yet after December 1991, the former Soviet republics of Central Asia had no choice but to assume the trappings, and the burdens, of sovereignty.

Not the least of these burdens is direct relations with other sovereign states. The failure of the August coup propelled the Central Asian republics from membership in a single tightly controlled state to membership in the uncontrolled international community of almost two hundred states. One of the inescapable consequences of the dissolution of the Soviet Union is the appearance of a set of international relations where none existed before. The international relations of Central Asia are the subject of this book.

THE REGION

The region of Central Asia, as defined here, is bounded, roughly, by the Russian steppe to the north, the Tien Shan mountains to the east, the Caspian Sea to the west, and the western part of the crescent of Islamic countries that stretches from Casablanca to Pakistan to the south. It comprises most—but not all—of what was historically known as Turkestan, so named for the prevalence of Turkic languages and people.[1] An older term for this general area is Inner Asia, which refers to landlocked parts of the Asian continent, including western China, Tibet, and Mongolia.

The five states are "central" as well in the sense that they lie between two distinct civilizations: Slavic Christendom to the north and the world of Islam to the south.

Central Asia may be said to be a single region for more reasons than geography. In demographic and economic terms all five states are part of the Third World. All have high rates of fertility, each one's population is disproportionately young, and life expectancy throughout the region is markedly lower than in the more developed world. All five countries have low per capita incomes, low rates of labor productivity, and a high proportion of their populations engaged in agriculture.[2]

All have experienced Russian colonial rule. Indeed, Russia's history in Central Asia bears a strong resemblance to that of Great Britain in India. Both imperial powers began their conquests in the eighteenth century by establishing a series of fortified encampments on the edges of the territories they ultimately subdued. During the next century each extended its rule by military conquest over all of the region. Similar motives drove the conquests in both cases: the ambitions of soldiers and adventurers; the hope of economic gain; and, not least, the fear in both capitals that the failure to push onward would cede ground to the other power, which was advancing from the other direction. Central Asia's neighbor Afghanistan was the site of what Kipling called "the great game," the nineteenth-century skirmishing between the Russians and the British in the no-man's-land between their Asian imperial possessions. Both the British in India and the Russians in Central Asia established systems of indirect rule, leaving local authorities in place under what was often loose supervision by imperial authorities.

The communist period in Central Asia in some ways continued tsarist rule, but in others broke with it and with the pattern of British and other European methods of imperial governance. The Bolsheviks were more ambitious, intrusive, and brutal. They aspired to reshape the societies they conquered after 1917. They tried to erase what they found and create something different in its place.

The tsars, for example, were content to leave Islamic observance untouched in Central Asia. The communists tried to eliminate it. The British introduced English into India and made it the official medium of communication but did not tamper with the local languages. The communists not only established Russian in Central Asia, they forced a change in the written form of the local languages from the Arabic to the Cyrillic alphabet.[3]

All periods of imperial rule bring change to the subject peoples. But the Soviet period had a particularly marked effect. Indeed, it had two distinctive, and opposite, effects: interruption and creation.

Moscow tried, with considerable success, to interrupt relations with the region from which Central Asia drew its basic cultural characteristics: the Islamic south. Those characteristics are deeply embedded in the social life of each of the five states, another common element among them that helps to define Central Asia as a distinct region.

The peoples of the region are of Turkish and Mongol stock. Their cultural patterns are of Turkish, Persian, and Arabic origins. Their languages belong to the Turkic family, with the exception of Tajik, which is Indo-European and closely related to the Farsi spoken in Iran; but even Tajik has some similarities to Uzbek.

The Islamic religion of Central Asia also came from the south, and the traditions absorbed from the south form part of the foundation of politics in the region. Underneath the communist apparatus imposed by Moscow, the power that local officials wielded often resided with clans and families.

By contrast, the political and economic institutions that the five states of Central Asia carry with them into independence were implanted during the communist period. What communism created there was also a common and defining feature of the region. Indeed, the political identities with which the five states entered the international community were created in Moscow. Communist officials drew the boundaries between and among them in the 1920s and 1930s, thereby defining the states that are now sovereign. The borders' origins are thus illegitimate, and they are disputed throughout the region, but they have nonetheless acquired a measure of acceptance both because they encompassed functioning administrative units under communist rule and because, after the collapse of communism, the rest of the world recognized them.

The communist period also replicated in each country, on a smaller scale, the political system that governed the whole country: at its center was the all-powerful Communist Party, which supervised both the government and the economy, and whose tentacles reached into every corner of organized social life.

Central Asia's status in the larger Soviet economy corresponded in important ways to the familiar definition of economic exploitation. The region produced raw materials—agricultural products and mineral resources—that were shipped to the metropolis to feed its industries. But if the pattern of intra-Soviet trade was classically colonial, the method of economic organization was classically Soviet. Central Asia was part of a Union-wide planned economy in which quotas for inputs and targets for outputs were set in Moscow and enforced by local officials.

Many of those officials were Russians. The communists continued—in some cases, accelerated—the tsarist practice of sending ethnic Russians to Central Asia. They held many of the most responsible jobs in the local economies. They also served as instruments through which Moscow exercised effective political control. The custom was for the first secretary of the republican Communist Party to be an Asian, but the second secretary, who often managed the security apparatus, to be a Russian. By the time the Soviet Union collapsed, the number of Russians and other Europeans in Central Asia far exceeded the number of British that had ever been in India; many were from families that had been established in the region for generations. Like the British in India, however, the Central Asian Russians lived separately from the non-Europeans, mainly in cities. Few ever learned the local language.

Russian and particularly Soviet rule did, however, produce local elites, which is another feature common to the five states of the region. These were people who learned Russian, joined the Communist Party, went through Russian and communist educational and party institutions, and came to occupy posts of real authority, if not ultimate power. It is they who have inherited responsibility for guiding the destinies of the Central Asian states in the immediate aftermath of independence. At the end of 1993, in every country save Kyrgyzstan, a leader from the communist era held supreme power.

Throughout Central Asia communist rule created societies that have some of the trappings of modernity: cities, factories, engineers. But if they are modern, they are not Western. Of all the parts of the former Soviet Union, Central Asia is the one where the presence of Western institutions and values is thinnest. It is the one most distant from the West both geographically and culturally. The new states have no experience of democracy and almost none with market economics. All parts of the former Soviet Union—the Baltic, the Slavic states, the Caucasus, and Central Asia—have embarked, at least according to the rhetoric of those who now govern them, on the path to Western political and economic practices. Central Asia is the region for which that path will be longest and hardest.

THE COUNTRIES

While they share a number of features in addition to location, the five new countries of Central Asia differ in important ways as well, and their differences bear on their relations with one another and with the rest of the world.

Kazakhstan is the largest of the five. It is large not only by the region's standards, but by the world's, larger than all of Western Europe. The Kazakh people were traditionally nomads. Only at the end of the nineteenth century did they move into settled communities in large numbers.

Often Kazakhstan has not been counted as part of Central Asia proper.[4] Not only is it far larger in area than any of the others, its economic structure is different. It has more industry, especially metallurgy, and contains significant deposits of petroleum. What most dramatically sets Kazakhstan apart from the rest of Central Asia, however, is its defining political feature: its relationship to Russia.

Kazakhstan is the only Central Asian country that shares a border with Russia. That border is one of the longest in the world between two countries, stretching some three thousand miles. Even more significantly, Kazakhstan is appreciably more Russian than the other four countries. An estimated 40 percent of the country is Kazakh and 38 percent Russian. (For the ethnic composition of each state, see Table 1.)

Kazakhstan's Russians are concentrated in the northern part of the state. (Its capital, Almaty, is not so much north as east: about 1,900 miles from Moscow, but less than 200 from China. By population and architecture the city is Russian.) To Russians in Russia their cousins in Kazakhstan are not "settlers" sent to live in the midst of a native population to assert the metropolitan claim to rule there, like the French *pieds noirs* in Algeria. The Kazakh Russians are considered "frontier Russians," whose communities extend the reach of Russia itself, like the Russians of Siberia and the Far East. In Russian eyes northern Kazakhstan is part of Russia in all but name.

In this sense Kazakhstan has less in common with the other countries of Central Asia than with Ukraine. Both new states have

TABLE 1.—POPULATION AND GEOGRAPHIC DATA: CENTRAL ASIAN REPUBLICS

Country	Population (millions)	Urban/Rural (millions)	Ethnic Composition (%)	Size (thous. sq. km)	Comparable-size Country (thous. sq. km)
Azerbaijan	7.1	3.9/3.3	Azeri 83/Russian 8	87	Austria (84)
Kazakhstan	16.7	9.5/7.2	Kazakh 40/Russian 38	2,717	Zaire (2,345)
Kyrgyzstan	4.4	1.7/2.7	Kyrgyz 52/Russian 22	199	Uruguay (176)
Tajikistan	5.3	1.7/3.6	Tajik 58/Russian 10	143	Nicaragua (128)
Turkmenistan	3.7	1.7/2.0	Turkmen 72/Russian 13	488	Spain (493)
Uzbekistan	20.5	8.4/12.1	Uzbek 71/Russian 11	447	Egypt (387)

Sources: World Bank, *Statistical Handbook: States of the Former USSR, 1992* (Washington, D.C.: World Bank, 1992); and Brian Hunter, ed., *The Statesman's Yearbook, 1991–1992,* 128th ed. (New York: St. Martin's Press, 1991).

a tenuous sense of identity, for neither ever before existed independently within its present borders. Each was tightly integrated into imperial and communist Russia. Each shares a long border with Russia and has a large Russian minority. Thus, both have a delicate political task: to craft an identity as a sovereign state that is distinct from Russia, while remaining on good terms with the Russian government, which could easily be moved to claim as its own Ukrainian and Kazakh territory on which ethnic Russians are concentrated. Each must become a successfully multinational state—an objective that has proven difficult for older, better-established political communities to achieve—or risk losing large chunks of its territory and population.

Compounding the delicacy of their relations with Russia is the fact that Kazakhstan and Ukraine both play host to nuclear weapons, which each pledged in 1992 to surrender to the Russian government but thereafter balked at giving up.

These relations are all the more difficult because both the Kazakh and the Ukrainian encounters with Russia and Russians have had bloody and terrible episodes. For the Ukrainians the Soviet period was by far the worst, the low point being the great famine of the 1930s, induced, perhaps deliberately, by Stalin's policy of agricultural collectivization.

The Kazakh disasters go back to the last decade of the nineteenth century, when the arrival of a flood of Russian peasants drove many off the land. Provoked by both anger at the Russian settlers and the stringencies of wartime rule, the Kazakhs staged an uprising in 1916, which the tsarist government brutally suppressed. The civil war that followed the Bolshevik seizure of power was fought partly in the Kazakh lands, bringing more death and destruction, and although the Kazakh elite sided with the Red Army, in the late 1920s most of that elite was purged. Kazakhstan suffered again during the period of collectivization.

While Kazakhstan is the largest Central Asian country by territory, Uzbekistan is the largest by population, numbering twenty million, as against Kazakhstan's seventeen million. Uzbekistan lies at the heart of Central Asia; it has common borders with each of the other four states.

The Uzbeks consider themselves the heirs of the great civilizations of the region. While the Kazakhs were nomads until a century ago, the Uzbeks became farmers, landowners, and city dwellers far earlier. Uzbekistan's territory encompasses the heart of old Turkestan, the land between the Syrdaria and Amu Darya rivers that includes the ancient city of Samarkand, a crossroads between East and West since the time of Alexander the Great and an important stop on the Silk Route, the main artery of trade between China and Europe. The country's capital is another historic city, Tashkent, an ancient commercial center on the caravan routes to Europe and Asia. Present-day Uzbekistan also includes much of the territory ruled by the strongest and most sophisticated regimes the Russians encountered in the nineteenth century: the khanates of Khiva, Bukhara, and Kokand.

Uzbekistan is the heart of what has come to be known as Central Asia's "cotton monoculture." Much of the labor force is devoted to growing and harvesting cotton. This dependence on a single crop has distorted the Uzbek economy. The environmental effects have been worse. Pesticides have poisoned the land and the people, who suffer from high rates of chemical-induced diseases and of infant mortality. The huge irrigation projects the communists constructed have likewise taken a toll. The Aral Sea, the world's fourth-largest inland lake, has lost 40 percent of its water to Soviet cotton.

Tajikistan is the smallest in area of the new states, and the one most distant from Moscow. It has the lowest standard of living. The Tajik language belongs not to the Turkic but to the Persian family. Perhaps Tajikistan's most conspicuous distinction is that it is the least stable country in Central Asia. A civil war erupted there soon after independence.[5] It is a sovereign state in name only.

Kyrgyzstan was promoted from oblast to union republic only in 1936. Like the Kazakhs, the Kyrgyz were nomads for most of their history. While they were nominally Muslim, their religious observance was spotty and their identification with the rest of the Islamic world—in contrast, for example, to the Uzbeks—was weak. Politically and culturally they traditionally looked eastward, to China.

Since independence, Kyrgyzstan has looked westward. It peacefully evicted its communist leadership from power and installed a prodemocratic physicist, Askar Akaev, as its president. It has followed the economic prescriptions of the International Monetary Fund (IMF) more faithfully than any of the others. In 1993 Kyrgyzstan became the first of the fifteen former Soviet republics to meet the requirements for an IMF loan.

Still, the country is not necessarily on its way to becoming an oasis of democracy and capitalism in the heart of landlocked Asia. Its location is a liability: Kyrgyzstan is wedged between a powerful and suspicious China; a Tajikistan in chaos; Kazakhstan, whose capital is less than 50 miles from their common border; and Uzbekistan, which has claims on its territory.

The fifth Central Asian state, Turkmenistan, has experienced the least change since independence. The communist leader, Supramurad Niyazov, remains in power. He permits no opposition. In the short term the country's economic prospects are bright. It has deposits of natural gas that could, if fully exploited, sustain a per capita income impressively high by the standards of the region. Turkmenistan has the potential, by some estimates, to be a Central Asian version of Kuwait. Its gas reserves aside, however, little distinguishes the country. Its territory is almost entirely desert. Before independence Turkmenistan was the Soviet Union's largest producer of silkworm cocoons.[6]

SCOPE OF THE BOOK

In what context are the international relations of these five states to be understood? The next four chapters present different perspectives.

The first, by Martha Brill Olcott, addresses relations between and among the Central Asian countries. Their common location and their similarities of culture, economics, and history draw them together. And another feature of independence turns them toward one another. Their common borders are frequently in dispute. Drawn by the Communists for the familiar imperial purpose of "divide and rule," they separate ethnic and national groups. Thus these boundaries, like others around the world drawn by colonial rulers, lack legitimacy. All of Uzbekistan's borders with its neighbors, for example, are in question in one way or another.

International relations within Central Asia are significant because what happens in one state affects the others, as Olcott's account of the ripple effects of the Tajik civil war and of the Kyrgyz effort to create its own currency demonstrates.

Moreover, as her essay shows, the idea of regional unity resonates among the leaders of Central Asia, although just what they mean by unity remains vague. In this way, the region may come to resemble the Arab world after World War II: there, the idea of Arab unity, although it was never achieved, had a powerful effect among states that, like those of Central Asia today, shared weak political institutions and an Islamic faith. It became a license for each Arab state to interest itself in the internal affairs of the others, and a pretext for leaders like Gamal Abdel Nasser of Egypt and Saddam Hussein to seek to expand their influence beyond the borders of their own countries. Similarly, as Olcott notes, either Kazakhstan or Uzbekistan or both may try to shape the region's affairs to its own specifications.

The thesis of Daniel Pipes's chapter is that Central Asia will, over time, return to the Middle East, where its cultural roots lie. The new states' most important international ties will be with countries to the south. Already Middle Eastern governments—those of Turkey, Iran, and Saudi Arabia—and different factions in Afghanistan are seeking to participate in the embryonic postindependence politics and economics of the region. A southward thrust in the international relations of Central Asia would resemble the way the countries of Central Europe—Poland, Hungary, and the Czech republic—once freed from Soviet domination, have gravitated toward what they consider their natural home in the West.

For the short term, at least, however, the five new states will be deeply engaged with their powerful northern neighbor. Central Asian relations with Russia is the subject of Graham Fuller's chapter. During the Soviet period the five were wards of Moscow. Powerful vertical ties bound them to metropolis, and were reinforced by the presence of so many Russians in Central Asia. By contrast, political and economic links with one another were sparse. The hypercentralization of the Soviet period will surely erode. It is already doing so. But the ties with the north will fade slowly. The elites of the region communicate with one another in Russian. The national armies have Russian officers. All but one of the new states initially chose to remain in the "ruble zone," which means that a major part of the economic life of each is controlled in Moscow. Here the states of the region resemble the countries of French West Africa that, decades after formal independence, continued to rely on Paris for political guidance, civil administration, and military protection.

Over time, it is possible that Central Asia will come to be tied to Russia in a different way. The predominant pattern of economic development and cultural transmission is from "cores"—centers of dynamism and learning—to peripheries—nearby lands and peoples that receive and absorb what is produced in the core regions by the benign processes of trade and travel, as well as through conquest. In the nineteenth and twentieth centuries, for example, the United States has played the role of core to Latin America's periphery. Germany has had a similar relationship with Central Europe, and Japan with Southeast Asia.

A Russia transformed by a successful transition to democracy and free markets, a Russia with a booming economy and a vibrant, open political system, could serve as a similar model and magnet for Central Asia. In such circumstances, Central Asian integration with, and political imitation of, Russia would be voluntary—not, as in the tsarist and communist periods, the result of coercion. Russia might, eventually, turn out to be the avenue along which Western politics and economics come to Central Asia.

As sovereign states, finally, the countries of Central Asia are part of the international community as a whole. They are thus connected, however tenuously, to the West. Those connections are the subject of Robert Cullen's chapter. The Central Asians are eager to multiply and deepen them. The West is, after all, the center of power and wealth in the world, and in the post–Cold War era membership in Western-designed and Western-dominated international organizations has come to be seen as the embodiment of sovereignty itself. All five Central Asian states, for example, joined the Conference on Security and Cooperation in Europe, to which the United States as well as all the countries of Europe belong, although all members commit themselves to standards of political conduct that are unlikely to be observed in Central Asia.

Thus far, Central Asia's interest in the West has been only modestly reciprocated. Under most circumstances, as Cullen observes, the region is likely to be of limited interest to Western Europe, North America, and Japan. The stakes the West has in what happens in Central Asia derive mainly from the region's effects on Russia and the Middle East, where, to be sure, Western interests are considerable. There is a parallel here to American policy toward the countries of Eastern Europe during the Cold War, which was defined not by the intrinsic importance of those countries, but by a powerful concern with their neighbors to the east and west, the Soviet Union and Western Europe.

Indeed, in this sense Central Asia today has something in common with much of the rest of the world, for American interests almost everywhere during the Cold War had their origins in the great rivalry with the Soviet Union. Because that rivalry was global in scope, virtually any conflict anywhere could be seen as part of it— and Washington did see many regional conflicts in that light. Now that the Cold War is over, this all-purpose source of political significance to the United States of far-flung corners of the world has disappeared without being replaced.

Each geographic context of the first four essays—the region itself, the Islamic south, the Russian north, and the international community as a whole—is relevant to the foreign policy of each Central Asian state. The international relations of the region is made up of the sum of all of them.

The international relations of Central Asia will also be shaped by the subjects of the last four chapters of the book. Economic developments within each country and in the region as a whole, which Shafiqul Islam discusses, will influence them. So will the disposition of military forces there, as Susan Clark's chapter demonstrates. The most important regional event thus far is the Tajik civil war, on which Barnett Rubin has contributed a chapter. Finally, the independent states of Central Asia will look not only inward, north, south, and west, but also east. Relations with the region's large and dynamic eastern neighbor, China, is the subject of the final chapter, by Ross Munro.

CONCLUSION

While the five landlocked Asian Islamic successor states of the Soviet Union may be said to be central in several ways, the region is peripheral in the political and economic calculations of the West.

Yet in certain circumstances Central Asia, or one or another of the states that constitute it, could capture the world's attention.

Such circumstances could involve nuclear weapons. Kazakhstan has 104 long-range missiles that could strike the West. Central Asia could become the site of trafficking in nuclear material to countries to the south. Iran is reportedly seeking its own bomb, and might be interested in the relevant technology and expertise that the region harbors.

Central Asia could also become a breeding ground for the kind of militant Islam, commonly known as fundamentalism, that has appeared in the Arab Middle East, in North Africa, and in Pakistan. Such a development is not likely. The region has a secular tradition, and in any case most Central Asian Muslims are of the Sunni branch of the faith, rather than the Shi'a variant, which predominates in the center of fundamentalism, Iran. Still, conditions of political collapse, economic disaster, and cultural disorientation—none a certainty, but all of them possible—could give rise to movements violently hostile to the West and ready to make common cause with those similarly disposed in other parts of the Islamic world.

Large-scale disasters, natural and man-made, attract international attention, most vividly through the medium of television. Such disasters have already occurred in Central Asia. Estimates of deaths caused by the Tajik conflict range up to 50,000, and the conflict has displaced as many as 500,000. The cotton monoculture has poisoned the land and the people of Uzbekistan. The Soviet nuclear test site at Semipalatinsk in Kazakhstan is dangerously toxic, as are the uranium mining and refining sites in Tajikistan. The rest of the world has thus far taken little notice of any of this; but that could conceivably change if any or all of these situations should worsen.

The border disputes within the region have also attracted little notice beyond Central Asia. But similar disputes with older, larger, better-established countries would have a far wider international impact. Nine million Azeris live in northern Iran, constituting fully a quarter of the Iranian population. On either side of the border between Azerbaijan and Iran, expression of the desire to unite all Azeris in a single state would alarm Tehran.

Similarly, all three Central Asian states that border on China—Kazakhstan, Kyrgyzstan, and Tajikistan—are home to people with ethnic kin on the Chinese side of the border. Some 60 percent of the fifteen million residents of the western Chinese province of Xinjiang are Turkic Muslims, including six million Uighurs and one million Kazakhs. Here is the potential for irredentist sentiment that Beijing would find unacceptable, if not threatening.

The likeliest way for Central Asia to affect the wider world is through its impact on its powerful northern neighbor. Russia might be drawn into the region to try to pacify it. Great powers intervening beyond their borders to enforce order are a familiar feature of international politics. Boris Yeltsin's government did dispatch a small contingent of troops to Tajikistan with the mission of pacification. Russia might also intervene to its south to protect Russians living there who felt subject to discrimination or threat. Indeed, discrimination against and threats to Russians have already appeared. Finally, a Russian government more rabidly nationalist than Boris Yeltsin's might see political profit and even justice, in annexing the largely Russian and mineral-rich northern part of Kazakhstan.

Russian intervention in Central Asia, depending on the scale and circumstances, could in turn re-create in the eyes of the world a Russia committed to expansion by military means, the Russia that the West was at pains to contain for much of the nineteenth and twentieth centuries. (The West seems likely to take more seriously what Russia does to its west than how it treats its new neighbors to the south. Intervention in Estonia to protect Russians would likely arouse a far stronger response than intervention in Uzbekistan for the same purpose.) A new and aggressive Russian foreign policy would feed back into the domestic politics of the Russian Federation. It would strengthen the authoritarian currents in Russian politics and weaken the democratic ones.

None of these circumstances in which Central Asia would intrude on the world's consciousness is desirable. All arise from the weakness and instability of the states of the region. They will be weak and unstable for a long time to come, as they struggle to build effective political structures and viable economies. That common struggle is likely to be successful to the extent that the populations and governments of the region channel their energies and resources inward—to the extent, that is, that what is most important in independent Central Asia is domestic development, not international relations.

NOTES

1. What is now the western part of China was also part of Turkestan.
2. For the argument that the states of Central Asia differ in important ways from Third World countries, see Shafiqul Islam's chapter in this volume.
3. They also imposed, or encouraged, Russian forms for local names. Thus the Azeri leader who sat in the Politburo in the Brezhnev era was known to the world as Gaidar Aliev, rather than by the Islamic form, Haidar Ali.
4. It was common, during the Soviet period, to refer to "Kazakhstan and Middle Asia." Kazakhstan is excluded from the definition of Central Asia in two books on the region published just before the collapse of the Soviet Union—Boris Rumer, *Central Asia: A Soviet Tragedy* (Winchester, Mass.: Unwin Hyman, 1989); and William Fierman, ed., *Soviet Central Asia,* (Boulder, Colo.: Westview Press, 1991).
5. For a discussion of the Tajik civil war, see Barnett Rubin's chapter in this volume.
6. Daniel Pipes's chapter deals with a sixth Soviet successor state: Azerbaijan. In geographic terms Azerbaijan is not part of Central Asia. It is located in the Caucasus, on the other side of the Caspian Sea. Culturally and politically, however, it has important affinities with the region. Like the five Central Asian countries, it is predominantly Muslim. Moreover, it is ethnically Turkish and, unlike the other five, has a common border with Turkey, and so may serve as an entry point for Turkish influence on the Islamic successor states to the Soviet Union.

Chapter 1

Ceremony and Substance: The Illusion of Unity in Central Asia

Martha Brill Olcott

A MONG THE HALLMARKS OF SOVIET PUBLIC LIFE WERE FREQUENT elaborate ceremonies meant to celebrate aspects of Soviet achievements that did not, in fact, exist—friendship among peoples, solidarity of workers, love of the people for the Communist Party. Indeed, the collapse of the USSR has demonstrated that a reliable guide to the trouble spots underlying the monolithic Soviet facade would have been precisely those ceremonies, since much of the intent of such gatherings was to attempt to make a desired condition *be* true by stating, stridently and repeatedly, that it *was* true.

The Soviet Union may have passed, but many of the habits of social conduct have continued; not surprisingly, for example, replacing the names of communist leaders on street signs has proven easier than replacing the effects those leaders had on society. As in the past, appeals to history are seen as a path to political legitimacy, save now the appeals are to different histories. Old ceremonies have been abandoned, and new ones have replaced them; but as before, they are designed not so much to mask as to transform one set of realities into another, more desirable possibility.

A case in point was the solemn assembly on Ordobasy hill, a sunbaked prominence outside of Chimkent, Kazakhstan, on May 28, 1993. The ceremony was convened by President Nursultan Nazarbaev and attended by about fifty thousand local Kazakhs, as well as by delegations from each of Kazakhstan's nineteen oblasts and the two administratively independent cities of Leninsk and Almaty. It was also honored by the presence of presidents Islam Karimov of Uzbekistan and Askar Akaev of Kyrgyzstan. After each president delivered a speech in his native language, and a Kazakh folk poet chanted the history of Ordobasy, there was a national folk fair, with exhibitions of folk dances, songs, crafts, and traditional sports. Mass horse racing concluded the evening.

The event this ceremony was to mark, commemorated by an as-yet-unconstructed monument, was the meeting in 1726 on that site of three local Kazakh elders, or *biis*—Tole Bi, Kazybek Bi, and Aiteke Bi—who were worried about the threat of invading Dzhungars and wished to reunite the three Kazakh hordes to mount a more effective defense. Certainly Kazakhstan's current climate of clan resurgence and regional struggles over resources gave reason enough for the search for symbols of unity. But Nazarbaev in his description of that meeting underlined the reason for which Akaev and Karimov had been invited by saying that the original three *biis* had been successful in getting Kyrgyz and Uzbek tribes to fight alongside them, uniting the Central Asian peoples to face a common enemy. The parallelism was further stressed in the drawings of the three *biis* published in the newspapers and on memorial souvenirs: they portray the three *biis* with nearly identical faces, each sporting the headgear of his horde, which was not unlike the current folkloric headgear of Kazakhs, Kyrgyz, and Uzbeks.[1]

Significantly, this was the meeting chosen to mark what has become Kazakhstan's official "unity day." Perhaps the choice was made to commemorate the first Ordobasy meeting because of Chimkent's proximity to Uzbekistan, thus making the celebration an affirmation of the Chimkent region's role in Kazakh history and the Kazakh role in Central Asian history more generally. Certainly, in terms of the Kazakhs' own history, other unifying events might have been a better choice to mark—such as Qasim Khan's successful unification of the three hordes in the sixteenth century—because in the end the meeting of the three *biis* at Ordobasy had very little effect. Indeed, in the late 1720s the Kazakh people were forced from their lands by Kalmyk invaders, beginning the Great Retreat, the greatest defeat the Kazakh people suffered until the twentieth century, when Russian and Soviet policies managed to kill 3.3 million Kazakhs, and drive another 1.2 million into exile.[2]

Clearly the point of this ceremony was not to honor the past, but to attempt to control the future, which in Kazakhstan and Central Asia, just as in the rest of the Commonwealth of Independent States, is increasingly turbid and difficult to read. In the murky world of Central Asian interstate relations, the very fact that Nazarbaev felt it necessary to create a celebration of Central Asian unity is an indication that such unity is probably further away now than it has been in many years. One president, Turkmenistan's Supramurad Niyazov, stayed home, while the three who met seemed to find little pleasure in each other's company, perhaps because just days before the meeting they had been involved in bitter arguing among themselves.

Myth and reality have always been intertwined in discussions of Central Asian unity. For most of the thousand years before the Russian conquest, unity was but a dream of Central Asia's leaders, achieved briefly in the thirteenth century by Chingis Khan's heirs, and again in the fourteenth century by Timur (whose name has sometimes been Westernized to Tamerlane), but denied to the Kazakh and Uzbek princes who succeeded him. Talk of a unified Central Asia—a single Turkestan or Turan—reflects either the dreams of Turkestani exiles in America and pan-Turkic nationalists in Istanbul, or the fears of Russian observers in Moscow eager to incite a Western defense against this new Islamic "threat." Neither the myth of Central Asian unity nor the fear of it is new. Unity was the ideal pan-Turks fought for at the time of the revolution, and the threat that led Joseph Stalin to carve the region up into five republics, none of which is ethnically homogeneous.

Though unity may never be attainable, it is a goal to which all of the region's leaders and peoples subscribe. Many, like former Mufti Muhammadsadyk Muhammad Yusuf, consider the Central Asians to be a single people, while others, such as the world-renowned Kyrgyz writer Chingis Aitmatov, talk of the Central Asians as a single family. However, people have multiple identities, and while most in the region consider themselves Central Asians, they also think of themselves as Kazakhs, Kyrgyz, Tajiks, Turkmen, or Uzbeks; as Muslims; and, until recently, often as Soviets as well.

While the Ordobasy ceremony may initially appear as a celebration of unity, a closer analysis of events in the region argues how little unity there is to celebrate. Central Asia is increasingly splitting, along fault lines that have lain deep within the region since the time of Alexander the Great. Central Asia has always been an arena of competition between different cultures and economic systems; what Ordobasy seems to suggest is that in this era of independence, these struggles are returning to the surface.

THE ARENA

The question of whether Central Asia is a distinct geopolitical unit is certainly open for debate. The territory of the five present-day Central Asian republics—Kazakhstan, Kyrgyzstan, Tajikistan, Uzbekistan, and Turkmenistan—occupies a poorly watered area about the size of the continental United States; it is bound on the east and most of the south by some of the world's tallest mountains. On the west the area is defined by the Caspian Sea, effectively enclosing Central Asia on three sides.

It has been Central Asia's misfortune that the region has no natural boundary to the north, where the steppes of northern Kazakhstan are indistinguishable from the steppes of southern Russia along what is today a border of more than three thousand miles. However, for much of the history of Central Asia, Russia was of little consequence, leaving the northern boundary as an endless hypothetical, against which a variety of Turanian, Mongol, Turkic, and Chinese conquerors pushed in various millennia, and with various levels of success. This huge bowl of open land, most of it far too dry to farm, cut by no rivers making their way to the open sea (unless one wishes to count the tributaries of the Irtysh, which flow eventually into the Arctic), has been inhabited since time immemorial, and has a recorded or traceable history distinct from that of Russia, China, Persia, or Afghanistan.

The identities and the languages of the peoples of Central Asia have changed over the millennia, as each fresh group of conquerors, usually from the East, has swept into this boundless, difficult-to-defend space. While unity has generally evaded the Central Asians, the maintenance of control of this territory, and its preservation intact, has been a constant goal of those living in the region. Although many individuals were undoubtedly killed in these waves of invaders, the predecessors were rarely forced out; rather, they were absorbed into the newcomers, in turn absorbing the newcomers as well, maintaining some aspects of their previous identity in their language, or in words they injected into their new language, in tribal identities and customs, blood ties and kinship patterns.

While archaeologists may disagree over the ethnic origin of Central Asia's ancient peoples, during the last two thousand years the region has been inhabited by Iranian peoples and Turko-Mongols. The Iranians were there first, living in agricultural oasis settlements, surrounded by growing numbers of nomadic and seminomadic Turkic and Turko-Mongol tribesmen, their numbers increased by Seljuk (Turkic), Karakhanid (Turkic), and Chingisid (Mongol) tribesmen who conquered and then stayed in the region.

The first cities in Central Asia were Persian; but by the twelfth century, Turkic culture was firmly established in the region as well. By the twelfth century, the Turkic city of Khwarazm (Khorezm) had replaced the Samanid (Persian) city of Bukhara as the center of Central Asian culture.[3] From that point on, the region's cities—Timur's fourteenth century Samarkand, the Astrakhanid's Bukhara, rebuilt in the fifteenth and sixteenth centuries—had a decidedly Turkic cast, and the countryside was dominated by Turkic and Mongol-Turkic tribesmen.[4]

The result over the ages was a complex pattern of interrelated peoples who maintained within their histories—most frequently oral—claims on territory being held by some other tribe, just as they retained glorifications of their own victories, in which they had seized land from others.

What remained constant throughout most of Central Asia's history was the manner of economy, for Central Asia always divided naturally into pastoral nomads and sedentary agriculturalists. This division was reinforced geographically by the difference between the relatively fertile conditions of the land between the Syr Darye and Amu Darya rivers (Transoxania), and the open steppe and desert land to the north; from the conquests of Alexander the Great until the conquests of the Russian Empire, these two areas of Central Asia had different histories and different evolutions. Among the differences were those created over the centuries by the requirements of the two types of economy in the natures of the societies they produced. Nomadic society placed great emphasis upon loose control over a vast expanse of territory, but cared little for the defense of any one piece of land, because the nomad was always able to move his band onward. Operating over huge territories in small, closely related units, the nomads developed loose governmental structures, requiring considerable consensus among individual authorities and permitting considerable autonomy. After all, within nomadic society, if conflict arose, there was always the option of simply moving on. The opposite was true within sedentary agricultural societies; dependent upon one specific piece of ground, which could grow only at the expense of someone else's land, the settled peoples required strong central control, to assure the stability of the entire group. The sedentary culture rewards submission of the individual to the needs of the group, and the group has a vested interested in tight monitoring and control of each individual within the community.

What Central Asian history has demonstrated repeatedly is that the manner of economy is a more powerful determinant of society than is ethnic composition. A case in point is the rivalry between Tajiks and Uzbeks. Seeing themselves as descendants of eleventh-century Samanids, today's Tajiks claim for themselves the distinction of being the "senior" people in Central Asia, with an ancient urban, sedentary culture that makes them "superior" to the Uzbeks, whom they regard as mere nomads—as indeed they were. However, the Uzbeks have been sedentarized since the sixteenth century, and have completely assimilated this sedentarization into their own culture. In fact, Uzbek self-identification has become so assertive that the roles have reversed, and many Uzbeks now argue that the Tajiks were Uzbeks "spoiled" by their Persian language.[5]

SOME HISTORY

The Tajiks aside and founding myths notwithstanding, the majority of Central Asia's titular nationalities were formed at approximately the same time. Crucial to present politics is the fact that the foundry for both the Uzbek and the Kazakh peoples was the Shaibani dynasty, established in the fifteenth century by Khan Abdul Khayr; although the dynasty gathered together a disparate group of tribes, Abdul Khayr was the inheritor of the Uzbek line, which under Timur and his grandson, Ulugh Bek, had made the Uzbeks the dominant people of the region. Abdul Khayr was able to recoup former losses and extend Uzbek control throughout most of present-day Uzbekistan, parts of Kyrgyzstan, and southern Kazakhstan. However, in the mid-fifteenth century, Janibek and Kirai, two sons of Abdul Khayr's predecessor, and rivals to the power they considered Abdul Khayr to have usurped, laid claim to territories on the northern edge of Abdul Khayr's lands, and began to gather followers from among other restless subjects. The Janibek-Kirai configuration gradually gained ascendancy, and the two are considered the first khans of the Kazakh people. The struggle between Uzbeks and Kazakhs continued for most of the rest of the century, until Kazakh success led to conquest of present-day Turkestan, and the conclusion of a peace that left the Kazakhs in control of the lands up to and including Tashkent (now Uzbekistan's capital). At that point the Uzbeks turned their attention south, conquering much of Transoxania, which is today most of Uzbekistan, as well as parts of Tajikistan and Kyrgyzstan. There they developed a mixed Turkic-Persian agrarian and urban culture, which was centered in a number of competing city-states; the westernmost of these, Khiva, bordered on and partially encompassed the nomadic Turkmen tribes.

Meanwhile, the Kazakhs spread north and west, coming by the end of the sixteenth century to control most of the territory of present-day Kazakhstan, where they continued to be pastoral nomads. Although they claim connection with another Turkic tribe of the same name who migrated from the Yenisei River area in the tenth century, today's Kyrgyz probably also are descended from a number of indigenous (as well as nonindigenous) Turkic clans and tribes who coalesced in the fifteen and sixteenth centuries and, while they did not swear fealty to the Kazakhs, were distinguished from them only by details of language, dress, and manner of nomadism.[6]

The split between Uzbeks and Kazakhs continued even after the collapse of their founding dynasties. Kazakh unity lasted until the end of the seventeenth century, when the Dzhungars (Mongols) moved westward from the Tarim basin in China and pushed the Kazakhs out of pasture lands that had been under Kazakh control for more than two hundred years, sending them on their Great Retreat. The Shaibani dynasty split into two competing successor dynasties in the sixteenth century; the khan of Khiva and the emir of Bukhara divided Transoxania between themselves, and the latter lost control of the Fergana Valley to a vassal khan in Kokand in the eighteenth century. After the Russians absorbed the northern half of the Kazakh territory (in the eighteenth and nineteenth centuries), the khans of Khiva and Kokand split southern Kazakhstan (and western Kyrgyzstan) between themselves, after encountering substantial local resistance.[7]

THE AGENDA

The age-old struggle for dominance in Central Asia was reshaped by the Russian conquests, and even more so by the imposition of Soviet rule, since Russia became the master of the area, transforming the region into a kind of contiguous Third World that supplied Russia with cheap raw materials and absorbed the generally low-quality goods Russia made from them. The waves of Russian conquest, and the conversion of the area to service of the Russian economy, transformed Central Asia into a periphery that lacked a single identity.

In the 1860s the Russians divided Central Asia into two administrative regions: the Steppe Region, which was acquired with relatively little bloodshed; and Turkestan, which was acquired through conquest. The cities of Bukhara and Khiva were made Russian protectorates and remained formally independent of Russia until the early 1920s.[8]

Russian colonial rule, the restrictions imposed by the colonizers, and contact with the empire's other colonialized peoples reshaped the political consciousness of Central Asians. As a result, on the eve of the revolution, the Kazakhs (termed Kirghiz by the Russians) were developing a secular elite, while the other Central Asian (Turkestanis, as they were known to the Russians) elites were divided between Islamic reformers and Islamic traditionalists.[9]

The February Revolution of 1917 plunged Central Asia into a state of confusion, which the October (Bolshevik) Revolution of 1917 exacerbated. While Central Asians could not agree on what they were for, they knew what they were against. Though the Kazakhs surrendered to the Red Army in 1920, it took the Bolsheviks until 1924—years after the civil war had ended everywhere else—to stabilize the political situation in Turkestan.[10]

The Central Asians' intense resistance to Bolshevik rule was certainly a major factor in Lenin and Stalin's decision to divide the region into even smaller territorial divisions than had the Russians, particularly since they questioned the loyalty even of Central Asia's communists. Although Lenin died before the pentapartite division of Central Asia became official, he undoubtedly approved of Stalin's decision, at least in principle.

Thus in 1924 the Turkestan and Kazakh republics (both territories within Russia) were reorganized, and the latter—still an autonomous republic of Russia, but now renamed Kazakh from its former Kirghiz—received two historically Kazakh districts from Turkestan. Turkmenistan and Uzbekistan were made full-fledged (Union) republics, the latter including the autonomous republic of Tajikistan (which received full republic status in 1929) and the Kyrgyz autonomous oblast (which became an autonomous republic of Russia in 1926). Both the Kyrgyz and the Kazakh republics became Union republics in 1936.[11]

None of these republics were mononational. Kazakhstan had a large Russian population, Kyrgyzstan had a somewhat smaller Russian population and a large Uzbek one. Though many Tajik intellectuals moved to Tajikistan, a large Tajik population remained in Uzbekistan; likewise, Tajikistan had a large Uzbek population. Although tribal, kin, and community-based identities were more important than were national identities when these states were formed, over the decades of Soviet rule the national identifications written on people's passports began increasingly to matter. All the Central Asians were Muslims, but this only united them against outsiders, as it did against the Bolsheviks at the time of the Revolution. However, for most Central Asians the region's common Islamic identity remained over time less important than their separate ethnic ones, although the shared religious identity undoubtedly helped produce a sense of shared historic fate among the region's various indigenous peoples.

By the 1980s, Russo-Soviet control of Central Asia was decaying, and the historical cycles of the region began to make themselves felt again, with Central Asia once again becoming an arena in which various peoples felt able to compete for dominance. Obviously, the current struggle is far tamer than were historic ones, and is still shaped in part by Russia's continuing, albeit diminishing, presence.

THE MODERN STRUGGLE FOR DOMINANCE

Part of the Soviet method of controlling the territory was to split it into five republics, each named for a people who had some claim to the land. Boundaries, however, were so drawn as to divide populations among two or more republics, while administrative and economic lines were created in a way that stimulated competition among the five republics for Moscow's attention and resources. Russian and Soviet rulers also moved more than fifteen million non-Asians into the territory, so that by the last Soviet census, in 1989, the non-Asian population of the various countries ranged from less than 10 percent, in Uzbekistan, to more than 50 percent, in Kazakhstan.[12]

Actively discouraged by Moscow from considering their republics to form a distinct regional subunit of the USSR, the Central Asian leaders did not convene as a group to discuss common interests until June 23, 1990, when Nursultan Nazarbaev, then first secretary of the Kazakh Communist Party, hosted fellow first secretaries Supramurad Niyazov (Turkmenistan), Kakhar Makhkamov (Tajikistan), Islam Karimov (Uzbekistan), and Absamat Masaliev (Kyrgyzstan) at a meeting in Kazakhstan's capital, Almaty.[13] That meeting was very much in line with Nazarbaev's growing influence within the Gorbachev administration. Although a Kazakh, Nazarbaev could not at that time be considered a nationalist; he was, however, a very strong regionalist, whose career in the Kazakh Council of Ministers had given him an excellent view of how much Moscow was taking from Kazakhstan, and how little the republic was getting in return.

The meeting unquestionably was sanctioned in Moscow, for the agenda was in the same mold as the economic and cultural maneuvering Gorbachev was engaged in as he tried both to cope with rising nationalism elsewhere in the USSR and to preserve the prerogatives of the center to control and direct use of resources. Another element was the growing recognition that Moscow, nearing bankruptcy, had ever fewer resources that it could direct back to Central Asia, which was facing a lengthening list of immediate and potential social problems.

Most of the declarations resulting from that meeting were about greater cultural contact and cooperation among the five nations; regional economic cooperation received not much more than lip service. It was, in fact, stated that the purpose of the meeting was not to foster separatism, but to improve regional performance within the wider whole. The Gorbachev buzzword of the period was *khozraschet,* or better financial management; by this, Moscow meant that Central Asia should ask less money from Moscow, and be less prodigal with what it got. However, after the Almaty meeting, the Central Asians began to understand that *khozraschet* could also mean that the region should begin to assert greater sovereignty over the resources on its territory, and to demand greater return from Moscow.

Much the same agenda was repeated a year later, when the five heads of state met again in Tashkent, on what turned out to be the eve of the August coup attempt.[14] However, some significant changes had occurred since the first meeting. One was that Kyrgyzstan was now represented by Askar Akaev, who had become president after Masaliev had been pushed out by his legislature;[15] unique among the leaders for having come up through the Academy of Sciences rather than the upper party ranks (Akaev was a Communist, just not as high-ranking a one as the others), Akaev was by the 1991 meeting pursuing a strong sovereignty line for Kyrgyzstan, and was already uncoupling its government from the Communist Party. Another difference was the absence of Olzhas Suleimenov, a Kazakh poet and Central Asian populist, who had been active at the first meeting, trying to organize the informal political movements of Central Asia into a broader Central Asian populist support group, much of the sort that Gorbachev had been attempting to enlist in public support for his reforms in Moscow.[16] Furthermore, the ethnic violence of 1990, and the ease with which mass movements could turn into nationalist blocs, had made clearer the difficulty, even danger, of harnessing public discontent, especially since in Central Asia there was always the danger that such a movement might take on a religious character.[17]

One of the paradoxes of the late Soviet period and of independence is that while it was generally agreed, both in the USSR and in the world, that the resurgence of the Russian Orthodox church was a positive sign, the parallel resurgence of Islam was greatly feared, not only by the West, but also by the leaders of the Central Asian countries themselves, who are all lifelong Soviet-era, Russified former partocrats (or in Akaev's case, technocrat). Of the present leaders, only Turkmenistan's Niyazov has wholly embraced his "historical religion," making hajj, dedicating mosques in his own honor, and erecting statues of himself on the way to Mecca. Although initially publicly devout, Uzbekistan's President Karimov has been more cautious, and Kyrgyzstan's President Akaev more cautious yet.[18] Kazakhstan's Nazarbaev has refused even to permit Islamic holidays to become state ones (which Akaev did), and has kept to a minimum his public observance of Islamic rituals.

The questions of how best to mobilize public support and, more precisely, how to encourage patriotism, soon became serious matters for Central Asia's leaders. Their next regional summit was called, again by Nazarbaev, for December 12, 1991, in Ashgebat, Turkmenistan. This was a much more hastily assembled gathering, with but one item on the agenda—how to respond to the trilateral dissolution of the USSR on December 8 by Russia, Belarus, and Ukraine.[19] Nazarbaev has subsequently reported that he was invited to join the meeting in Belo-Vezhsky on December 8, but refused because he had been given too little time to study the documents he would have to sign; it was lost on no one at the Ashgebat meeting, however, that the three Slavic presidents had pointedly excluded the four Turkic presidents (plus one Tajik), unceremoniously flinging all five Central Asian republics out into independence.

Although the formal declarations of that meeting were similar to those of the Almaty and Tashkent meetings—about the necessity of regional cooperation and the desirability of establishing some sort of regional structure—the atmosphere was very different, because all of the leaders present were conscious that the Slavs had suddenly orphaned them.

Again the representation of the five republics, and what they represented, differed significantly. Karimov, Akaev, and Niyazov remained in power, but all three had already declared their nations to be independent of the USSR: Akaev had done so as early as August 30, and Uzbekistan's declaration came just two days later. Tajikistan had also declared independence, but was now represented by Rakhmon Nabiev, the Brezhnev-era ruler of the republic, who had been pushed out by Gorbachev in 1985. Forging a short-lived union with Tajikistan's democrats and Islamic fundamentalists, Nabiev had succeeded in ousting Gorbachev's man, Makhkamov, and had set out to follow a strongly nationalist line, initially with some religious overtones.

Odd man out at the Ashgebat meetings was Nazarbaev, who was still trying desperately to keep some form of transnational union alive.[20] Perhaps precisely because of the awareness he had gained as head of the Kazakh Council of Ministers of the degree to which the republics were economically nonviable as separate units, and most certainly fearful of the political implications of the Kazakhs' being less than a majority in their titular homeland, Nazarbaev had emerged in the last years of the Soviet Union as a strong advocate of the Union treaty. Throughout the fall of 1991 he continued to push the other republic leaders together, so that the December 8 meeting had been a particularly pointed rejection of Nazarbaev's position, that there had to be some sort of post-Soviet, supranational successor entity.

Even though he had just been popularly elected president of Kazakhstan (on December 1, with almost 99 percent of the vote), Nazarbaev still had not declared his country independent. His arguments at the Ashgebat meeting were to create a Central Asian, primarily Turkic, organization as a countervalent to the new Slavic entity that had been declared in Belarus. The public posture was that such a union could survive, even flourish, without the Slavs, but Nazarbaev's intent seems to have been to raise the specter of the age-old Slavic-Turkic confrontations, as a way of inducing the Russia-Belarus-Ukraine trio to widen the constitution of what soon became the CIS.[21]

If that was indeed the purpose, then Nazarbaev's goal was achieved on December 21, 1991. On that date, five days after Nazarbaev had declared Kazakhstan's independence, the presidents of the three Slavic republics, the five Central Asian republics, Armenia, Azerbaijan, and Moldova assembled in Almaty, and the original all-Slavic composition of the USSR's successor was recast, to compose the CIS.

The next meeting of the Central Asian leaders, exclusive of other CIS leaders, came in Bishkek, Kyrgyzstan's capital, on April 23, 1992.[22] This time Tajikistan was not represented at all, because the country was in the first stages of a civil war. The goal of this meeting was to seek greater economic cooperation and coordination among the five republics, but a telling detail was the presence at the gathering of Russia's foreign minister, Andrei Kozyrev. This underscored the continuing truth of the evolution of the post-Soviet states, that Russia remained the dominant determinant in interrepublic relations. The Russian-Soviet legacy continued to shape regional developments in a number of important ways; for example, since intraregional transportation was still almost nonexistent, it remained easier to get to Moscow than from one end of Kazakhstan to the other, or from Ashgebat to Almaty. Certainly contact with the outside world, even by telephone, was still largely through Moscow. Trade and supply lines, too, remained much as they had been, tying Central Asia to the foundering Russian economy.

When the Central Asian leadership met in early January 1993, in Tashkent, on the eve of a CIS meeting in Minsk, the question of the region's continuing economic interdependence with Russia was already a subject suitable for debate. The leaders of the Turkic states remained as they had been at the last meeting, but again the Tajik representative, Imomali Rakhmonov, was new, because of the bloody civil war that had been fought in Tajikistan through most of 1992.[23]

Although practical results of that meeting were as few as they had been at earlier meetings, a number of important and telling symbolic changes occurred in Tashkent. The purpose of the gathering was to begin to explore the possibility of creating a unified Central Asian economic space, on the model of the European

Community, in which goods could move about without hindrance, taxes would be reduced to a minimum, customs checks and duties within the region would be removed, and a common currency would be put in place. Significantly, the group chose at that meeting to change the name of the region from Middle Asia and Kazakhstan to Central Asia, thus claiming that Kazakhstan was integral to the area, and so creating in words what Central Asia increasingly clearly was not—a single political and economic space.

CLEARING THE FIELD

By January 1993, it was obvious that Turkmenistan's Niyazov was beginning to carve a path for his republic independent of both the CIS and smaller, regional identifications. Blessed with a lightly populated republic that more or less floats on an ocean of natural gas, Niyazov has created a sort of post-Soviet emirate in Turkmenistan, imposing extremely tight political control, in exchange for which the citizens are shielded from Russian inflation. For example, since January 1, 1993, Turkmenistan has used its vast wealth to supply its citizens with free water, gas, and electricity, as well as to continue subsidies of basic foods, which have kept consumer prices almost as low as in Soviet times. On the periphery of both the CIS and Central Asia, Turkmenistan is increasingly able to define its own (self-defensive and unambitious) course. One stark demonstration of this was Niyazov's decision simply not to come back from lunch at the May 1993 CIS meetings in Moscow to participate in the group press conference, demonstrating that while Russia was still an economic and military power of sufficient importance to shape Turkmenistan's development, Boris Yeltsin could no longer dictate Supramurad Niyazov's appointment schedule.[24]

Kyrgyzstan and Tajikistan had also been shunted to the periphery of Central Asia and the CIS, although for quite different reasons. Both nations remain prominent in the Central Asian configuration, but now as problems. At the time of independence, these two smallest nations of Central Asia were in very similar positions: both are mountainous, both had powerful regional clans greedy for enhanced political and economic power, both are extremely remote (even by Central Asian standards), and, most important, both began independence with more debts than obvious assets. However, since independence, the two have followed quite different paths.

Kyrgyzstan leaders have tended since independence to explain the vigorous flourishing of democracy in their republic as a product of the Kyrgyz nomadic culture, which accepts a wide latitude of human behavior. Another explanation may be the character of Akaev, who is the least personally ambitious of any of the Central Asian leaders. Whatever their source, the intellectual and political freedoms of Kyrgyzstan are very real: the country has a free press that rivals anything in Moscow—or, indeed, Warsaw or Prague—and a vigorous political opposition.

In the bright dreams of early independence, Kyrgyzstan had hoped to capitalize upon its freedom, to make the country what Akaev called "an Asian Switzerland," a haven for foreign money and foreign thinkers. What happened instead is that Kyrgyzstan's economy collapsed; in 1992 productivity dropped 25 percent (against a previous year that had already seen a large decline) and the wholesale price index rose 1,800 percent.[25] Bound to the plummeting Russian ruble, wholly dependent upon outside sources for petroleum and natural gas, Kyrgyzstan by the January 1993 meeting was facing an economy in which the projected cost of basic energy imports alone was going to be larger than the entire state budget. With the country's airport virtually shut by a shortage of jet fuel—or, more properly, by a lack of funds to buy fuel—the situation had become so desperate in one city (Naryn) that municipal authorities even replaced the city buses with horse-drawn omnibuses.

Tajikistan also collapsed in 1992, but with far bloodier consequences. Seriously unstable even before independence, the country continued to unravel throughout most of 1992, as Nabiev turned on his democratic and Islamic allies, who in their turn forced him from office, installing a religiously oriented government of their own. Even before that group was able to establish power, however, they were attacked and driven from Dushanbe, the capital. In late 1992 the Tajik parliament abolished the post of president, making the speaker of the parliament, Imomali Rakhmonov, the head of government. With strong support from the Russian troops already stationed there, and the Uzbek troops Karimov had dispatched in fall 1992, Rakhmonov has achieved a brutal "stability" in Tajikistan, killing or imprisoning political figures deemed to be from the opposition, and forcing thousands into exile. Many of the refugees have fled into Afghanistan, where some are reported to be training for a *mujahedeen*-style war against Rakhmonov; others—a much smaller number—have fled into Kyrgyzstan, creating disturbances along the border and, far more worrisome to the Kyrgyzstan government, setting up the possibility of government "security incursions" from the Tajikistan side.[26] It is not reassuring to the Kyrgyzstan government that Tajikistan, alone among the Central Asian governments, has refused to recognize the existing borders.

TWO PRESIDENTS, TWO MODELS

Thus by the January 1993 meetings, the major actors of Central Asia had essentially been reduced to two, Uzbekistan and Kazakhstan, which increasingly have recapitulated the centuries-old struggle for dominance of the region, albeit this time in a peaceful competition for influence within Central Asia and its broader international environs.

At the time of independence, Kazakhstan's Nazarbaev seemed clearly to be the preeminent figure in Central Asia. He enjoyed great political standing, within his own country, in the former USSR, and in the West. Enhanced by his continued support for Gorbachev through the fall of 1991, and then by his generally compliant attitude toward his nation's sudden status as a "nuclear power," Nazarbaev looked to be the ideal postcommunist national leader, who would be able to oversee his country's transition to capitalism in a balanced, judicious way—as the title of his widely circulated book, *Without Right or Left*,[27] suggested. Nor did it hurt Nazarbaev's status that Kazakhstan appeared to be a new El Dorado, with potential oil reserves rivaling those of Saudi Arabia, which would give Kazakhstan the material footing to become the bridge of which Nazarbaev dreamed, joining East and West, Islamic and Christian cultures, Russia and Asia.

The goals of Nazarbaev's program are clear, although the details of how Kazakhstan will reach these goals are sometimes vague. Kazakhstan is eager to make a rapid transition to a market economy, complete with private ownership. It aims to do this by offering generous terms to potential foreign investors. Nazarbaev believes that economic recovery cannot occur if political stability is sacrificed. But he also believes that the republic will fail to recover economically if it attempts to reach the market through autocratic policies. While Nazarbaev is no Jeffersonian Democrat, he accepts the argument that Kazakhstan must make steady movement toward becoming a democratic society if it is to become an international actor of note.[28] However, the ever pragmatic Nazarbaev also recognizes that Kazakhstan's independence depends on Russia's recognition of that independence. Russia will not accept a threat on her southern border, which Kazakhstan would be if it were to become an Islamic or nationalistic, anti-Russian state.

By contrast, Uzbekistan's President Karimov had little all-Union presence and was unknown in the outside world. His first appearances on a world stage did not increase his authority abroad, and only the most careful editing increased it at home. In the first months of independence, Karimov would return from each of his visits—to Turkey, to Saudia Arabia (where he made *hajj*), to Singapore—with the proclamation that his latest destination was now the model of development his nation should follow.[29]

With 25 percent of the USSR's gold reserves, a huge cotton crop, some oil, and the largest population in Central Asia, Uzbekistan had an economic potential that was not as great as that of Kazakhstan, but was worthy of attention. This potential is great enough that Karimov has felt that Uzbekistan should not be beholden to its foreign partners, either for investment or for instructions on how Uzbekistan's development should proceed.

A model was one thing, but the Uzbeks—and especially Karimov—must be free to decide how best to apply any model that was chosen to the republic's own specific conditions, which included its Asian and Muslim temperament.[30] The market and democracy were admirable ideals, but to pursue either too rapidly was to risk exciting the Uzbeks' Asian temperament and push the republic toward Islamic fundamentalism, plunging the country and the region more generally into turmoil.[31]

General world opinion was that Kazakhstan was the more likely of the two to become the power to reckon with in the region; one indicator of that was the decision by Lufthansa Airlines to bring the first direct European air service to the region into Almaty, rather than Tashkent. However, the course of events since independence has greatly shifted the balance between Nazarbaev and Karimov, and the nations they lead. Part of the cause is internal to Central Asia, but an enormous portion of the blame for Nazarbaev's slide in influence lies with the failure of the CIS, which he has backed so strongly, to develop into anything of substance. Almost as destructive has been the collapse of Russia, both economically and politically.

As the leader of a country with an economy that depends upon Russia for 70 percent of its activity, a population that is almost half Slavic, and a border of three thousand miles separating areas (and populations) that are almost identically "Russian," Nazarbaev has probably had no choice but to continue to press for a real functioning CIS, and to work with Yeltsin as much as he is able. One crucial measure of Nazarbaev's support is that Kazakhstan remained within the ruble zone as long as it possibly could, until November 1993, and even afterward continued to accept the argument that a unified economic space is necessary.

Increasingly Nazarbaev has become one of the few politicians, or indeed even citizens of the former USSR, who is still articulating a view of the body politic that stresses the contributions of various sectors—republics, peoples, or classes—to a whole; much more common, both within the various nations and among them, are arguments pressing demands for rights and benefits that groups feel they are "due," without any awareness of the needs or demands of a larger whole. A case in point is Kazakhstan's political spectrum, which includes Kazakhs who feel that, having suffered under the Russians in the past, they should not have to reckon with Russian sensibilities now; Russians who, more than any of the other "stranded" Russians of Central Asia, are quick to take as violation of their "human rights" the slightest suggestion that they should submit to Kazakh authority, learn any Kazakh language, or serve in a Kazakhstan army; and Cossacks who claim (with historical justification) that parts of northern Kazakhstan have been theirs for more than four centuries. Kazakhs and Russians share an obvious political center, but how large and how firm it may prove to be is a subject for conjecture.[32]

Such exclusively defined self-interest has been one of the root causes of the failure of multinational political movements to coalesce. Olzhas Suleimenov's efforts to mobilize Kazakh and Russian opposition to Soviet nuclear testing in Semipalatinsk had seemed in 1990 a promising model of a multiethnic democratic movement in the Soviet Union, for which reason it received a great deal of official support. For a variety of reasons, however, that movement proved the sole exception in a political landscape dotted with religious and nationalist groups, of all nationalities, who were arguing increasingly narrow, and mutually exclusive, agendas.

Now President Nazarbaev is himself trying to create his multinational movement—SNEK, the Peoples Unity Party of Kazakhstan—which he hopes will dominate the March 1994 legislative elections and ensure his own political future and that of the multinational republic more generally. As those Americans involved with organizing "democratic initiatives" in Kazakhstan will attest, Nazarbaev fears that the rapid introduction of a fully free press and a Western-style pluralistic party system would threaten the survival of his new state. However, for all his displeasure at public criticism, Nazarbaev has taken great pains to distinguish his far more passive treatment of political opposition groups from the far more aggressive stance of Uzbekistan's President Islam Karimov.

While Karimov likes to justify his policies as necessary to counter the violent spontaneity of his Asian population, until the fall of 1992 and the outbreak of all-out fighting in Tajikistan, Karimov's harsh internal policies seem to have undercut his influence within the leadership of Central Asia, particularly with Nazarbaev and Akaev, who want to present a very different Central Asia to world attention. Although he had originally permitted the activities of nationalist opposition groups like Birlik and Erk, in the spring of 1992 Karimov began to crack down, with a directness and severity that was reminiscent of the Andropov-era KGB.[33] Important opposition figures have been forced into exile or silence, as have his former rivals from within the Communist Party, and the press, media, and parliament have been taken into close control. Karimov has moved to control the religious hierarchy as well, replacing the head mufti, Muhammadsadyk Muhammad Yusuf, and bringing charges against him. However, the bloody devastation of the civil war in Tajikistan and Karimov's role in reimposing "stability" there have greatly enhanced the Uzbekistan president's standing.

FIRST CRISIS

One important difference between Nazarbaev and Karimov emerged in October 1992, when the Central Asian leaders agreed that the Tajik problem was becoming a threat to all of Central Asia, and so must be dealt with. Karimov, Nazarbaev, and Akaev endorsed a proposal to mount a joint expeditionary force, with Russian involvement. If successful, this operation would have been an important demonstration of the ability of Central Asia to act in a concerted manner (whatever the wisdom of the precedent such a force would have set for intervention in the political affairs of neighboring states).

However, unlike Karimov, who enjoys a rubber-stamp parliament, neither Nazarbaev nor Akaev was able to secure the permission of his parliament to use national troops as peacemakers—and in Kyrgyzstan's case the mere question of sending them became an extremely divisive issue.[34] Thus only Karimov sent soldiers into Tajikistan, in the process defining their mission more broadly than was initially intended, so that the well-armed and well-trained Uzbek army played an important role in securing the installation of the Rakhmonov government. The ex-Soviet troops in Tajikistan, now under Russian command, also played a large role, but mostly in defense of a tightly defined set of Russian interests, paramount of which is keeping the old USSR border with Afghanistan sealed against gun and drug smuggling. Uzbekistan has a much wider range of interests, including the age-old battle over whether "Tajiks" per se even exist, and Karimov has therefore been able to gain significant influence over the conduct of Tajikistan's business, while using the example of his neighbor's instability as a justification for tightening political control within his country. Not insignificantly, the provision of "fraternal assistance" in Tajikistan has also given Karimov's army extremely valuable experience as a republic-controlled fighting unit.

Karimov's standing within Central Asia has been steadily rising since Tajikistan's civil war began, because the threat that similar instability may occur elsewhere terrifies the Central Asian leadership. Even Akaev, the most democratically minded of the five leaders, has spoken more frequently than before of the need to preserve stability in Central Asia. Increasingly Karimov has demonstrated that he has both the will and the power to do so.

Without a common border with Tajikistan, and with his worries directed north, to the long border he shares with a disintegrating Russia, Nazarbaev was not as intimately concerned with the problems in Tajikistan as was Karimov. His neighbor, both by geography and by culture (Kyrgyz and Kazakh being almost indistinguishable in language and practice), is Kyrgyzstan. The two countries, and many of the problems they face (including having a large Russian minority), are sufficiently similar that Nazarbaev seems to have been content to let Kyrgyzstan's experiments with liberalism continue without comment, because they removed pressure on him. The free press of Kyrgyzstan and the possibility to use Bishkek as a nearby venue (it is four hours by car from Almaty) for human rights conferences and other exercises in democracy have given Nazarbaev an important safety valve for Kazakh nationalism; it has seemed an easy enough trade-off to let Bishkek use Almaty as Kyrgyzstan's de facto portal to the world, after the collapsing economy meant that international air service to Kyrgyzstan all but ceased.

For much of 1992 and the beginning of 1993, Central Asia was evolving into a contemporary version of its age-old configuration, with Kazakhs and Kyrgyz in a rough alliance along the north, while the Uzbeks clasped the Tajiks in a tight embrace along the south.

However, the economy in Kyrgyzstan has collapsed so totally that by May 1993, the country had acquired the freedom of utter desperation; with nothing to lose, Kyrgyzstan was the first of the CIS countries to bolt from the ruble zone, by introducing its own currency, the som. This action was designed to free Kyrgyzstan from Russia's galloping inflation and to allow the republic to draw upon International Monetary Fund currency stabilization funds and international economic development credits.

SECOND CRISIS

Each of the Central Asian countries had spoken before May 1993 of introducing a separate currency (the tenga in Kazakhstan, the menat in Turkmenistan, and the som in Uzbekistan; all were introduced in the fall of 1993. However, Kyrgyzstan's decision actually to do so—warning its neighboring states, but not coordinating this introduction with their economies—set off the second internal crisis of the new Central Asia, one that left lingering economic effects long after it ceased to be front-page news.[35] Since Kazakhstan and Uzbekistan felt compelled to back out of the planned currency union with Russia, plans have gone forward to establish a Kyrgyz, Kazakh, and Uzbek free trade zone by 2000, but for now trade within the region remains in considerable disarray.

Though by no means as life-threatening to the regimes of Central Asia as the war in Tajikistan, the introduction of the som can be seen as a genuine regional crisis. Some of its effects are as much symbolic as they are real. The presence of the som makes the creation of a common Central Asian market that much more unlikely, just as Akaev's unilateral decision to introduce this currency demonstrates the fiction that Central Asia has anything like a unified approach to the problems of transition. In fact, the only Central Asian leader who defended Kyrgyzstan's action, Turkmenistan's Niyazov, argued that as the leader of a sovereign state, Akaev had the right to introduce a national currency unilaterally if he chose to do so.

Other effects, however, are more substantive. As the ruble remains Central Asia's trading currency, introduction of the som irrevocably disrupted regional trade: Uzbeks and Kazakhs were no longer free to trade their goods in Kyrgyzstan, and those in Kyrgyzstan were no longer free to trade in their neighboring states. Kazakhs and Uzbeks had no use for the som, while Kyrgyz had real difficulty getting rubles, and there were not nearly enough dollars anywhere in the region to permit regional trade to "dollarize." As a result, the market in Kyrgyzstan dried up throughout the spring and summer of 1993, creating even greater shortages and forcing up prices in the private shops of Kyrgyzstan. At the same time, Uzbek farmers were left with large amounts of unsold foodstuffs. Central Asians who traveled to Kyrgyzstan to vacation (the republic's Lake Issyk Kul is a major resort site for the region) also found themselves in serious straits, when the July 1993 embargo on pre-1993 rubles left many Russian and other vacationers literally without the means to obtain a return ticket, since Bishkek was not on the list of republics eligible to receive new rubles. Similarly, those hoping to emigrate from Kyrgyzstan have found themselves facing new and strict ruble export regulations.[36]

The effect on interrepublic trade was no less profound. Kyrgyzstan is estimated to have had fifty-five billion rubles in circulation, of which only six billion were exchanged for som. With the ruble now outlawed for use in Kyrgyzstan, those additional forty-nine billion rubles became a palpable threat, because Kyrgyzstan's citizens could take their rubles to neighboring states and buy up the already scarce goods, thus adding further inflationary pressure to a situation that even without the Kyrgyz rubles was teetering between hyperinflation and totally uncontrolled inflation.

Characteristically, Karimov was the first to react, immediately closing the borders between Kyrgyzstan and Uzbekistan, and introducing local regulations that made it impossible for non-Uzbekistan citizens to use their cash. He subsequently shut off air service between the two countries, then refused to allow natural gas to be piped through his republic if its destination was Kyrgyzstan, thus leaving the southern oblasts of Kyrgyzstan without fuel. These actions would have been sufficiently hostile by themselves, but the presence of a large Uzbek population in southern Kyrgyzstan—six hundred thousand people, or about one-third of Osh oblast—makes the situation uncomfortably reminiscent of analogous European regions, like Sudetenland or Alsace-Lorraine. Even more alarming was Karimov's assertion of the right (echoing that declared a year earlier by Russian Vice President Aleksandr Rutskoi for Russia and Russians) to defend the rights of Uzbeks, "wherever they might live," a warning made more ominous by the memories of fighting between the Uzbeks and Kyrgyz of Osh in the summer of 1990.

Karimov had already shown his contempt for Kyrgyzstan's sovereignty in December 1992, by ordering his KGB to arrest three Uzbekistani dissidents (two Uzbek, one Tajik) on a Bishkek city street during an international conference on human rights. Thus President Akaev was probably wise, in the short run, to fly to Tashkent, where he offered a humiliating public apology to Karimov, for the distress suffered by Uzbeks at the introduction of the som; Akaev is said too to have agreed to redeem (presumably in scarce dollars) the currency Karimov claimed had been dumped in his republic (which the Uzbekistan president insisted was fifty-two million rubles). Akaev's action managed to get the pipelines turned on (although payment must now be in hard currency) and the borders reopened, but the precedent set would seem ominous. Unsettling, too, are reports from late May 1993 that Akaev informed his parliament that a part of the republic's revenues from gold concessions was being spent on arms, as a demonstration of which he is said to have brandished a rifle.

For all of Karimov's obvious fury, though, it is Nazarbaev who was most seriously damaged by the som. Northern Kyrgyzstan is as intimately connected to Kazakhstan as southern Kyrgyzstan is to Uzbekistan, so that the forty-nine billion rubles presented as large an economic threat to him as they did to Karimov. Nazarbaev's public reaction was less bellicose than was Karimov's, but his actions were very similar; tighter border checks for commercial traffic were put in place, and interrepublic trade restrictions reportedly are being enforced, while the past practice of allowing Kyrgyzstan's residents to pay rubles for air and train tickets for travel from Kazakhstan was ended. Now all journeys originating in Kyrgyzstan must be paid for in hard currency, which will be a further blow to a nation that has had virtually no international air service of its own (even to Moscow) since December 1992. Akaev reportedly apologized to Nazarbaev as well (though not so publicly), and promised to make good "his" rubles there, but the currency regulations remain in place, effectively stranding Kyrgyzstan in the middle of the Asian landmass.

The real damage to Nazarbaev, however, is that Akaev's action has forced Kazakhstan's president even deeper into a corner, from which there are no obvious exits. Nazarbaev has struggled since 1989 to make the various parts, first of the USSR, then of the

CIS and Central Asia, behave in a mutually responsible manner, because from his point of view the alternative is disaster. It is indicative of Nazarbaev's position that the question of currency for Kazakhstan has never been primarily financial; the republic is sufficiently wealthy to be able to survive with its own currency. Indeed, as Nazarbaev himself has pointed out, the republic would be better off in some ways if it did not use the ruble, as long as Russia refuses to control the emission of its money or to give the other ruble nations a role in ruble zone financial decision making.

Like most issues in Kazakhstan, the question of currency is largely ethnic. The republic's move to a currency other than that which Russia uses, has added yet another straw to the uncertain camelback of Russian nationalism. If a Kazakhstan currency were to make life on the Kazakhstan side of the border better than it is on the Russian side, then the risk immediately emerges that the Russian side might attempt to absorb its "irredentist" population; if life on the Kazakhstan side were to become worse, then the temptation for Nazarbaev's Russians might be to press for their inclusion in Russia. Even without that threat, the use of different currencies would complicate yet further the exchange of funds between Russia and Kazakhstan, whose economies are as interwoven, and as dangerous to separate, as Siamese twins.[37]

Thus, although it was not so intended, Akaev's introduction of the som was seen by many to be a slap in Nazarbaev's face, which must sting all the more because of the degree to which Kazakhstan has served as Kyrgyzstan's "big brother," providing goods and services the tiny republic needs but cannot supply for itself. At the same time, however, Nazarbaev cannot afford to allow the Kyrgyz to suffer too greatly, or he risks having his own nationalists accuse him of behaving like Karimov, siding with the Uzbeks against the Kazakhs' "little brother."

CONCLUSION

For all his very tenuous commitment to Western democratic ideals, Nazarbaev does not want to rule with the same iron hand that Karimov does. Both leaders accept the necessity of a strong central administration; where they differ is on the degree of centralization, and the manner in which it is achieved. Karimov has argued since the beginning of Uzbekistan's independence that the stresses of the transformation to a market economy require a strong hand, which he has shown both the willingness and an increasing ability to supply, particularly as the stresses have grown greater, and the transformation ever more distant. Although Karimov's KGB so far lacks the technical capacity to monitor all aspects of Uzbekistan's daily life, the will to do so is clearly present. Karimov has interpreted "opposition" in ever broader terms, so that now even a neutral absence of enthusiastic support for his government can be defined as illegal dissent.

Nazarbaev's Kazakhstan is much more relaxed politically, with a press that is diverse, if not actually free, and with laws that permit a broad range of opinion and activity critical of the government. In part because of the ethnic fractures running through every aspect of his society, but in part too because of personal inclination—perhaps because he witnessed the bloody aftermath of the attempts of his predecessor, Gennadii Kolbin, to suppress political opposition by force—Nazarbaev has given fairly wide latitude to the expression of political disaffection in his country. Although the new constitution includes severe penalties for any liberties taken with the "dignity" of the president (penalties that in fact were invoked in at least one court case), Nazarbaev has been willing to endure considerable criticism, as well as a certain amount of resistance from within Kazakhstan's parliament. The result, if not democratic in the Western sense, is a society that by most criteria is more pluralistic than it was in the past, with Kazakhstan a nation that has so far managed to contain a wide diversity of ethnic groups, economic communities, and political philosophies.

Unfortunately, though, the course of developments in Central Asia is beginning to suggest that at least some of the historical determinants of the region remain true, and are beginning to reassert themselves. Increasingly it is becoming clear that President Nazarbaev has a society over which he can exercise only a limited amount of direct control. The imposition of much more central rule than currently exists is not feasible: Kazakhstan is simply too large and too empty, with too many different populations whose interests are not only not shared, but often mutually exclusive. For too much of Kazakhstan, it remains far too easy for disaffected groups to, in effect, simply move elsewhere; as the governor of Uralsk has pointed out, his city is nearer to Paris than it is to Almaty.[38]

Thus Nazarbaev's options for the future remain all too uncomfortably like those before the three *biis* whose meeting he was attempting to commemorate at Ordobasy. The dangers facing Central Asia are manifest—economic collapse, an ever more imponderable and unpredictable Russia, and internecine quarrels that have the capacity to erupt into Tajikistan-scale fighting, not only within but between republics. The wisdom of joining forces to meet those dangers is clear.

President Nazarbaev would have Central Asia join forces because of a reasoned recognition of shared interest. Both within the republics and among them, such a recognition would create a unity that allows various communities, or nations, to preserve their separate identities, even as they ally. However, Central Asia's forces may be joined in another way, as both Nazarbaev and Karimov understand, and as Karimov has already demonstrated, both within his own society and in Tajikistan. For the time being, President Nazarbaev's skills of persuasion are so great, and the possible consequences of the failure of his approach so alarming, that Central Asia is likely to continue trying to surmount its problems, internal and external, through consultation and consensus. However, if the problems continue to mount, and Nazarbaev's range of possible responses continues to shrink, then President Karimov's method of uniting Central Asia, under an Uzbek army that he controls, remains a distinct and growing possibility.

NOTES

1. *Kazakhstanskaia pravda,* May 29, 1993.
2. See Martha Brill Olcott, *The Kazakhs* (Stanford, Calif.: Hoover Institution Press, 1987), esp. ch. 1.
3. See Richard Frye, *Bukhara: A Medieval Jewel* (Norman, Okla.: University of Oklahoma, 1965).
4. For an account of the problem of dating the Turkic ascendancy, see Yuri

Bregel, "Turko-Mongol Influences in Central Asia," in Robert Canfield, ed., *Turko-Persia in Historical Perspective* (Cambridge: Cambridge University Press, 1991), pp. 53–73.

5. On the ethnogenesis of these various peoples, see V. V. Bart'old, *Four Studies on the History of Central Asia,* trans. by V. Minorsky and T. Minorsky (Leiden: E. J. Brill, 1956–1963), esp. vol. 1.

6. See Edward Allworth, *The Modern Uzbeks* (Stanford, Calif.: Hoover Institution Press, 1990), esp. ch. 1.

7. A history of this unrest is found in E. Bekmakhanov, *Kazakhstan v 20–40 gody XIX veka* (Almaty, 1947). Bekhmakhanov was arrested and jailed for this book, which described resistance to both the Russian and the Kokandi conquests of the Kazakhs and Kyrgyz.

8. For a history of the conquest, see Richard A. Pierce, *Russian Central Asia 1867–1917* (Berkeley: University of California Press, 1960).

9. For a description of the various movements in Central Asia and their publications, see Alexandre Bennigsen and Chantel Lemercier Quelquejay, *La Press et le Mouvement National chez les Musulmans de Russie avant 1920* (Paris: Mouton, 1964).

10. For details of the civil war in Central Asia, see Martha Brill Olcott, "The Basmachi or Freeman's Revolt in Turkestan 1918–1924," *Soviet Studies,* vol. 33, no. 3 (July 1981), pp. 352–369.

11. Kh. T. Tursunov, *Obrazovanie Uzbekskoi Sovetskoi Sotsialisticheskoi Respubliki* (Tashkent: Izdatel'stvo Akademii Nauk Uzbekskoi SSR, 1957), offers a detailed account of the various negotiations and boundary decisions.

12. *Soyuz,* no. 32 (August 1990).

13. *Kazakhstanskaia pravda,* June 25, 1990.

14. *Kazakhstanskaia pravda,* August 16, 1991.

15. *Sovetskaia Kirgiziia,* October 25, 1990.

16. *Kazakhstanskaia pravda,* June 27, 1990.

17. See Helene Carrere D'Encausse, *The End of the Soviet Empire* (New York: Basic Books, 1993), pt. 2.

18. *Nezavisimaia gazeta,* January 7, 1992.

19. *Izvestiia,* December 16, 1991.

20. *Vremiia* (Ostankino television, Moscow), December 10, 1991.

21. This interpretation is consistent with Nazarbaev's later reflections on those days. See *Nezavisimaia gazeta,* July 28, 1993.

22. *Izvestiia,* April 25, 1992.

23. *Izvestiia,* January 7, 1993.

24. *Vremiia* (Ostankino television, Moscow), May 7, 1993.

25. *Kommersant,* no. 8 (1993).

26. For a summary of the events of Tajikistan's first two years of independence, see *Nezavisimaia gazeta,* September 9, 1992.

27. Nursultan Nazarbaev, *Nursultan Nazarbaev: Bez pravykh i levykh* (Moscow: Molodaia gvardia, 1991).

28. *Ekonomika i zhizn'* (Almaty), no. 8 (1992).

29. *Izvestiia,* September 21, 1991.

30. Islam A. Karimov, *Uzbekistan svoi put' obnovleniia i progressa* (Tashkent: Uzbkeistson, 1992).

31. Interview with Ostankino television. Foreign Broadcast Information Service, Republic Affairs, June 6, 1993.
32. *Nezavisimaia gazeta,* August 28, 1993.
33. *Narod i demokratiia,* no. 7–8 (1992).
34. *Slovo Kyrgyzstana,* October 14, 1992.
35. *Slovo Kyrgyzstana,* May 14, 1993.
36. *Slovo Kyrgyzstana,* July 27, 1993.
37. This discussion reflects the situation as of the summer of 1993. Russian financial policies forced the introduction of national currencies in Central Asia in October and November 1993.
38. K. K. Dzhakupov, personal communication, May 1993.

Chapter 2

The Event of Our Era: Former Soviet Muslim Republics Change the Middle East

Daniel Pipes

THE EMERGENCE OF SIX MOSTLY MUSLIM REPUBLICS FROM THE former Soviet Union has prompted much concern about their falling under Middle Eastern influence. But Middle Eastern states have attained little power over those republics; ironically, the impact goes the other way. The independence of republics in the Trans-Caucasus (Azerbaijan)[1] and Central Asia (Kazakstan, Kyrgyzstan, Tajikistan, Turkmenistan, and Uzbekistan) has profound implications for the Middle East, and especially for their four immediate neighbors—Turkey, Iran, Afghanistan, and Pakistan. Süleyman Demirel, Turkey's former prime minister, exaggerated only slightly when he called the independence of these states (henceforth called the ex-Soviet Muslim republics or the Southern Tier) "the event of our era."[2] Indeed, the Southern Tier's resumption of history may well have enormous consequences for the Middle East.

MIDDLE EASTERN IMPACT ON THE SOUTHERN TIER

Reporting from Central Asia and Azerbaijan since late 1991 has concentrated on the competition for influence over them among Middle Eastern states. The rivals are primarily Turkey and Iran, as well as Saudi Arabia and Pakistan. Ankara sees success at wooing the Southern Tier as a means of advancing Turkish secularism as a model, while Iran's success would win support for that country's anti-Western Islamic model.

To be sure, this competition does exist: Many Middle Eastern states saw an opportunity in about 1990 to gain influence in what seemed a virgin territory. Turks swooned at the prospect of leading a substantial bloc of Turkic speakers. Iranians jumped at the opportunity to reassert their historic cultural influence, now laced with Khomeinist Islam, over the Southern Tier. Pakistanis looked to Central Asia as a place to do business and establish a strategic hinterland versus India. Some Tajik and Uzbek Afghans looked to the region for allies. Saudi Arabians quickly geared up their Islamic apparatus to operate in a new region. Both Israelis and Syrians actively sought out friends in the Southern Tier. The ensuing competition had political, strategic, economic, ideological, and cultural dimensions. All these states dispatched diplomats to the Southern Tier; signed cultural, trade, or security protocols; beamed radio and television broadcasts; provided loans; and trained students.

But activity alone does not guarantee influence. Indeed, the Middle Eastern states have so far exerted little real authority in any area of Southern Tier life, from military affairs to religious practice. This generalization holds especially in Kazakhstan[3] and Uzbekistan, the Southern Tier's most populous and powerful states; it also applies to Azerbaijan and Tajikistan, where Turkey and Iran, respectively, enjoy greatest strength.

Why so little impact? Because Middle Eastern states are weak and divided, while the Southern Tier is proud and wary.

Middle Eastern Weakness

Turkey, Iran, Saudi Arabia, and Pakistan all suffer from severe limitations. Not one of them has the cultural, economic, or military means to carve out a sphere of influence. In addition, each state has its own special shortcomings. Although Iran's location will surely mean commercial and transportation links to the Southern Tier, the country's international isolation much reduces its attraction for states just emerging from three generations of colonialism and political quarantine. Also, its severe, unremitting

Islamic order puts off peoples accustomed to secularism. Saudi Arabia competes, but its flimsy manpower base, remote location, and alien religious customs make it a less than formidable contender. As for Pakistan, it suffers from perpetual instability and wrenching poverty, and so can neither project power nor serve as a convincing model for others.

Of all the Middle Eastern actors, Turkey has the most active program for the Southern Tier and is widely seen as the most plausible influence over that region; its weaknesses therefore deserve more detailed consideration. Western notions to the contrary ("Turkey has the strongest historical and cultural links"),[4] not only is Turkey geographically remote from Central Asia, but it enjoys few historical or cultural ties to that region. Istanbul never ruled Central Asia, and Central Asia ruled Anatolia only momentarily (under Tamerlane) six centuries ago. Ottomans concentrated attention on their vast empire from Hungary to Yemen, not on distant Turkestan. Consequently, they had little cultural impact there until the decades just before World War I. The Soviets broke communications between the two areas, so that Kemal Atatürk's Westernizing reforms in Turkey during the 1920s and 1930s had almost no effect in the Southern Tier.

Turkish politicians sometimes portray their country as a middleman between the former Soviet republics and the West. Turks hope their Western orientation will strongly appeal to peoples emerging from three generations of totalitarianism. But how well can Turks[5] serve this function if they themselves have not been let into the European Community? And even if they can, why should the newly emerging states look to a peripheral member of the West rather than approach the key players directly?

Anecdotal evidence suggests that Central Asians find disappointment in Turkey. Students report poor conditions for study, businessmen find capital limited, and religious figures do not care for the country's secularism. All of them encounter a language more difficult to understand and a culture more remote than expected. And while the Turks have extended their media—television and newspapers especially—to the Southern Tier, they do not custom-design materials for these new audiences. Once the novelty of the media fare wore off, this severely restricted its appeal.

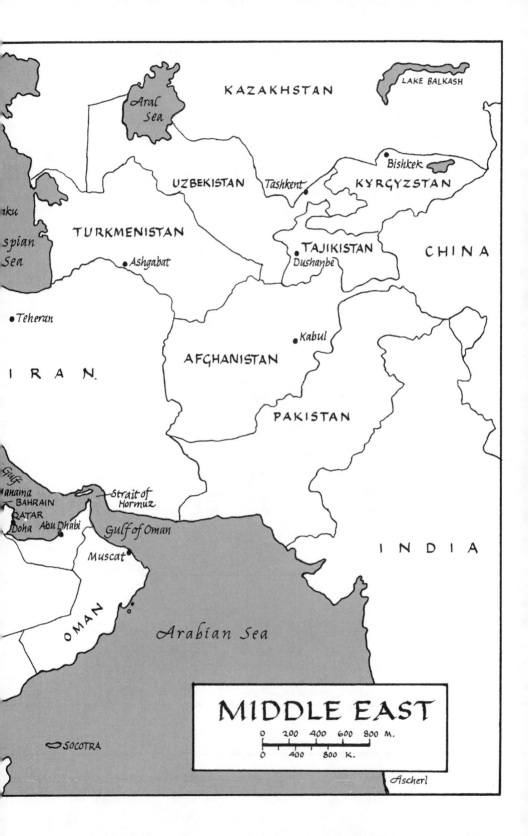

Turks lack the capital to carry through on their ambitious economic plans. Utbank, a joint Turkish-Uzbek commercial bank established in Tashkent, Uzbekistan, to considerable fanfare, had a meager $2 million capitalization. In by far the biggest deal so far, the Turkish company BMB signed an $11.7 billion deal to operate four oil fields in Kazakhstan. But a few months later it was reduced to making a public appeal for an $800 million loan over four years ("and $200 million of it very urgently") because its own funds would not permit it to carry through the contracted prospecting in Kazakhstan.[6] In general, Turkish entrepreneurs have become active in small-scale efforts (commerce, training, transportation), but have forfeited the larger undertakings (in oil, gas, gold) to Western and Asian corporations.

Further, the business that has actually transpired is pretty paltry: in 1992 Turkey's total trade (imports and exports) with the five republics of Central Asia amounted to a mere $300 million. Nor is it likely to increase much soon, for the two sides produce many of the same goods. Turkey neither offers much of a market for Southern Tier products nor supplies what the Southern Tier most wants to buy.

By late 1992, Southern Tier republics had begun complaining about Turkish activities. For example, the Azerbaijani authorities disliked the fact that Turkish joint ventures were attached not to manufacturing but to—as in the old, bad Soviet days—exporting raw materials. In December 1992 Kazakhstan's ambassador to Turkey accused Turkish businessmen of "lacking the courage to initiate investment,"[7] though he may have been confusing courage with capitalization. More broadly, as Patrick Clawson of the National Defense University argues, the Turkish example does not inspire ex-Soviet Muslims:

> The "Turkish model" looks rather uninviting to those who see Turkey as at best a second-class economy, with profound problems—a foreign debt that has had to be rescheduled several times in recent decades, a growth record well below that in East Asia, continuing macroeconomic imbalances (budget deficits and inflation), etc.[8]

Assessing Turkey's current economic capabilities, William Ward Maggs holds that it cannot "do much more than ship typewriters and television programs" to the Southern Tier.[9] In Martha

Brill Olcott's words, Turkish efforts have proven to be "more air than action."[10] The new "great game" for power in Central Asia, Boris Rumer comments, brutally but accurately, "is unfolding not so much among the old colonial powers as among their former minions, many of whom are themselves just emerging from colonial domination and seeking to define their roles."[11]

Then there is the Azerbaijan fiasco. As the Southern Tier republic closest to Turkey both spatially and culturally, Azerbaijan served as a showcase for Turkish efforts to help ex-Soviet Muslims leave the Russian sphere of influence and find their way to stable democracy. But Ankara did little to help Azerbaijan in its war with Armenia. The Turks warned Yerevan in 1992 that Armenia's attacks on Azerbaijan forces "would inevitably affect Turkish politics, and could even destabilize the country."[12] A year later, as Armenian aggression intensified, so did Turkish rhetoric, with Prime Minister Demirel going so far as to warn the Armenians, "If you are enemies of Azerbaijan, so you become enemies of Turkey."[13] Many observers[14] expected that fighting between Azeris and Armenians would spur Ankara to come to the aid of its brethren. Heated words aside, however, Ankara basically stayed out of the conflict; it strenuously asserted that "not a single Turkish soldier serves in the Azerbaijan armed forces"[15] and admitted only to sending humanitarian aid and training Azeri officers. For its part, Baku acknowledged just Turkish deliveries of fabric for Azeri troops' field uniforms and a retired Turkish general of Azeri origins.[16]

The election of Ebulfez Ali Elçibey as president of Azerbaijan in June 1992 brought a passionately pro-Turkish politician to power. Elçibey hung a portrait of Atatürk in his office, appointed Turkish citizens to high positions in his government, and spoke ardently of Turkey as a "light of hope for all Central Asia Muslims and Turks."[17] His comments even took on a maudlin quality, as when he explained how Azeris become "tearful when Turkey is mentioned. These tears are the tears of estrangement and longing of a hundred years."[18] Turks replied to these extravagant statements in kind. For example, President Turgut Özal told Elçibey: "This is your second country and Azerbaijan is our second motherland."[19] When Haydar Aliyev removed Elçibey from power in

June and July 1993, however, Ankara did not lift a finger to rescue Elçibey's presidency. Turkish politicians merely pointed out the illegality of Aliyev's rule and fretted about his "Stalinist" methods.

This combination—not protecting Azerbaijan from Armenian predations or swaying Azerbaijan's domestic politics—drastically reduced Ankara's reputation as a force to be reckoned with in the Southern Tier.

Lack of Interest

The Western press contains many statements to the effect that Southern Tier countries are looking to the Middle East for a model to follow. In a typical assertion, Colin Barraclough held that the "Central Asians are searching the outside world for a model for change."[20] Middle Easterners also promote this notion. Umut Arik, chairman of the Turkish Cooperation and Development Agency (TIKA), which doles out Turkish aid to the Southern Tier, contended that the new republics are "in search of a model."[21]

But a close examination of sentiments among the ex-Soviet Muslims suggests they are not looking to the Middle East. To begin with, they recognize the weakness of their neighbors. With some disdain, they dismiss as "secondhand" the technology proffered them by Turks and Iranians, pointing out that it really comes from Germany or some other Western country.

Southern Tier leaders also express skepticism about coming under the sway of another state. "We reject foreign influence, whether Turkey's or Iran's, in our lives and politics," Foreign Minister Khudoyberdy Kholiqnazarov[22] of Tajikistan has asserted. "After years of Russian imperialism we just want to live free in an independent country called Tajikistan."[23] Ex-Soviet Muslims have plenty of diurnal problems without getting involved in faraway regions. Falling right back under what Southern Tier residents consider the tutelage of another distant capital holds out few charms for them. And visionary schemes of any sort have little appeal for peoples emerging from decades of corrupted ideology.

Ties to Russia remain strong; indeed, in many respects the independence of the Southern Tier states is more formal than real. And Russia shows keen and growing interest in reasserting its influence over the former Soviet republics (now known as the "near abroad"). To associate too closely with Middle Eastern states, then, could make trouble with Moscow.

Finally, ex-Soviet Muslims take pride in their own accomplishments. They see themselves as no less civilized than their southern neighbors and reject notions that they need to learn from the latter. Where are infant mortality rates lower and literacy rates higher? Who hosts a space center and advanced military industries? And which countries until recently contributed to the Soviet superpower? Southern Tier Muslims feel culturally and technologically at least the equal of Turkey. Azimbay Ghaliyev, a Kazakh demographer, sees the balance this way:

> Turkey is a developing country. Internal conditions and internal stability are inadequate; religious and nationalist fundamentalism and powerful Kurd and Arab nationalities are increasingly important factors. The light and food industries and tourism are well developed in Turkey. On the other hand, non-ferrous metallurgy, chemistry, and machinery construction technology are just now becoming established. Sectors such as space research, astrophysics, nuclear physics, mathematical physics, and chemical medicine are mostly nonexistent. They are striving to learn these from us. Likewise, it would be more suitable for us to learn the banking system from the United States, Germany, and Japan. In this area, we must look at the Turkish example with critical eyes.[24]

Symbolic of the ex-Soviet Muslims' pride, Tashkent in August 1992 announced the granting of a hundred scholarships for Turkish students to study in Uzbekistan, signaling that aid will not go in just one direction. At the same time, the Uzbekistanis[25] (and Kyrgyzstanis) took advantage of only some of the two thousand spots awarded their students at Turkish institutions.

Azerbaijan's experience confirmed the hesitations of ex-Soviet Muslims about Turkey in another way. Elçibey's extravagantly pro-Turkish policies and statements led to criticism that he had replaced the Russian "big brother" (starshyi brat) with a Turkish one (agabey).[26] The pro-Turkish program alienated so many constituents that by the time Elçibey faced a military rebellion in June 1993, he lacked a strong base. His old-guard opponents easily overthrew him, brought in communist-era practices, and replaced the Turkish orientation with a Russian one.

Nevertheless, Southern Tier leaders are willing to play along with Middle Easterners—for a price. The Southern Tier urgently needs capital and training; flattery is a small price to pay for these benefits. As Maqsudul Hasan Nuri puts it, referring to the states of the Southern Tier, "these 'six brides' are going to use all their charms and wiles and guile to extract maximum aid and the best business terms for themselves."[27] The apparatchiks yet running the Southern Tier made their way up the slippery hierarchy of the Communist Party by pleasing their superiors, and they have few scruples about pleasing new potentates. It is simply a matter of adapting their verbiage: democracy takes the place of socialism, Islam replaces atheism, the market replaces central planning, Turkish and Persian languages replace Russian. Reality changes very little, however.

Thus, the deputy prime minister of Uzbekistan had no problem appealing to Turks, "Teach us the Turkish language and culture."[28] Islam Karimov, the tough ex-communist leader of Uzbekistan, referred unblushingly to "the holy land of Iran" on arrival in Tehran.[29] If Turks wish to suffuse their politics with emotions, Southern Tier Muslims happily respond in kind. When Demirel told a Central Asian audience, "Your name will be registered in a golden page in the history of the great Turkic community," Uzbekistan's president replied with a rousing "Long live the unity of Uzbeks and Turks."[30] The right prize will prompt almost any words. On the other hand, these words will cease if suitable rewards are not forthcoming.

SOUTHERN TIER IMPACT ON THE MIDDLE EAST

If Middle Eastern states have little influence over the Southern Tier, influence emanating from the latter has greatly affected the Middle East. In the language of social science, the causal arrow goes from Central Asia to the Middle East. Opinion polls confirm this observation. Southern Tier residents consistently show great curiosity in and high expectations of the West and Russia, and much less of both concerning Turks, Iranians, Arabs, and Pakistanis. When asked in January 1992 which country they would like to visit, a representative sampling of almost nine hundred adults living in the Uzbekistan capital of Tashkent placed the United States a strong first, followed by India, Japan, and Turkey. The same poll revealed that six in ten Uzbekistanis want Western countries to help them "build democracy."[31] In contrast, a sampling of one thousand Turks in November 1992 revealed very strong interest in Central Asia; for example, more Turks sought social and cultural relations with Central Asia than with Western Europe, the Middle East, or the United States.[32]

Southern Tier independence has already had a variety of consequences for the Middle East. For example, the Iranians had planned to construct a pipeline across Turkey to Europe, but scuttled this plan in April 1992, choosing instead to lay the line via Azerbaijan, Russia, and Ukraine. This change in route (which is yet to be financed) clearly reflected the Iranian rivalry with Ankara for influence in the Southern Tier. Turks understood this change of mind in light of that competition and threatened to retaliate by encouraging Turkmenistan not to build a pipeline through Iran, but instead under the Caspian Sea, then through Azerbaijan and along the Armenia-Iran border. Ankara raised the stakes in August 1993 when it retaliated for Iranian obstructionism by charging 1,600 German marks for each Iranian truck crossing through Turkey. The Turks made it clear that they would rescind the charge if given access to Azerbaijan via Iranian territory.

Most consequences are larger and vaguer than this, however. The remainder of this chapter looks at two especially dangerous theaters, the Azeri and the Tajik-Pashtun, and assesses the ways in which they can disrupt the Middle East. Then it considers Turkey and the other Middle Eastern states affected by Southern Tier independence. It concludes with some speculations for the long-term future.

BACKGROUND

Muslims of the former Soviet Union number some fifty-five million and live primarily in six southern republics, one in the Trans-Causasus (Azerbaijan) and five in Central Asia (Kazakhstan, Kyrgyzstan, Tajikistan, Turkmenistan, and Uzbekistan). Muslims make up a majority in all these Southern Tier republics except for

Kazakhstan, where they constitute just 42 percent of the population (Russians constitute about 36 percent). Uzbekistan and Kazakhstan have by far the largest populations (20.7 and 16.8 millions, respectively), followed by Azerbaijan (7.2 million), Tajikistan (5.4 million), Kyrgyzstan (4.4 million), and Turkmenistan (3.7 million).

Fifty million residents of the Southern Tier speak various forms of Turkic, some quite intelligible to a resident of Istanbul, others not. The languages of Azerbaijan and Turkmenistan present him with few troubles, but Kazakh is another matter. A native of Istanbul can communicate basic ideas in Kazakh, but little more. Conversing requires several months of residence and study. While it is true, as Paul Henze of the Rand Corporation points out, that *su* means "water" from the Adriatic to China, most other words change across that vast distance. The gradations of difference might make it possible, however, for the Kazakh to pass on his message via a Kyrgyz to an Uzbek, to an Azeri, then to the Istanbul native.

The other five million Muslims of the Southern Tier speak Tajik, an Iranian language intelligible to Tehran's residents. Tajik closely resembles Dari, the Persian language of Afghanistan.

Russian conquest of the Southern Tier began with the conquest of Azerbaijan by 1828. The tsar's forces then needed another forty years to conquer Central Asia, from 1847 to 1885–which was about the same time as the British and French empires reached their maximum extents in Africa and Asia. Indeed, Russian settlement in Central Asia resembled that of the British in Rhodesia or the Portuguese in Angola. But it most closely mirrored French control of Algeria. Algeria and the Southern Tier are both lands of ancient civilization and high Muslim civilization. Like the French in Algeria, Russians settled in Central Asia in substantial numbers. They built new European cities alongside the old Muslim ones. They appropriated the best land and monopolized the key jobs. The main differences are three: Russians used far more brutal methods than the French or any other European colonial power; blue water divides Algeria from France, while the Southern Tier is connected by land to Russia, thereby obscuring the colonial quality of Russian rule; and the Soviets gave colonialism a modern cast, turning it into a seemingly altruistic enterprise for the sake of "younger brothers" in the Southern Tier.

During the Soviet period, and especially before 1980, this colonized Muslim body experienced a nearly total isolation from its coreligionists to the south. With very few exceptions, borders were completely closed. This meant, for example, that travel between Baku and Tehran, just 350 miles apart, required going via Moscow's Sheremetyevo airport, a detour of 2,400 miles. (In American terms, that is like going from Boston to Baltimore via Houston.) Moscow manipulated scripts to reduce communications, imposing the Cyrillic alphabet to distance Soviet Turcophones[33] from the Latin script used in Turkey and the Arabic script used elsewhere in the Muslim Middle East. Bombarded by Marxism-Leninism, Soviet Muslims could not participate in the culture of Islam. Only a handful of them made the pilgrimage to Mecca or studied at Islamic institutions of higher learning in Cairo or Fez. At the same time, glossy propaganda featured peoples called "Muslims of the Soviet East," and a steady parade of Third World delegations was routed through Tashkent to witness the wonders of Soviet civilization in Islamic garb.

Seventy years of isolation (and 150 years of Russian dominance) came abruptly and unexpectedly to an end in late 1991 with the collapse of the Soviet Union.[34] One anecdote captures the astonishing speed of this transformation: On his arrival in Turkey on the morning of December 16, 1991, President Islam Karimov of Uzbekistan received no official honors, for Ankara viewed his republic as part of the Soviet Union; that very afternoon, the Turks recognized all the Soviet republics as independent states, changing Karimov's status. On leaving Turkey three days later, he received the twenty-one-gun salute reserved for heads of state.

Liberation and independence came not only quickly, but also nearly unasked for. Soviet Muslims did very little to bring about the end of communism or to break up the USSR; they simply benefited from actions taken elsewhere. Bakhadir Abdurazakov, a Soviet ambassador of Uzbek origins, captured the general astonishment this way: "The disintegration of the empire was God's gift. Really, it is enough to make one believe."[35] Not only were the Southern Tier leaders not involved in winning their independence, but in many cases they did not even welcome it, remaining loyal to the old order longer than did the Russians themselves! Kazakhstan's government, for example, never declared its withdrawal from the Soviet Union. As Martha Brill Olcott writes, "Few peoples of the world have ever been forced to become independent nations. Yet that is precisely what happened to the five Central Asia republics."[36]

These unusual circumstances explain why the new Southern Tier governments were so woefully unprepared for sovereignty. Abdurrahim Pulatov, leader of the opposition in Uzbekistan, ruefully looks back on this experience and declares, "Independence came to Central Asia too quickly and too easily."[37] A Central Asian economist expressed this even more strongly, comparing the new republics to "a baby who has lost his parents."[38] The apparatchiks who still make most decisions knew how to execute economic and social orders from Moscow, not how to incubate a free market or solve ethnic problems; and they certainly have little experience in making foreign policy.

The abruptness of Central Asian independence spawned many problems. Thus far, two stand out as the most dangerous, one concerning Azeris, the other Tajiks.

TWO DANGEROUS THEATERS

Azeris and Tajiks have several features in common. Both populate and control small republics at the edge of the former Soviet Union. Both connect linguistically and religiously to several neighboring countries, and Iran in particular. Both are in the throes of violent upheavals that threaten their entire regions.

The Azeri Theater

While the travails in the Caucasus impinge on many countries—Russia, Georgia, Armenia, Turkey, Iran—they center on Azerbaijan for two main reasons. Twice as many Azeris live in Iran as in Azerbaijan, raising acute tensions between Tehran and the newly independent government in Baku; and Azerbaijan's war with Armenia tempts Turkey and Iran to intervene, with potentially cataclysmic results.

Iranian Azerbaijan. Azerbaijan is a nation divided in two, with the independent Republic of Azerbaijan (capital, Baku) in the north and the traditional Iranian province of Azerbaijan (capital, Tabriz) in the south. A mere six million Azeris live in independent Azerbaijan, versus some twelve million in Iran (where they constitute by far that country's largest ethnic minority).[39] Moscow conquered northern Azerbaijan by 1828; from then until January 1990, the two halves of Azerbaijan had no serious hope of uniting, except in 1945–1946, when Stalin controlled Iranian Azerbaijan.

Baku's emergence as an independent capital has fundamentally changed the equation, inspiring Tabriz to dream of independence and union. With the election of Ebulfez Ali Elçibey as president of Azerbaijan in June 1992, nationalist Azeri ambitions to unite Azerbaijan increased dramatically, only to decline a year later when Elçibey lost power. Elçibey referred to his country as "northern Azerbaijan"[40] and regularly called for the cultural autonomy of Azeris living in Iran, the uniting of the Azerbaijani region of Iran with his country, and even the overthrow of the Islamic Republic of Iran.[41]

Especially during the Soviet era, Azeris living in Iran had little desire to join their northern confreres. ("When the Tabriz residents interviewed in 1952 were asked about sentiment for union with Azerbaijanis now in the Soviet Union, their . . . unanimous response was one of incredulity.")[42] Even today, they feel unsure of their identity—Turcophones who happen to live in Iran or Iranians who happen to speak Turkic. But the emergence of an independent Azerbaijan has an impact. If ex-Soviet Azeris are politically independent of Moscow, why do those living in Iran remain subject to Tehran? Nationalist appeals coming from Baku resonate. Northerners fleeing their troubles move south and take with them nationalist ideas. They win rapturous receptions in the south, especially when the two sides connect culturally (for example, through poetry) or politically (through anti-Armenian slogans).[43]

Even with Elçibey out of power, the Iranian authorities rightly worry that independent Azerbaijan will eventually try to wrest away Iranian Azerbaijan. Loss of this area would have several major consequences for Iran. It would reduce the country's population by about one-fourth. It would provide a land bridge between

Turkey and northern Azerbaijan, now separated by Armenia, strengthening the Turcophone bloc to the north. It might inspire Iranian Kurds and Turkmens (also known as Turkomans) to break from Iran to join their brethren across the border, leading to a breakup of the Iranian polity.

To protect against these developments, Iranian leaders strongly denounced Elçibey and helped the opposition forces in his country. They moved Nakhichevan, an autonomous and geographically separate portion of Azerbaijan, toward the Iranian orbit by maneuvering politically and building up trade relations. They helped Haydar Aliyev topple Elçibey in June 1993. More defensively, they split Iranian Azerbaijan into two provinces (Sabalan and East Azerbaijan, with capitals in Ardebil and Tabriz), in an apparent effort to reduce a sense of Azeri nationhood. These efforts succeeded in containing Azeri nationalism to the point that Tehran felt confident enough to relax long-standing prohibitions against Azeri Turkish in 1992, allow an Azerbaijan consulate in Tabriz in June 1993, and open a direct Tabriz-Baku flight one month later. But it could yet lose control.

War with Armenia. War between Azerbaijan and Armenia poses even greater dangers. Fighting began in early 1988 when the Armenian leadership in Yerevan, sensing the decline of Moscow's power, launched a military campaign to seize control of Nagorno-Karabakh, a mountainous area populated by Armenians but located within Azerbaijan's borders. Azeris resisted, and the conflict escalated into a brutal struggle of mutual sieges, embargo, and massacre. While Armenians have suffered terribly from hunger and cold, their forces have fared well on the battlefield; by late 1993, they held nearly 20 percent of Azerbaijan's territory.[44]

Turks have a strong visceral sympathy for Azeris, an emotion that Azeris reciprocate. The two speak almost the same language and have a history of close relations. Symbolic of this, Azeris (alone of the ex-Soviet Muslims) have actually taken steps to adopt the Latin alphabet, have chosen to be represented abroad by Turkey, and have asked Ankara "to be a center for our country's relations with the outside world."[45] They proclaimed an adherence to "Atatürk's way."[46] Also, Turks and Azeris share a history of conflict with Armenians. In addition, Turkey counts many citizens of Azeri origins.

Not surprisingly, Turkey's leaders feel strong popular pressure to join the battle on Azerbaijan's side. Mustafa Necati Özfatura, a pan-Turkic nationalist, pushed for alliance with Azerbaijan, stating that "an attack on Azerbaijan would be considered an attack on Turkey."[47] Özal called for Turkey to help Azerbaijan fight the Armenians. A May 1992 poll showed one-third of the Turkish electorate supporting armed intervention. Pressure also came from Azerbaijan, where leaders use a kind of code, calling on Turkish support to help the Azerbaijanis "consolidate" their independence—that is, control the territories contested by Armenians.[48] Prime Minister Tansu Çiller subsequently warned that "if one spot of Nakhichevan is touched," she would ask parliament to authorize war on Armenia.[49]

Although 1,600 Turkish military experts were sent to Azerbaijan (where they were joined by two hundred pan-Turkic militants of the Nationalist Action Party),[50] Turks generally maintained what Demirel characterized as a "coolheaded approach,"[51] resisting the temptation and the pressure to intervene. They did so for very good reasons. In the first place, Turkey needs Armenia for access to Azerbaijan and Central Asia—be it transportation links or oil pipelines. Second, Turkey has enough problems with neighbors (Aegean islands and Cyprus with Greece, ethnic Turks with Bulgaria, water with Syria, Kurds with Iraq and Iran) without needing another hostile state. Third, siding with Azerbaijan could jeopardize Turkey's carefully nurtured relationship with the U.S. government. When arguing for restraint, Demirel explicitly acknowledged the danger of an erosion in his country's international position:

> When I was received by U.S. President Bush in Washington on 11 February [1992], I told him that if the United States and Western countries back Armenia in this conflict, then we will have to stand by Azerbaijan, and this will turn into a conflict between Muslims and Christians that will last for years.[52]

On another occasion, Demirel commented, "The world will move against Turkey if we close all our doors and move against Armenia."[53] To this, Foreign Minister Hikmet Çetin added: "The people in the United States would create an uproar if the Armenian people die of hunger and cold."[54]

Fourth, the Caucasus could explode if Turkey joined Azerbaijan's war against Armenia. Russia, Iran, and some Western countries might respond by assisting Armenia. Russia, the Armenians' traditional protector, explicitly raised the possibility of intervention. In a May 1992 statement, Marshal Yevgeny Shaposhnikov of the Commonwealth of Independent States (CIS) warned that were Turkey to join the conflict, "we shall be on the brink of a new world war."[55] While exaggerated, this threat did have a sobering impact in Turkey. For good measure, the Armenian foreign minister two days later threatened to take recourse to its CIS security pact if Turkey intervened militarily in the Caucasus. To prevent a Russian-Turkish confrontation, Çiller traveled to Moscow in September 1993, and the two sides set up a hot line.

These reasons impelled Turkey's leadership to exercise admirable restraint toward Armenia. It has even made goodwill gestures, such as supplying one hundred thousand tons of grain, thus helping that country circumvent the economic blockade imposed by Azerbaijan. More surprising yet, Turkey contracted in November 1992 to sell three hundred million kilowatt-hours of electricity to the Armenian energy grid at a lower rate than that paid by Turkish consumers. (The electricity was to be supplied, ironically, via power lines installed during the 1980s to carry Soviet electricity to Turkey.) Foreign Minister Çetin justified this aid by arguing that it shows "Ankara is not Yerevan's enemy."[56] In addition, Turks worried that, cut off from outside supplies of energy, the Armenians would reactivate their Chernobyl-style nuclear reactor at Medzamor. But Azeris vehemently objected to this sale, calling it a "stab in the back" and a "betrayal" of their cause,[57] and their Turkish partisans protested loudly. In the end, the Turks sent heating fuel to Armenia, though these supplies (and all other humanitarian aid) were cut as a result of Armenia's breaking out of the Nagorno-Karabakh area in March 1993 and capturing large amounts of Azerbaijani territory.

Armenia also had compelling reasons to maintain good relations with Turkey. Having lost its historic Russian protector and being nearly surrounded by Turcophone Muslims, it needed to get along with the strongest of its neighbors. Also, Turkey provided its best access to the outside world. In gratitude for Turkey's goodwill gestures, the Armenians offered "to open all our roads" for transporting humanitarian aid to Azerbaijan.[58] To encourage Turkey to remain neutral, Yerevan ignored the vehement anti-Turk sentiments of its own population[59] and downplayed the issue of genocide during World War I. When asked about the latter, Deputy Foreign Minister Arman Kirakosyan replied, "Armenia wants to look forward in its relations with Turkey. Genocide does not concern the Armenia government. . . . Any incidents took place before the republic in Turkey was established."[60] Yerevan even asked its diaspora brethren, much to their annoyance, to ease up on the anti-Turkish campaign. Strangely, then, the Caucasus war has so far led to an improvement in Turkish-Armenian relations, a testimony to the maturity of the leaders on both sides, and enhanced Turkey's lagging reputation in the West.

Unfortunately, the strength and patience of moderates has limits. Should atrocities against Azeris continue or Armenians succeed in taking more and more of Azerbaijan's territory, Turkey could intervene militarily, with disastrous results for nearly everyone. On the Armenian side, continued war, isolation, and impoverishment reduces the appeal of President Levon Ter-Petrosian's middle course, while winning support for the extremist Dashnak Party.[61]

As for Iran, it formed a quasi-alliance with Armenia, helping this Christian nation against its Muslim neighbor. This may explain why Armenian forces pushed their offensive toward Azerbaijan's border with Iran in August 1993. Tehran moved extra troops to the area of its border with Turkey and sought to undermine Azerbaijan's control of Nakhichevan. The Iranians did so because they share key concerns with Armenians about Turkey and Turcophone unity, though for different reasons. They also can help each other. For example, Armenia's leaders offer themselves as a bridge to the West and make their scientists available for Iranian employment. James M. Dorsey claims, with only some exaggeration, that the Armenian-Iranian alliance "could reshape the political map of the Middle East."[62]

Because fighting in the Caucasus so closely touches on Turkish and Iranian interests alike, it could embroil them in a conflict neither seeks. "If there is to be a major war between these two," William Ward Maggs writes, "it will come in Armenia and Azerbaijan, where their interests will most actively collide."[63] In sum, while Azerbaijani independence creates problems for both Turkey and Iran, it also presents opportunities for the former.

The Tajik Theater

Central Asia is a cauldron of real and potential troubles. Afghanistan's civil war began in 1979 and continues; Tajikistan's civil war began in 1992. Border problems could cause as much trouble in Central Asia as in the Caucasus; ten territories are in contention. One observer calls these a "time bomb" for the region.[64] Religious, ethnic, and ideological problems afflict the region. Religion's cutting edge concerns Sunnis and Shi'ites. Leading ethnic groups include Kyrgyz, Uzbeks, Tajiks, and Pashtuns. The first three came to blows in Osh, a corner of the Fergana Valley. The second three are engaged in Afghanistan. As for ideology, fundamentalist Islam constitutes the main force. It comes in several varieties (Khomeinist, Pakistani, Tajik). Communism used to offer an alternate vision, but with the collapse of the Soviet Union, it is now reduced to the common background of a self-interested group that benefited from the old system.

These conflicts threaten the stability of the entire region between Iran and China, but we concentrate here on the impact on Afghanistan and Pakistan.

Afghanistan. As in the Caucasus, ethnic mixing bedevils politics in the Tajik-Pashtun theater. From the birth of Afghanistan in the eighteenth century until the Soviet invasion, Pashtuns (also known as Pathans and Pukhtuns) constituted more than half of the population and ruled the country. As a result of massive emigration during the 1979–1989 war, mostly to Pakistan, today they make up just one-third of Afghanistan's population, or about five million. In contrast, Pakistan now hosts twice that number of Pashtuns, though they constitute less than 10 percent of Pakistan's population.

Similarly, more Tajiks live in Afghanistan (about 5 million) than in Tajikistan (about 3.3 million), although they make up a smaller proportion of the population in the former (35 percent vs. 62 percent). Additionally, some million Tajiks live in Uzbekistan, one hundred thousand in Kazakhstan, and thirty thousand in Xinjiang Province of China.[65]

These figures point to two main sources of trouble. First, the imbalance in populations (Afghanistan hosts more Tajiks than Tajikistan, Pakistan hosts more Pashtuns than Afghanistan) is a surefire recipe for instability. As elsewhere (Iran hosts more Azeris than Azerbaijan, more Turkmens than Turkmenistan; Jordan hosts more Palestinians than "Palestine"), a national group that lives primarily outside its own primary region is virtually foreordained to irredentism.

Second, Tajiks hope to take advantage of their new numerical strength in Afghanistan to wrest power from the Pashtuns. Each of these peoples constitutes about one-third of Afghanistan's fifteen million inhabitants;[66] the rest of the population divides among Hazara (about 15 percent), Uzbeks (12 percent), and Turkmens (5 percent). Afghanistan's civil war has produced military leaders from the two largest ethnic groups and from the Uzbeks.

Gulbuddin Hekmatyar, the leader of Hizb-i Islami, represents the Pashtun determination not to cede power in Afghanistan. As is so often the case with nationalist leaders, he was born outside his ethnic heartland, in the predominantly Tajik area of Kunduz. Though he is widely seen in the West as a fundamentalist Muslim extremist, Hekmatyar's record reveals him to be an opportunist of the first rank. The Pakistani government, working through the Interservices Intelligence (ISI), found Hekmatyar an ideally pliable agent of its power during the war and used him as a way to bring the *mujahedeen* under its control.

Ahmed Shah Masud, the hero of the anti-Soviet resistance and defense minister of Afghanistan, represents the ethnic Tajik intent to win power from Pashtuns. Although an immensely capable leader who united the Tajiks under his command and made common cause with Uzbeks, he has been unable to extend his ministry's mandate to the Pashtun areas; also, he has repeatedly lost ground to Uzbeks. Indeed, Masud could not even hold on to Tajik regions. Again, Masud's reputation in the West belies reality; though widely seen as religiously moderate, he is the genuine fundamentalist.

Gen. Abdurrashid Dostam ("the most powerful man in Afghanistan today")[67] represents the interests of the largest people in Central Asia, the Uzbeks. And, as befits a former military leader fighting for the Soviet-sponsored regime, he represents the forces of antifundamentalism. For both these reasons, Dostam has particularly close relations with Karimov of Uzbekistan; his family lives in Tashkent, and the two leaders have discussed his going independent. This is a realistic possibility, for, based in the northwestern Afghan city of Mazar-i Sharif, Dostam has managed to carve out for himself "virtually a separate state" or "a state within a state."[68] Indeed, Mazar-i Sharif already boasts consulates of Iran, Uzbekistan, and Pakistan.

Rival forces have thus effectively divided Afghanistan into three zones: Pashtuns under their chieftains and Hekmatyar control the south of Afghanistan; Uzbeks under Dostam rule the north; and the government of Iran enjoys predominant influence in the west, where it controls a grouping of Shi'ites, the Hizb-i Wahdat. (Tajiks under Masud have been restricted to the northeast, largely squeezed out of the country's power politics.) Each of these powers looks to bring its region of Afghanistan in closer association with a state beyond the border—Uzbekistan, Pakistan, and Iran, respectively. (And the Tajiks look to Tajikistan.)

The civil war in Afghanistan directly affects surrounding countries. For example, the fall of Afghanistan's President Najibullah to fundamentalist Muslims in April 1992 inspired fundamentalists in Tajikistan just a month later to bring down their own communist ruler, Rakhmon Nabiev.

Afghanistan's northern border has been highly porous for a decade. During wartime, official Afghanistan forces virtually ignored the formal lines separating their country from the Soviet Union, and the *mujahedeen* imitated them, laying mines in Soviet territory and recruiting among Muslims in the Soviet Union. The *mujahedeen* also directed radio broadcasts to the north. Today, the old border hardly exists, as Dostam's ethnic Uzbek militia routinely crosses into Tajikistan to protect fellow Uzbeks there. The authorities in Uzbekistan blame the proliferation of weapons among ethnic Tajiks in their country on smuggling from Afghanistan. Going in the other direction, over one hundred thousand Tajiks have braved the frigid waters of the Amu Darya to flee the war in Tajikistan and seek refuge in Afghanistan. On arrival, the young men among them are armed, and some return to battle the government in Tajikistan.

This disappearing border gives substance to the hope of many Tajiks, including Masud, to join northern Afghanistan and Tajikistan in a unified Tajik state. As my colleague Khalid Durán notes, the process is fairly far along: "the reunification of Tajikistan—one Afghan, the other formerly Soviet—has progressed considerably since 1988, even though it did not make headlines as Germany did."[69] In all likelihood, such a state would enforce an extreme fundamentalist Islamic vision of society comparable to that in Iran—but in this case Sunni.

The fate of Tajikistan influences the course of events in Afghanistan, which in turn influences politics in Pakistan. To the north, Tajikistan influences Uzbekistan, which influences Kazakhstan, which has a potentially major bearing on Russia. In a sense, then, Tajikistan stands at a pivot, capable of creating problems from the Indian Ocean to the North Pole. For these reasons, Boris Rumer rightly suggests that a Greater Tajikistan "must be a nightmare for [Uzbekistan's President Islam] Karimov. But such prospects ought to disturb [Russia's President Boris] Yeltsin as well. Indeed, such prospects ought to be unsettling for Western states."[70]

Peace and stability in the region depend in large part on Afghanistan, and its future will be determined largely by developments in Tajikistan. Protracted civil war in Tajikistan means Central Asia will burn.

Pakistan. Conceptually, Pakistan lies distant from Central Asia. Geographically, however, it is a near neighbor. Pakistan's capital city, Islamabad, is closer to Tashkent than to its own port city of Karachi; Lahore is closer to Dushanbe than to Karachi. Pashtuns and other peoples of the country's north look more to Central Asia for trade and culture than to India.

Pakistan has substantial interests in Central Asia. Fundamentalist Muslims from Pakistan have their own variant of Islam to promote; the radical group Tabligh-i Jama'at is especially active in Central Asia.

As other doors have closed, Central Asia has taken on major importance as a place for skilled Pakistani emigrants to exercise their talents. They operate as traders, professionals, and executives in Central Asia, a culturally familiar environment in which they feel at ease. As Russians departed, Pakistani entrepreneurs quickly found niches for themselves, especially connecting Central Asia to the outside world. They opened banks and hotels, trained business personnel, and established an airline. They work as doctors and college instructors. In one display of raw financial power, Pakistanis responded to a request from Kazakhstan's prime minister by raising a $100 million loan within three days.

Yacub Tabani, a young entrepreneur, may head the list of Pakistanis active in Central Asia. He helped set up Uzbekistan Airlines and provides management assistance to nearly all the new airlines of the region. Tabani handled fertilizer, chemicals, and cotton for the governments; he set up garment and cigarette factories; and he built a hotel in Tashkent.[71]

Finally, the Pakistan state has a perceived need to develop strategic depth against India; Central Asia offers geographic vastness and a sizable population. This defensive concern may imply grand nationalist ambitions, as Hafeez Malik of Villanova University explains: "Pakistanis have started to speculate that Pakistan's natural habitat includes Turkey, Iran, Afghanistan, and the Central Asia Republics."[72] Sometimes called "Islamistan," this region gets counterpoised against the Arabic-speaking south.

The Pakistani government has tried hard to establish close relations with the Southern Tier states through diplomacy and transportation links. By late 1991, Islamabad had offered unconditional support for Azerbaijan's cause against Armenia. It recognized the Southern Tier republics just days after Turkey did, then sent a large delegation to Central Asia to establish cultural and economic ties. The Pakistani authorities strenuously tried to establish special relations with Kyrgyzstan. To win favor in oil-rich Turkmenistan (dubbed by some "the second Kuwait"), Islamabad offered $10 million in credit.

Pakistan's government plans ambitious transport connections to Central Asia. It has proposed building a railway across Afghanistan to link up to the trains of the former Soviet Union. A new road along the Amu Darya connects Mazar-i Sharif in north Afghanistan with Chardzhou, the second-largest city in Turkmenistan, but unsettled conditions have much reduced traffic. For now, once-weekly PIA flights to Tashkent and Almaty (Kazakhstan's capital) constitute the sole transportation link between Pakistan and Central Asia. This air connection does not suffice, however; for Pakistanis fully to exploit the Central Asian connection, they need a land route via Afghanistan.

A land link in turn implies the need for peace in Afghanistan, which partially explains why Pakistan's policy dramatically changed in late 1991, when Islamabad abandoned Hekmatyar. (Another imperative for seeking a settlement was to induce the Afghan refugees to go home.) With Hekmatyar in power in Kabul, the Pakistani government would have gained its long-sought strategic hinterland. But Islamabad diminished its support for Hekmatyar because it had an eye on Central Asia. As Central Asia beckoned, using Hekmatyar to establish a military hinterland lost priority.

In sum, Central Asia's independence has fundamentally altered the civil war in Afghanistan, adding new elements and altering Pakistan's calculations.

IMPACT ON TURKEY

"Turkey is like a strong castle in a tempestuous sea," President Özal confidently declared in late 1991.[73] But the abrupt independence of tens of millions of Muslims in Central Asia, the Caucasus, and the Balkans[74] has caused some leakage in the Republic of Turkey. The stolid pro–North Atlantic Treaty Organization course of recent decades is giving way to an unfamiliar excitement and confusion. The Southern Tier's independence has affected politics in Turkey, with large and unpredictable consequences, making this country particularly deserving of attention.

Changed Politics

Thanks to the Soviet bloc's collapse, a new and excited tone pervaded the Turkish body politic in 1991 and 1992. "Heady days for Turks, these."[75] The Turkish population got engaged in foreign policy in new ways, and the government adopted an unheard-of activism. Mainstream politicians articulated ideas about pan-Turkic nationalism that had been the exclusive preserve of the fringe right. In all, the situation led Turks to see themselves as a more active force in the world.

Foreign Policy Activism. For decades, Ankara avoided taking foreign policy initiatives, preferring to follow its allies. This held doubly true in policy vis-à-vis the Soviet Union. The Soviet collapse inspired Turks quite suddenly to see themselves as a major regional power, relatively stable, militarily potent, and economically strong, roles enhanced by the Turkish role in Operation Desert Storm. They variously portrayed Turkey as the natural leader of the Balkans, the Black Sea area, the northern Middle East, and world Turcophones. The Turkish decision of mid-December 1991 to recognize all the republics of the former Soviet Union as independent states, possibly the most daring Turkish choice in decades, marked the emergence of this new confidence. One newspaper commentary viewed this as the first time Turkey had ever acted "without considering the decisions of other countries."[76]

A stunning series of regional initiatives also occurred in 1992. President Turgut Özal announced that "three important areas, the Balkans, the Caucasus and the Middle East, have opened in front of Turkey,"[77] and the government followed up on this vision. Ankara conceived the Black Sea Economic Cooperation Zone and hosted a summit meeting of member states in June. It hosted a summit conference of Turcophone leaders in October, not coincidentally on Turkey's independence day. And it hosted a Balkan summit in November. Further, the Turks infused new life into the Economic Cooperation Organization, which links Turkey to Iran, Pakistan, and other states. Perhaps most interesting were the attempts to reach out to long-time adversaries (Greece, Armenia, the Kurds), inspired both by a practical need to improve the country's diplomatic position and international reputation and by a sense of power that implied largesse.

Turkish diplomacy took on a slightly frenzied quality—new embassies, huge delegations traveling to many countries, and lots of visitors. On a single day in January 1992, for example, no fewer than three presidents—those of Albania, Serbia, and Azerbaijan—found themselves in Ankara. Some guests came from places only Ankara cared much about, such as Tatarstan. After years of acceding to Arab wishes, Ankara boldly invited Israel's President Chaim Herzog to participate in the quincentennial anniversary of the arrival of Sephardic Jews from Spain in 1492.

The 1993 dispatch of a Turkish unit to Somalia and the appointment of a Turkish general to the mission constituted a small but revealingly far-flung endeavor of a sort that would have been unlikely in previous years.

But then the mood passed almost as quickly as it arose. An October 1992 summit of Turcophone leaders in Ankara signaled the troubles ahead; Kazakhstan's President Nursultan Nazarbaev refused to go along with the Turkish agenda out of concern not to upset Moscow. The June 1993 collapse of Elçibey's government finally punctured the romance with the new states. Turkish leaders realized the limits of their influence and retreated to a more passive foreign policy.

Ethnic Identification. In this century alone, substantial numbers of immigrants have come from Bosnia, Albania, Greece, Bulgaria, Cyprus, Iraq, Iran, the Russian empire/Soviet Union, Afghanistan, and China. Numbers are hard to come by and are probably exaggerated: Turks of Azeri origins, for example, are said to number six million, while nearly ten million Turks trace their origins to the Balkans. Taking inflated figures into account, the descendants of these immigrants probably number about twelve million, or one-fifth of the Turkish population.

While immigrants assimilated into Turkish life, they yet remembered their ancestry. During the Cold War, the authorities in Ankara suppressed connections to the old countries for the simple reason that most of them had communist governments. The Soviet bloc's collapse ended that suppression and raised the specter of heightened ethnic consciousness within Turkey. As Caucasian peoples like the Abkhaz, Chechen, and Ossetians asserted their identity, Turkish citizens of such origins found their ethnic affiliations newly important. Graham Fuller notes that "in 1991, for the first time ever, Turks began to start talking about their own various geographic origins as Turks from diverse areas."[78]

In one case, that of Bosnia, an actual ethnic lobby emerged in 1992. Serbian efforts at "ethnic cleansing" suddenly gave the four million Turkish citizens who trace their origins to Bosnia (twice as many as the Muslims in Bosnia itself) a special political cause of their own. From the time the war began in early 1992, "they lived with the rhythms of combat in the ex-Yugoslavia, crying for the deaths, indignant about the general indifference for their former patrimony, and trying to soften the lot of refugees stranded in the former Ottoman capital."[79] Folk dancing gave way to refugee absorption efforts. Özal referred to Balkan immigrants, creating a "bridge of obligation" between Turkey and their lands of origins.[80] Even the loss of the Serbo-Croatian language did not dim the sense of ethnic solidarity. The mother of Mesut Yilmaz,[81] a former prime minister, came from Bosnia, which helps explain why he was especially vocal on the situation in ex-Yugoslavia. Indeed, Çetin repeatedly mentioned the Bosnian element as one of the reasons his government took special interest in former Yugoslavia.[82]

This fracturing of the Turkish body politic seems likely to continue and to gain in importance.[83]

Worries about Immigration. Turmoil in the Balkans, the Caucasus, and Central Asia sent waves of emigrants into Turkey. The Bulgarian campaign of assimilation in the late 1980s prompted 320,000 of its Turkish population to move to Turkey. (With the fall of the communist regime, however, half of these returned to Bulgaria.) In 1992 the Turkish assembly unanimously accepted fifty thousand Meskhetian Turks from southern Georgia and indicated a readiness to take in the Akhista (or Akhaltsikhe) Turks of Kyrgyzstan. By November 1992, fifteen thousand Bosnians had newly arrived in Turkey, of whom fully fourteen thousand settled near relatives. Serbian aggression could cause these numbers to multiply many times; Muhammad Çengic, the deputy prime minister of Bosnia-Herzegovina, announced in May 1992 that about one million Bosnians hoped to emigrate to Turkey.[84]

Like Germans, many Turks feel "the boat is full" (that is, their country has reached full capacity) and actively try to discourage future immigrants by subsidizing them in their places of origins. Ankara is explicit about this: "We aim to provide incentives for Turks to stay where they were born," acknowledged Minister of State Orhan Kilercioglu.[85] Toward this end, it provides courses on marketing, management, and public administration, and it encourages Turkish businesses to invest in Bulgaria.

Changed Ideas

In the course of establishing the Republic of Turkey, Kemal Atatürk explicitly renounced two types of claims: to form a union with distant Turcophones and to regain the lost Ottoman Empire. His doctrine of disengagement from international affairs ("Peace at home, peace in the world") guided Turkish politicians for seventy years. But the collapse of the Soviet bloc has suddenly opened the possibility of a more ambitious foreign policy. Some Turks have thought through the possibilities of pan-Turkic nationalism and reasserting Ottoman connections. Together, these ideas have created a new sense of Turkey's importance in the world.

Pan-Turkic Nationalism. Pan-Turkism, the belief that Turkic speakers from Albania to the farther reaches of Siberia constitute a single people and should form some kind of union, has been rediscovered. Extremist figures like Alparslan Türkeş of the National Work Party (MCP) found themselves relegated to virtual irrelevance during the era of Soviet strength. But in 1992 his call for Turcophone countries to unify on the basis of "Unity in language, idea, and work"[86] found a new, larger audience.

Süleyman Demirel, the former prime minister, hardly issued so direct an appeal, but he did occasionally echo Türkeş. As the Turkish leader most affected by the prospect of Turcophone emancipation, he sometimes got carried away with an uncharacteristic enthusiasm. Here is a small sampling of Demirel's statements:

- Returning from a tour of the Turcophone republics: "My head is turning. I am very excited."[87]

- Meeting a leader of the Crimean Tatars: "You were never alone, and you are not alone now; we are all together."[88]

- Addressing an audience in Kazakhstan: "Your name will be registered in a golden page in the history of the great Turkic community."[89]

- Dedicating a new bridge between Turkey and Nakhichevan: the bridge meant "the two countries became one again."[90]

Demirel announced that "a new Turkic world has emerged" or, even more ambitiously, "a new world has emerged and a new map is taking shape."[91] He proclaimed that Turcophones inhabit an area of ten thousand square kilometers and noted that "five new flags with crescents have been added to Turkey's crescent-and-star flag. The great Turkic world extending from the Adriatic to the China Sea should intermingle."[92] Demirel enjoyed his new role as chief Turcophone leader. After Islam Karimov of Uzbekistan called him "big brother" *(agabey)*,[93] a highly pleased Demirel often repeated this title.[94]

Of course, Demirel did not alone feel excitement about Turkey's Turcopone hinterland. "We were all alone; now there are five others," a senior Turkish official explained.[95] To which an intellectual added: "It has been a great thrill for Turks to realize that they are no longer alone in the world."[96] This thrill, more than dreams of glory, lay behind the statements of Demirel and other politicians. It is also important to underline that these statements did not have operational consequences.

Neo-Ottomanism. Nostalgia for empire grew noticeably with the Soviet collapse. After three generations of living the prosaic reality of the Turkish Republic, memories of the Ottoman Empire revived and appear to exert a strong, if slightly illicit, allure. Dreams of recapturing the grandeur of the old empire found new expression. Çengiz Candar, who dubbed these sentiments "neo-Ottomanism,"[97] stated, "The time has come to reconsider [Atatürk's] policy. We cannot stick to the old taboos while the world is changing and new opportunities are arising for Turkey. We have to think big."[98]

Many in Turkey echoed this view. Özal announced that "current historical circumstances permit Turkey to reverse the shrinking process that began at the walls of Vienna [in 1683]."[99] He saw the inhabitants of former Ottoman lands outside Turkey as "children of those who yesterday were our countrymen and the kinsmen of our present countrymen." Reestablishing relations with them is "a natural right and duty." Özal asked, "How could it be otherwise, when we have lived 800 to 900 years together and have been cut off from each other only for the last 70 or 80 years!"[100] Nur Vergin of Bilkent University eloquently captured the sense of longing for empire:

> Place names that we sealed away in our subconscious as a result of collective amnesia and which we tried to remember as ordinary geographic areas have begun to reappear in our daily lives: Bosnia, Macedonia, Kurdistan, the Caucasus, and beyond that, Transoxiana [Central Asia].[101]

Even a pan-Turkic nationalist like Özfatura incorporated elements of neo-Ottomanism. On the grounds that the former Ottoman subjects look to Turkey as their liberator, he called on Turkish troops to intervene in Nakhichevan, Nagorno-Karabakh, Bosnia-Herzegovina, Kosovo, and Macedonia.[102]

Turkey's Importance. Turkish politicians, with Süleyman Demirel again leading the way, made audacious statements about Turkey's new importance. Demirel asserted that "the presence of an additional five flags beside the star and crescent boosted our prestige and that of the Turkic republics."[103] "A new world is being born," he declared, "and Turkey is a window on it. . . . This is a centuries-old dream."[104] "Everyone has to take Turkey more seriously," he told Azeribaijanis in Baku.[105] In part, the prime minister premised these assertions on economics. "When we take a collective view of the economic potential of our [Turcophone] region we can see that it is one of the world's most promising regions . . . if we pool our resources then there is no obstacle we cannot surmount."[106] Demirel let his imagination get carried away when he declared that "the oil and natural gas reserves in Central Asia and the Caucasus are bigger than all the world's reserves,"[107] an obviously false assertion.

Nor was Demirel alone in these grandiose declarations. Özal asserted in his 1993 New Year's message: "Turkey's region is the most critical region in the world."[108] The writer Attila Ilhan stated,

"Turkey can extend its region of influence all the way to the Yellow River [in China]."[109] Husamettin Cindoruk, speaker of the Turkish Grand National Assembly, announced that "Turkish unity will bring peace, tranquility, and stability to the world."[110] In perhaps the most extravagant statement of all, Kamran Inan, a minister of state, averred that "Turkey is a candidate to be the strongest state in the West in the period following the year 2010."[111]

Turks not only made lofty statements about the future, but sometimes convinced themselves that Turkey had already attained more than was the case. Just as Mikhail Gorbachev announced the demise of the Soviet Union, Hikmet Çetin declared:

> Turkey is no longer the peripheral country it used to be during the cold war. It has gained a more central position on the map. . . . Indeed, in an area that extends from the Atlantic to the Chinese border, Turkey is at the focal point of the sensitive balances.[112]

Çetin also made the astonishing statement that "if you look at world problems, you can see that none of them could be tackled without Turkey."[113] State Minister Ikram Cayhun declared that Turkey's progress in the 1980s made it "one of the developed states of the world,"[114] which it plainly did not.

So far, this rhetoric about pan-Turkic nationalism, a revived Ottoman sphere, and Turkey's importance has not caused any problems. Quite the contrary, realistic policies and sober actions have been the order of the day. Further, Prime Minister Çiller has been almost silent on these topics. There is no immediate danger that Turks, taking inflated statements by politicians to heart, will get carried away with a sense of their own power, leading to serious errors. But these statements sow seeds that, while not harmful in themselves, could unsettle Turkey in the future. Many problems surround Turks and involve them—Bosnia, Greece, Armenia and Azerbaijan, northern Iraq, Syria, Cyprus—so the stakes are very high. An unnamed Western diplomat in Ankara summed up this concern: "We're heading into uncharted waters. It's very difficult, very dangerous and alarming."[115]

OTHER EFFECTS ON THE MIDDLE EAST

Turkey's connections to the Southern Tier are fairly obvious, having to do with the Turkic language, immigrants, and customs (such as a shared cuisine). Iran's connections are deeper but also more subtle, and so call for more explanation.[116] The Arabs and Israel have also become involved, at least at the margins.

Iran and the Turko-Persian Tradition

History. Central Asia and the Trans-Caucasus have for a thousand years been included in the "Persianate zone,"[117] a large cultural area marked "by the use of the New Persian language as a medium of administration and literature, by the rise of Persianized Turks to administrative control, by a new political importance for the *'ulama* [Islam's rabbis], and by the development of an ethnically composite Islamicate society."[118]

The Southern Tier had for millennia participated integrally in the development of Iranian culture. The Shahnameh, Iran's national epic, takes place mostly on what later became Soviet territory; the region's cities have a larger presence in the classics of Persian poetry than do those of Iran proper. Bukhara and Marv are two of the oldest and most important cities of Iranian civilization. Samarkand boasts the Gur Emir, Tamerlane's tomb, as well as many other great Islamic structures. Tashkent hosts ancient schools. Medieval figures such as the philosophers Alfarabi and Avicenna, the geographer Albiruni, the poet Ali Sher Navai, and the astronomer Ulugh Beg all lived in what we term the Southern Tier.

The Turko-Persian tradition developed in the Seljuk period (1040–1118) and reached its fullest florescence in the sixteenth to eighteenth centuries, when it prevailed in an area stretching from Anatolia to southern India, from Iraq to Xinjiang.[119] The Ottoman, Safavid, Chagatay, and Mughal empires all subscribed to this civilization. Their prestige caused it to spread even beyond their boundaries—for example, to Hyderabad in southern India. The Turko-Persian tradition declined in the eighteenth century, when Europeans began to encroach and land trade declined. Still, Persian remained the language of culture in the Central Asian cities until the Russian Revolution.

Islam set the parameters in the Persianate zone, Turcophones ruled, and Iranians administered. As this implies, each of the three classical languages of Islam had a distinct function: Arabic belonged to religion; Turkish to the military; and Persian to administration, polite society, and the arts. In short, the Turko-Persian tradition featured Persian culture patronized by Turcophone rulers. This mix led to unlikely juxtapositions: for example, shortly after 1500, the Iranian ruler Shah Isma'il wrote poetry in Azeri Turkic (under the pen name Khata'i) while his Ottoman counterpart in Istanbul wrote poetry in Persian.

The elites had much in common, from education to home life to styles of dress. But that was not all, as Robert L. Canfield of Washington University in St. Louis explains:

> People on many levels of the society had similar notions about the ground-rules of cooperation and dispute, and in other ways shared a number of common institutions, arts, knowledge, customs, and rituals. These similarities of cultural style were perpetuated by poets, artists, architects, artisans, jurists, and scholars, who maintained relations among their peers in the far-flung cities of the Turko-Persian Islamicate ecumene, from Istanbul to Delhi.[120]

Today. The Southern Tier's connections to Iran would seem to be moribund, overtaken by the delimitation of nation-states, Russian colonization, the Soviet experiment, and the Islamic Republic. But they are not: on both sides of the old Soviet border with Iran, the Turko-Persian tradition lives on.

On the northern side, the Turko-Persian tradition remained a source of pride and hope through seven decades of Soviet rule. In 1967 Olaf Caroe, the British administrator and author, explained that "it would be a profound mistake to imagine that the Sovietization of Central Asia and its populations has wiped clean the earlier drawings on the slate."[121] In 1990 Graham Fuller reiterated the point: "the Persian legacy still runs deep in those republics, profoundly shaping their basic culture."[122] Ex-Soviet Muslims have various connections to Iran. Tajiks share with it ethnic and linguistic bonds; Azeris share the Twelver Shi'ite religious tradition; Armenians look to it for a potential balance to the Turcophones; and the whole region celebrates Nowruz (the Iranian New Year's festival in March). Much else—music, cuisine, crafts—is also similar. Today, dispirited by the devastation about them, many ex-Soviet Muslims see Persianate culture and Iran as sources of hope. Symbolic of this, the Tajiks have replaced a statue of Lenin with one of the poet Ferdousi, author of the Shahnameh. Turkmeni-

stanis considered changing their currency unit to the dinar or tu-
man, though they eventually settled on the menat. Turkmenistan's
President Supramurad Niyazov told the foreign minister of Iran
that he was "personally interested" in learning Persian and would
facilitate its teaching in his country.[123] On a visit to Iran, Kazakhstan's Minister of Culture Yerkegeliy Rahkmadiyev referred
to the two countries' thousand-year relations and declared, "We
consider Iran as our own home."[124]

While today's republics have won a utilitarian acceptance, the
old khanates of Bukhara, Khiva, and Kokand live on in the imagination. The Great Ariana Society in Tajikistan advocates a Greater
Khurasan, which would incorporate a Persian-speaking belt from
the far end of Afghanistan to the Persian Gulf. Graham Fuller spec-
ulates that such a unit could become a counterpoise against a Turcophone belt to the north.[125]

On the Iranian side, too, the Turko-Persian tradition survives.
Government officials are generally cautious in their public state-
ments, disclaiming interest in political influence, seeking only a
softer kind. According to Foreign Minister Ali Akbar Velayati,
"the export of revolution means the export of culture and ideas, no
more."[126] As a sign of the kind of influence Iranians hope to have,
Velayati himself delivered a lecture at the Turkmen Academy of
Sciences on the poet and thinker Mahdum Kuli. President
Hashemi-Rafsanjani contented himself with bland statements.
"The newly independent countries to the north are very dear to
us," he declared in late 1992.[127]

Still, indelicate expressions—betraying Iranians' excitement—
sometimes get articulated. Velayati spoke of Central Asia's "Iranian identity" and noted that it is impossible to look at the region
"without making reference to Iranian culture and to the Iranian
language."[128] The religious leader of Isfahan, Ayatollah Taheri,
held that "some of the newly independent republics of the former
Soviet Union do not agree to the ignominious Turkmanchay Treaty
between Iran and the former Soviet Union [actually Russia] and
consider themselves part of Iran and regard the esteemed leader
[Khamene'i] as their own leader."[129] An Iranian journalist explains
this impulse: "In our heart of hearts, we know that Azerbaijan and
Turkmenia [Central Asia] were once part of the Persian empire."[130]

Some Iranians explicitly say as much; a former minister of labor predicted that independent Azerbaijan would eventually "become part of Iran."[131] The prayer leader of Mashhad echoed, "The Treaty of Turkmanchay expired several years ago, and these countries are now parts of Iran."[132]

Interestingly, Iran's political "moderates" articulate these dangerous dreams more than its "radicals." That is because the radicals have only Islamic aspirations, while the moderates have Persian nationalist ones as well.[133] For the latter, Shahram Chubin notes, the new states "could in theory become a new constituency or audience, widening the strategic depth of the Islamic republic and deepening its base."[134] Powerful elements within Iran, in short, appear to want to create a sphere of influence that includes Azerbaijan and Central Asia.

In asserting their claims, these Iranians dismiss Turkey's claimed connections to Central Asia and Azerbaijan. Iran's deputy foreign minister reacted with scorn when asked about possible rivalry between Turkey and Iran in the area: "What rivalry? Turks have nothing in the area but local idioms close to Turkish. History, civilization, culture, literature, science—everything is Iranian."[135]

The Arabs and Israel

Saudi activities in the Southern Tier consist in large part of building mosques, distributing Qur'ans, finding local agents, subsidizing pilgrimages to Mecca, and establishing a range of Islamic institutions. Tajikistan had just sixteen working mosques in the mid-1980s; thanks to Saudi largesse, some five hundred mosques a year were built over the next four years. According to *The Washington Post*, Riyadh has spent over $1 billion just on Islamic centers and efforts to promulgate the Arabic language.[136] The response was mixed. Kyrgyzstan declined an invitation to the Saudi-dominated Organization of the Islamic Conference in October 1991, but a year later signed an accord to accept aid and an Arab information-cultural center. Realizing the weakness of their position, the Saudis quickly deployed their resources best to block Iranian influence over the Southern Tier by supporting Turks. As Khalid Durán observes, "These days the Saudis appear pleased when the Turks defeat the Iranians, and it doesn't matter if the Turk is a Kemalist or a Wahhabi"[137]—a secularist or a fundamentalist.

The Syrians joined the fray by establishing connections to Armenia. It helped that President Ter-Petrosian was the son of a Communist Party leader in Syria, but a shared hostility to the Republic of Turkey provided the real basis of cooperation. The Armenians opened an embassy in Damascus during the depths of Yerevan's siege in April 1993. In turn, Syrian President Hafiz al-Asad promised seven thousand tons of fuel oil gratis to the starving Armenians. In early 1993 Azerbaijan's President Elçibey announced that five hundred terrorists had arrived in Armenia from Lebanon, while his ambassador in Ankara asserted that Syrian citizens fought with Armenia against Azerbaijan.[138] The Turks permitted a scheduled Aleppo-Yerevan flight until early April 1993, when Armenian aggression in Azerbaijan caused the Turks to cancel this and all other flights between the two countries. Accordingly, when the Armenian foreign minister visited Syria a few days later, he traveled via Paris.

Southern Tier independence has stirred much interest in Israel, including a hot debate as to whether it is a positive or negative development. Chief of Staff Ehud Barak expressed a pessimistic view about the emergence of the Southern Tier states: "new Muslim republics in Asia don't seem . . . something that will add to our health, at least in the long term."[139] When fundamentalist Muslim demonstrators took to the streets of Tajikistan in April 1992 carrying Khomeinist signs proclaiming "Death to Israel," this worry seemed to be borne out.

But this agitation proved to be very much the exception. Most voices from the Southern Tier insisted that religious differences or the Arab-Israeli conflict not obstruct good relations with Israel. For the leaders, ties with Israel symbolized an antifundamentalist orientation. A pro-Israel outlook was understood to enhance one's standing in the West. Jewish immigrants from the Southern Tier were expected to invest in their countries of origin. For their part, Israelis responded with alacrity. In addition to the usual reasons for seeking good relations, they particularly welcomed warm ties with predominantly Muslim states; and they looked ahead to setting up networks for the day when the region's two hundred thousand Jews might need to leave in a hurry.

Ties flourished. An Israeli cabinet minister visited Baku even before the August 1991 coup attempt. Azerbaijan, Kazakhstan, Kyrgyzstan, and Uzbekistan established full diplomatic relations with Israel; in turn, Jerusalem opened embassies in all but Kyrgyzstan. In September 1992 Kazakhstan's Prime Minister Sergei Tereschenko paid an official visit to Israel. President Askar Akaev of Kyrgyzstan visited Israel in January 1993—becoming only the second Muslim head of state ever to visit the capital of the Jewish state. Most remarkably, he agreed to establish an embassy in Jerusalem, though this notion got quickly scuttled. (Only two states, Costa Rica and El Salvador, have embassies in Jerusalem; all other embassies are in Tel Aviv.) He also stated that "Jerusalem cannot be divided."[140]

So pleased were the Israelis that in early 1993 the parliament voted a credit for Kazakhstan, the first time it had voted for credits to a specific state. At the same time, Jerusalem got a bit blasé about these new connections—for example, not placing an ambassador in Azerbaijan for many months after diplomatic relations had been established.

LONG-TERM PROSPECTS

The long-term implications of Southern Tier independence are as unclear as they are momentous. The Southern Tier polities are too new, untried, and unpredictable for informed speculations about the distant future. We have insufficient experience with Rip Van Winkle states to guess intelligently what they might do upon waking.

Still, we can try: In the very long term, Muslims of the Southern Tier are likely to leave Russia's orbit and rejoin the Middle East. The experience of other ex-colonies and the history of Muslim-Christian relations support this conclusion. Stripping away the rhetoric and the superstructures, Muslim republics during the Soviet period were essentially colonies of Moscow.[141] Like other ex-colonies, they will eventually move away from the imperial center. Of course, Russia differs in important ways from other European colonizers, having unique strengths (a greater willingness to use force, closer ties, and contiguity) and weaknesses (the Marxist-

Leninist System, a poorer economy). Nevertheless, Russia seems likely to follow the same general pattern as Britain, France, and the others. Intense ties with the former colonies will continue for years to come, but the prospects of reasserting true imperial control appear dim. Russians have not yet come to terms with the end of empire; their minister of finance, Boris Fedorov, noted in late 1993 that "most people, even here in Moscow, still fail to realize that Kazakhstan, say, is a foreign country. To them, its independence is make-believe."[142] This attitude may cause enormous problems.

Religious differences will play a major role. Muslims invariably insist on ruling themselves and in the long run resist living under the control of non-Muslims. This autonomist impulse runs deep through history; it is apparent today in such diverse places as Cyprus, Israel, and Kashmir. With time, as the new republics become real polities, they will turn away from Russian as their international language and the ruble as their currency. Institutional connections to Russia will atrophy, and those to the Middle East and Asia will grow, in terms of studies abroad, media influence, and trade and investment.

Russian efforts to dominate the southern "near abroad" may work for a while, but they cannot succeed in the long term. As Turkic- and Persian-speaking Muslims, the Southern Tier peoples will eventually repudiate Moscow; of this there can be no question. However, Kazakhstan and Kyrgyzstan will retain more ties to the old metropolitan center than the other four countries (Azerbaijan, Turkmenistan, Uzbekistan, and Tajikistan) because they share a border with Russia and host much larger Slavic populations. Interestingly, both are developing important trade and cultural links to China, which might balance the old ties to Russia.

In brief, the map eventually will change: the Middle East will include six new countries and some sixty million new people. Turcophones will become more important in the Middle East, and Arabophones less so. What used to be the Northern Tier—Turkey, Iran, Afghanistan—will stand at the heart of the Middle East.

This northward movement of the Middle East's boundaries will eventually affect virtually every aspect of Middle Eastern political life. Shahram Chubin rightly judges that the new, predominantly Muslim states "could change the balance of political power in Islam and affect the tenor of politics in the Islamic world, especially if they were to act collectively or in unison. They could alter the predominant tone of Islamic gatherings, give impetus to radical, or anchor moderate, tendencies, and alter prevailing alignments."[143]

Many political factions and religious groups in the Middle East look to the former Soviet citizens as their lifeblood, believing their own future to be largely determined by the outlook of the former Soviet citizens. Were ex-Soviet Muslims to adopt pan-Turkic nationalism, their politics could become as unsettled as Arab politics was in the 1950s. The proliferation of independent states using Turkic languages could cause Turkey to accelerate its move away from a European orientation and toward a pan-Turkic one. Pan-Turkism also might mobilize Turkic populations in other countries, especially Iran and Afghanistan, to become politically active. Ironically, the example of Turcophone independence could also spur Kurdish nationalism in eastern Turkey.

When it comes to religion, the fact that ex-Soviet Muslims lived for seven decades under an atheistic regime makes them needy for contact with their coreligionists in the Middle East. (In this, too, the Southern Tier most closely resembles Algeria.) They look to the Middle East for heritage, knowledge, and ideas. These include a return to the Arabic script, a hunger for Saudi-donated Qur'ans, the need for religious teachers, and admiration for Ayatollah Khomeini. But the ex-Soviet Muslims are more than passive consumers of Middle Eastern religiosity. They have major decisions to make, and the way they turn will have a great impact on religion throughout the Middle East. Should ex-Soviet Muslims accept Turkish-style secularism, this will be the first major boost for Atatürkism in many decades. If the new countries turn toward the Iranian version of fundamentalist Islam, they provide an enormous hinterland for Tehran's lagging movement, greatly strengthening Tehran's hand. If they turn toward Pakistan, they willy-nilly enter the Indo-Pakistani political system.

The opening of the Southern Tier introduced a new arena of Arab-Israeli competition. Will ex-Soviet Muslims, like so many of their ex-nationals, adopt a pro-Israel policy out of reflective distaste for the old regime's anti-Israel animus? Or will Muslim solidarity prompt them to adopt an anti-Israel policy? The rise of

Turcophone power could alarm the Arab world and turn its attention away from Israel; or fundamentalism in the Southern Tier might dramatically expand the threat to Israel's existence.

The profusion of new oil and gas production could either harm the Persian Gulf exporters (by expanding the supply) or help them (by concentrating yet more energy clout in the Middle East); it all depends on politics.

The Southern Tier could become a new Balkans, leading to shifting and competitive relations between would-be hegemons, then to skirmishes and small wars, and possibly even to a larger conflagration. Efforts by the Southern Tier states to define their geopolitical orientation, Boris Rumer argues, "threatens to alter political and military equations from China to the Persian Gulf."[144]

Speculating even more freely, such problems could cause the existing state order suddenly to collapse. Should southern Azerbaijan break away from Iran, Kurds and Turkmens might take advantage of the turmoil to win their independence from Iran, leaving Tehran the capital of a rump state. Alternatively, were Iran to incorporate independent Azerbaijan, the Persian nature of that country would come under doubt. Were Tajiks to secede from Afghanistan, Pashtuns and Baluch could follow suit. Both peoples would presumably seek to unite with their brethren in Pakistan, perhaps splitting Pakistan and destroying it. Separatist tendencies in India, already strong, would likely be encouraged by these developments, possibly leading to its breakup.

The Economist is probably right to describe Central Asia as "one of the most unstable parts of the world over the next decade,"[145] in which case it will export a wide range of problems. The emergence of an independent Southern Tier has, in other words, one common implication for neighbors: it complicates their politics. We cannot tell whether it will have deep consequences, but the potential is vast. The map from Turkey to Bangladesh could undergo drastic changes on short notice.

NOTES

1. Azerbaijan is included in this study because from a Middle Eastern viewpoint it and Central Asia form part of a single unit, and because it makes no sense to exclude Azerbaijan when discussing the impact of the ex-Soviet re-

publics on Turkey and Iran. Unless otherwise defined, "Azerbaijan" refers to the northern half of Azerbaijan—tsarist, Soviet, or independent Azerbaijan, depending on the era—and not the southern (or Iranian) half.

2. TRT Television, April 30, 1992. Note: References to radio and television broadcasts derive from the Foreign Broadcast Information Service [FBIS], *Daily Report,* as do some news agency and newspaper reports. I have occasionally amended FBIS translations for purposes of style.

3. In Russian-language usage, Kazakhstan is usually excluded from Central Asia; in English usage, it is normally included. We follow the latter practice.

4. *Economist,* December 26, 1992–January 8, 1993. Westerners are not alone in making this mistake about a long tradition of Turkish influence over Central Asia. President Supramurad Niyazov of Turkmenistan, for example, incorrectly refers to the Turkish efforts as a "revival" of its historical contacts (*Turkmenistan,* August 8, 1992).

5. As used here, "Turks" are citizens of Turkey and other lands formerly under Ottoman control who speak the form of Turkic called Turkish.

6. Reuters, April 5, 1993.

7. Quoted in Kenneth MacKenzie, "Turkey's Circumspect Activism," *The World Today,* February 1993, p. 26.

8. Patrick Clawson, "The Former Soviet South and the Muslim World" (unpublished), p. 19.

9. William Ward Maggs, "Armenia and Azerbaijan: Looking toward the Middle East," *Current History,* January 1993, p. 8.

10. Martha Brill Olcott, "Central Asia and the New Russian-American Rapprochement" (unpublished), p. 11.

11. Boris Rumer, "The Gathering Storm in Central Asia," *Orbis,* Winter 1993, p. 89. For more on this subject, see Philip Robins, "Between Sentiment and Self-Interest: Turkey's Policy toward Azerbaijan and the Central Asian States," *Middle East Journal,* Autumn 1993, pp. 593–610.

12. *Le Monde,* May 21, 1992.

13. *Turkish Daily News,* March 16, 1993.

14. For example, Sami Kohen, writing in *Milliyet,* quoted in *Turkish Times,* September 15, 1991.

15. Under Secretary of Foreign Affairs Özdem Sanberk, quoted in *Hürriyet,* July 19, 1992.

16. Anatolia, April 8, 1993; Türkiye Radyolari, January 26, 1992; *Literaturnaya gazeta,* October 7, 1992; and *Türkiye,* February 22, 1993. Armenia accused Turkey of providing much more to Azerbaijan, including materiel and military instructors.

17. Anatolia, November 2, 1992.

18. Türkiye Radyolari, November 2, 1992.

19. Türkiye Radyolari, November 4, 1992.

20. Colin Barraclough, "Asian Republics a Turkish Delight," *Insight,* November 23, 1992.

21. *Turkish Times,* November 15, 1992.

22. The Russian and Soviet authorities Russified Muslim names by turning the *h* sound (absent in Russian) into *g* or *kh;* adding the Slavic suffic -*ev* or -*ov* to distinguish the family name from given names; and using the Russian

patronymic *-ovich*. Gasan Gasanov, in other words, is the Russified version of Hasan Hasan.

With time, ex-Soviet Muslims are de-Russifying their names—for example, by dropping *-ovich* in favor of the Turkic *-oglu* or *-ogly*. Their changes have political overtones. Two Azeri politicians with the same family name symbolize this point: The Azeri nationalist Ebulfez Aliyev became Ebulfez Ali Elçibey, while the old Stalinist Gaidar Aliyev has gone only so far as Haydar Aliyev.

In this chapter, we drop the change from *h*, but if an individual retains the *-ev*, *-ov*, or *-ovich*, we do, too.

23. *Al-Majalla*, November 4–10, 1992.

24. *Ana Tili* (Almaty), January 7, 1993.

25. To distinguish between an ethnic Uzbek and a resident of Uzbekistan, we call the former an Uzbek and the latter an Uzbekistani. Uzbekistanis include Russians, Tajiks, and many other nationalities. The same nomenclature applies to the other republics (e.g., Azeri, Azerbaijani). This said, we should add that the notion of an ethnic Uzbek (or Tajik, and so on) dates back only to the Soviet reorganization of the 1920s, and so is a somewhat superficial identity.

26. "Elder brother" was the term Russians applied to themselves and used for decades to justify their hegemony over non-Russian peoples; using the Turkish equivalent of that concept today carries unfortunate associations with the Russian past.

27. Maqsudul Hasan Nuri, "India and Central Asia, Present and Future," *Regional Studies*, Winter 1992–93, p. 88.

28. *Tercüman*, September 21, 1991.

29. Voice of the Islamic Republic of Iran, November 24, 1992.

30. TRT Television, April 29, 1992; and *Izvestiya*, April 29, 1992.

31. Sharen M. Shackleford, *People of Uzbekistan View the United States Positively*, USIA Opinion Research Memorandum (Washington, D.C.: Office of Research, United States Information Agency, 1992).

32. B. Susan White, *Turks Prefer Close Ties with Central Asia or Western Europe over Middle East or U.S.*, USIA Opinion Research Memorandum (Washington, D.C.: Office of Research, United States Information Agency, 1993).

33. As used here, "Turcophones" are peoples (Azeris, Kazakhs, Turks, Uzbeks, and so forth) who speak forms of Turkic other than Turkish.

34. Also, it should be noted that Soviet Muslims were the last substantial body of Third World people under European control; their independence in December 1991 closed the chapter on five hundred years of European colonialism in a dramatic but unheralded fashion. It could be that the American-led intervention in Somalia a year later opened a new chapter.

35. *The Middle East*, March 1993.

36. Martha Brill Olcott, "Central Asia's Catapult to Independence," *Foreign Affairs*, Summer 1992, p. 108. The same applies to Azerbaijan.

This reticence comes as a great surprise to outside observers. As early as 1919, a British Foreign Office report concluded that "Russia having fallen to pieces, Central Asia will be the first to break away." See Great Britain, Foreign Office, *The Rise of the Turks; The Pan-Turanian Movement* (London: His Majesty's Stationery Office, 1919), p. 16. As late as 1989 this author wrote about the Central Asian leaders that "it seems inevitable . . . [they] will demand independence." See Daniel Pipes, "The Third World Peoples of Soviet Central Asia," in *The Long Shadow: Culture and Politics in the Middle East* (New Brunswick, N.J.: Transaction, 1989), p. 59.

37. October 15, 1992, quoted in Martha Brill Olcott, "Central Asia on Its Own," *Journal of Democracy,* January 1993, p. 92.

38. Quoted in Rumer, "Gathering Storm," p. 100.

39. Estimates of the Azeri population in Iran vary widely, from six million to twenty million. The estimate of twelve million derives from David B. Nissman, *The Soviet Union and Iranian Azerbaijan: The Use of Nationalism for Political Penetration* (Boulder, Colo.: Westview, 1986), p. 2.

40. *Iran Times,* July 10, 1992.

41. Islamic Revolution News Agency, November 8, 1992.

42. Richard W. Cottam, *Nationalism in Iran* (Pittsburgh: University of Pittsburgh Press, 1964), p. 133.

43. For an example of a northern Azeri's emotional experience in the south, see Sekhavet Ismayylov's account in *Azerbayjan Muellimi* (Baku), July 24, 1992.

44. Azeris fared so poorly on the battlefield in part because, as Muslims, they tended to fill noncombat positions in the Red Army (construction brigades, support operations, and the like). In contrast, Soviet leaders trusted Armenians and trained them in ways that proved useful from 1988 on.

45. *Milliyet,* August 12, 1992.

46. *2000 Ikibin'e Dogru,* January 28, 1990, quoted in Reiner Freitag, "Aserbaidshan und die Türkei: Die internationale Dimension des Nationalitätenkonflikts im Transkaukasus," *Orient,* vol. 31 (1990), p. 548.

47. *Türkiye,* September 11, 1991. In expressing these views, Özfatura undoubtedly had his Azeri readership in mind, for *Türkiye,* like many of the Turkish national papers, has been available in Azerbaijan.

48. *Christian Science Monitor,* September 23, 1991.

49. *Philadelphia Inquirer,* September 5, 1993.

50. Aydinlik, September 3, 1993.

51. TRT Television, April 13, 1993.

52. TRT Television, May 2, 1992.

53. *Sabah,* January 6, 1993.

54. *Sabah,* January 12, 1993.

55. *Philadelphia Inquirer,* May 21, 1992.

56. *Tercüman,* November 30, 1992. Armenians in the United States responded in their usual hostile fashion, calling Turkey's promises of aid to Armenia "an expensive public relations campaign to improve its image." See Lorig Titizian, government affairs director of the Armenian National Committee, letter to *Los Angeles Times,* February 20, 1993.

57. *Hürriyet,* November 24, 1992.

58. Supreme Soviet Chairman Babken Ararktsvan, quoted on TRT Television, February 25, 1993.

59. A June 1992 poll reveals 91 percent of Armenians seeing Turkey unfavorably and just 5 percent favorably disposed. Only Azerbaijan does worse (96

percent vs. 2 percent). See Rachel Halpern, *Armenians View U.S. and Iran Favorably, Azerbaijan and Turkey the Opposite,* USIA Opinion Research Memorandum (Washington, D.C.: Office of Research, United States Information Agency, 1992).

60. *Milliyet,* December 10, 1992.
61. Sharen M. Shackleford, *Armenian Moderation Ebbs as Fighting Intensifies,* USIA Opinion Research Memorandum (Washington, D.C.: Office of Research, United States Information Agency, 1992).
62. *Middle East International,* December 4, 1992.
63. Maggs, "Armenia and Azerbaijan," p. 6.
64. Igor Rotar, writing in *Nezavisimaya gazeta* (Moscow), December 25, 1992. For a listing of the ten disputes, see Gregory Gleason, "Uzbekistan: From Statehood to Nationhood," in Ian Bremmer and Ray Taras, eds., *Nations and Politics in the Soviet Successor States* (Cambridge: Cambridge University Press, 1993), p. 350.
65. Uzbeks are also dispersed, though not quite so dramatically. Some 15 million live in Uzbekistan, 1.6 million in Afghanistan, 1.3 million in Tajikistan, and 300,000 in Kazakhstan.
66. Reference books typically list Afghanistan's population as eighteen million, but this ignores the millions who emigrated during the 1979–1989 war.
67. *Far Eastern Economic Review,* February 18, 1993.
68. *New York Times,* January 14, 1993; and *Far Eastern Economic Review,* February 18, 1993.
69. Khalid Durán, "Afghanistan: Slicing Up a Traditional Buffer State: Regional Repercussions of the Mujahidin Takeover in Kabul," *The World & I,* December 1992, p. 603. I have relied heavily on Durán's article for this section on the Tajik theater.
70. Rumer, "Gathering Storm," p. 95.
71. On Tabani, see *Asiaweek,* May 12, 1993.
72. Hafeez Malik, "New Relationships between Central and Southern Asia: Regional Politics of Pakistan," *National Development and Security* (Rawalpindi), November 1992, p. 58.
73. *Turkish Times,* January 1, 1992.
74. We include the Balkans when dealing with Turkey, for its impact on Turkish politics parallels and augments that of the Southern Tier republics. On this general issue, see Gareth Winrow, *Where East Meets West: Turkey and the Balkans* (London: Insitute for European Defence and Strategic Studies, 1993).
75. Ali Ferda Sevin in *Turkish Times,* September 1, 1992.
76. *Hürriyet,* December 19, 1991.
77. *Turkish Times,* January 1, 1992.
78. Graham E. Fuller, *Turkey Faces East: New Orientation toward the Middle East and the Old Soviet Union* (Santa Monica, Calif.: Rand, 1992), p. 11.
79. *Le Nouvel Observateur,* January 28–February 3, 1993.
80. Anatolia, February 15, 1993.
81. The computer lacks the Turkish undotted *i,* so we use *i* in its stead.
82. *NRC Handelsblad,* August 17, 1992; and *Le Figaro,* February 3, 1993.
83. In a related development, the Turkish government reversed a decades-old

policy in 1991 when it acknowledged the existence of a Kurdish ethnicity and permitted Kurds the right to speak their own language. These mild concessions had a tremendous impact, for they made legitimate the largest, most contentious subnational identification in Turkey.

84. Türkiye Radyolari, May 22, 1992.
85. Anatolia, January 6, 1993.
86. *Turkish Daily News,* May 11, 1992.
87. *Le Monde,* May 6, 1992.
88. TRT Television, February 6, 1992.
89. TRT Television, April 29, 1992.
90. TRT Television, May 28, 1992.
91. *Turkish Times,* May 15, 1992; and TRT Television, October 31, 1992.
92. TRT Television, February 9, 1993; and TRT Television, August 4, 1992. Demirel varied his wording, sometimes referring to "a big Turkic world" (TRT Television, May 2, 1992) and sometimes extending its reach only as far as the Great Wall of China.
93. *Turkish Daily News,* December 20, 1991, repeated by Deputy Prime Minister Muhammad Karabaev of Uzbekistan (Anatolia, February 27, 1992). With more restraint, President Nazarbaev of Kazakhstan referred to Demirel as "my brother Süleyman Bey" (TRT Television, April 29, 1992).
94. *Der Spiegel,* February 10, 1992; and TRT Television, November 12, 1991.
95. *New York Times,* June 27, 1992.
96. Quoted in Fuller, *Turkey Faces East,* p. 39.
97. See *Nokta,* June 21, 1992.
98. *Washington Post,* February 24, 1993.
99. *Der Spiegel,* December 23, 1991.
100. *Al-Hayat* (London), December 29, 1992.
101. *Nokta,* June 21, 1992.
102. *Türkiye,* May 13, 1992.
103. *Tercüman,* February 14, 1993.
104. TRT Television, November 12, 1991.
105. *Washington Times,* May 12, 1992.
106. TRT Television, October 30, 1992.
107. TRT Television, March 9, 1993.
108. TRT Television, December 31, 1992.
109. *Nokta,* June 21, 1992.
110. TRT Television, September 30, 1992.
111. *Milliyet,* March 30, 1992.
112. TRT Television (Ankara), December 25, 1991.
113. *Türkiye,* December 14, 1992.
114. *Pravda vostoka,* April 18, 1992.
115. *Middle East International,* May 29, 1992.
116. In addition, Iran worries about such practical matters as refugees flooding in from the Caucasus and Tajikistan; Iran already hosts some four million refugees, mostly from Afghanistan and Iraq, and does not relish more.
117. Marshall G. S. Hodgson, *The Venture of Islam: Conscience and History in a World Civilization* (Chicago: University of Chicago Press, 1974), vol. 2, p. 293.

118. Robert L. Canfield, "Introduction: The Turko-Perisan Tradition," in *Turko-Persia in Historical Perspective* (Cambridge: Cambridge University Press, 1991), p. 6.

119. Just as Europe has for centuries been divided into the Latin and the Germanic cultural zones, with almost no movement in boundaries, so the Muslim world has been divided into Arab and Turko-Persian components. In this sense, the Iraq-Iran border resembles the the French-German border.

120. Canfield, "Introduction," pp. 20–21.

121. Olaf Caroe, *Soviet Empire: The Turks of Central Asia and Stalinism,* Second ed. (London: Macmillan, 1967), p. 31.

122. Graham E. Fuller, "The Emergence of Central Asia," *Foreign Policy,* Spring 1990, p. 50.

123. Islamic Revolution News Agency, January 30, 1993.

124. Islamic Revolution News Agency, June 17, 1993.

125. Graham E. Fuller, *Central Asia: The New Geopolitics* (Santa Monica, Calif.: Rand, 1992), p. 66.

126. Quoted by V. Skosyrev in *Izvestiya,* October 9, 1991.

127. IRIB Television, October 21, 1992.

128. *The Middle East,* March 1993.

129. *Kar va Kargar,* about February 25, 1992, quoted in Patrick Clawson, *Iran's Challenge to the West: How, When, and Why* (Washington, D.C.: Washington Institute for Near East Policy, 1993), p. 42.

130. *Christian Science Monitor,* September 23, 1991.

131. September 6, 1991, quoted in *Turkish Daily News,* January 15, 1992.

132. Mullah Abaii, quoted in Mohammad Mohaddessin, *Islamic Fundamentalism: The New Global Threat* (Washington, D.C.: Seven Locks Press, 1993), p. 79.

133. On this difference and its implications for Iranian foreign policy, see Clawson, *Iran's Challenge to the West,* ch. 1.

134. Shahram Chubin, "The Geopolitics of the Southern Republics of the CIS," *Iranian Journal of International Affairs,* Summer 1992, p. 318.

135. Quoted in George I. Mirsky, "Central Asia's Emergence," *Current History,* October 1992, p. 337.

136. *Washington Post,* March 22, 1992.

137. Khalid Durán, "Islamische Kolonisierung Zentralasiens: Wettkämpf und Bombengeschäfte," *Schweizer Monatshefte,* July/August 1992, p. 556.

138. Interfax, April 15, 1993; and *Türkiye,* February 22, 1993.

139. Israeli Television, September 11, 1991.

140. Interfax, January 25, 1993.

141. For an argument making this case, see Pipes, "Third World Peoples," pp. 50–57.

142. *Economist,* September 18, 1993.

143. Chubin, "Geopolitics of the Southern Republics," p. 317.

144. Rumer, "Gathering Storm," p. 89.

145. *Economist,* December 26, 1992–January 8, 1993.

Chapter 3

Russia and Central Asia: Federation or Fault Line?

Graham E. Fuller

THE COLLAPSE OF THE RUSSIAN EMPIRE, THE STUNNING POLITICAL event of the latter half of this century, is a process whose implications are still only beginning to be fully apprehended on the global level. Russia itself is still passing through an extraordinary period of internal transition. The end of an empire of several hundred years' standing has given birth to a new, truncated Russia living within arbitrary borders that have never before existed in history. Territorial change has been matched by ideological change: the end of Marxist-Leninist communism as an overarching doctrine, guide, and pretext for action has not only radically altered the internal power structure and character of the Russian state, but also induced sharp change in Moscow's foreign policy.

Even the very term "foreign policy" has taken on a new complexity for Russians, for the state borders are now vastly different—shrunken—from what they were in 1991. Russia today is closed off from nearly all of its old international borders, except for that with North Korea and a severely reduced border with China. Most of the former republics now represent the "external" borders of the Russian state. But psychological acceptance of this fact comes hard for even the most liberal-minded Russian. The permanence of this situation has not been fully accepted, as the existence of the Commonwealth of Independent States (CIS) suggests:

Russians in their hearts cling to the concept that the final status of these states in relation to Russia has not yet been finally resolved. They may be right. The clearest representation of this fact lies in the use of the term "near abroad" (*blizhnee zarubezhie*) to designate a distinct kind of "foreign policy" with these newly independent states, different from that with the former border states of the old USSR.

The independence of the Central Asian republics represents overwhelmingly Russia's largest territorial loss, even if it evokes less psychological and cultural distress than the loss of Ukraine, the very heartland of ancient "Rus'." The Russian-Ukrainian relationship is also perhaps the most important factor in the evolving new geopolitics among Russia, Eastern Europe, and Germany, and hence of signal importance to the West as a whole. In similar fashion, Russia's relations with the Central Asian republics are important for their effect on Russia's ability to expand its influence to the south and the broader Muslim world.

But Russia's future relationship with Central Asia also presents an unstable and possibly troubled picture. First, Central Asia constitutes a vast region of five new independent Muslim states, none of which existed before as part of the modern international state structure; a lot of shaking down within them and in their relations with each other will be inevitable. Second, unlike Ukraine and Belarus, the Central Asian region is culturally sharply distinct from European culture because of its Islamic orientation and rapidly renewing ties with the rest of the Muslim world and China—a dramatically different political environment.

Third, those external Middle Eastern and South Asian states to which Central Asia is contiguous are themselves threatened with major political change, partly in reaction to events in Central Asia. The virus of nationalist separatism is already infecting Afghanistan, with potential impact on Pakistan and India. China, as one of the last remaining large empires of the world, will surely face the specter of ethnic separation and breakup—as its sclerotic communist nomenklatura bites the dust in the coming years—mostly in the Inner Asian areas of Tibet and Xinjiang (former Chinese Turkestan). Iran, meanwhile, could be sharply affected by changes in the Caucasus, especially Azerbaijan. All these changes will have

OCEAN

Bering
Sea

Kamchatka

Sea of
Okhotsk

S I A

Mongolia

Sea of
Japan

Korea

CHINA

Ascherl

PACIFIC
OCEAN

impact on Russia's near environment, and Central Asia will inevitably be the cockpit within which these changes in Inner Asia
play themselves out. Critical years of internal political evolution
thus lie ahead for the Central Asian states as they sort out their unresolved identities and their internal and regional conflicts and
policies, and as they confront an intimidating external world—all
surrounded by the potentially unstable nuclear powers of Russia,
China, India, and Pakistan.

THE RUSSIAN NATIONAL INTEREST

No discussion of Russia's future role and involvement in Central
Asia is possible without an understanding of what constitutes the
new Russian national interest there. But determination of Russia's
relations with Central Asia is only part of a larger process of the
redetermination of the entire scope of Russia's new national interests. Guided and formed by Marxist-Leninist doctrine and the
global Cold War, the Soviet/Russian perception of national interest over the last century had come to be highly distorted; literally
any place on the globe could be transformed into a potentially critical locus of confrontation on the grand East-West chessboard.
With the end of empire and ideology, Russia plunged into complete
conceptual confusion regarding what the "true" national interest
is all about.

Determination of the national interest is not, of course, some
simple objective process on which all might agree, but rather a direct reflection of the differing subjective values, philosophies, and
orientations of a variety of beholders. Not surprisingly, we witness
a broad spectrum of views in the Russian national debate on the
topic. Introduction of the concept of the "near abroad" further
complicates that debate. Indeed, tension between concepts of
"near" and "far abroad" makes up one of the fundamental dilem-
mas of Russian foreign policy today.

Basically Russia will have to resolve the character of its relations with the former republics—the near abroad—before it can
establish external relationships on a firm footing. How Russia gets
along with the near abroad will inevitably exert immense impact
on the nature of Russian domestic politics overall, on the degree of

its liberality, openness, and ability to adjust to new national and international realities. A failure to manage its relationships with the near abroad will lead to tensions and hostilities that can even push these former republics into defensive postures—whereby they may end up serving as instruments of influence for major external powers against Russia. Such a situation can only enhance Russia's general predisposition to fear "encirclement." Yet in reality most states are "encircled" by others—the concept says nothing about geography, but everything about the character of political relationships, which need not automatically be hostile.

Nineteenth-century Russian history provides a long and fascinating debate over Russia's basic "national character" and the future of its political orientation. Is Russia part of the "West" or "Asian" in character? Each of these terms contained complex philosophical visions about the nature of the Russian state and the role of Russia in history—and among other Slavic nations. While the Bolsheviks preempted the argument, and forcibly imposed their own answer on both the Russians and the world as to the character of Russia's geopolitical role in the world, the issue was never "permanently" resolved, even after three-quarters of a century. The ultimate failure of the Bolsheviks' anti-Western and messianic vision of foreign policy would now seem to restore balance to the argument once again, allowing the grand debate in Russia to begin anew in a different world environment.

NOSTALGIA FOR THE OLD EMPIRE

Debate over Russian foreign policy today encompasses several schools, most notably the "Atlanticists," the "Eurasianists," and the "imperialists." We will examine these schools of thought later, in discussing Russian policy toward the external world. But reality intrudes. Debate over Russia's mission and goals in the world today must deal first of all with the concrete reality of Russia's new immediate neighbors—those peoples whose fate it was to be forcibly included within the borders of the tsarist and Bolshevik empires—the near abroad. Here there are roughly three ways of responding to the breakup of the empire: acceptance of the reality of the new delimited Russian nation-state; search for a new form of confederal relationships with the former republics of the Soviet Union, this time on a voluntary and equal basis within a new commonwealth of states; and a quest for the reestablishment of former empire by whatever means it takes, including guile and even force. Let us look at the character and implications of each of these positions.

- *A new democratic Russian nation-state.* This vision openly rejects Russia's imperial past. It clearly sees linkage between the form of government and the character of its concomitant foreign policy. Under the tsars, the imperial tradition placed Russia in competition with Western imperialist powers. Worse, when the imperial tradition was linked with Bolshevik totalitarianism, it placed Russia on an ideologically predetermined and highly dangerous course of political and military confrontation with the West. This imperial past must therefore be rejected on several grounds. First, empire imposed over basically unwilling subjects clearly foreordains Russia itself to an authoritarian rule that ultimately saddles its Russian masters as fully as their non-Russian subjects. Second, this kind of empire runs contrary to Western political values and thus must be inherently anti-Western; such a stance deprives Russia of a place in the ranks of the economically most advanced nations of the world, where democratic governance is the norm. Third, it isolates Russia in a broader sense from the community of nations, condemning it to struggle for maintenance of empire in an era in which empires are an obsolete political form and increasingly unsustainable. The new Russian state instead seeks to operate on a democratic basis within the democratic community.

- *New confederal relations with the former republics of the USSR.* The breakup of empire has meant more than simply psychic shock to the Russians; it has spawned an economic crisis between Russia and the former republics. The economic relations of the Soviet period, the argument goes, had come to be sanctioned by time and experience, and need to be resuscitated on a new and more rational and egalitarian basis, in the interests of all participants, in an effort to salvage what was good and mutually beneficial from among the past imperial relations. Security relations and military policy in this new period can also be handled in a confederal framework. The CIS will thus serve as the primary vehicle to direct these relationships on a flexible, consultative, and equal basis, covering economics, security relations, and some elements of foreign policy. The theoretical framework for these new relationships essentially exists within the CIS, but the CIS itself seems to be foundering as a meaningful structure, and its principles are variously accepted or not accepted on a smorgasbord basis by each state in accordance with its own shifting perception of its national interests.

- *A neo-Russian empire*. According to this view, Russia must re-create its old empire, which is sanctioned by centuries of intimate interrelationships among its constituent peoples. Zealous and shortsighted nationalists must be isolated and politically neutralized in the republics; an unraveling of the old empire will otherwise not stop with the loss of the republics, but will follow an inevitable course leading to the breakup of the Russian Federation itself. Furthermore, the breakup of the empire has been economically disastrous to all. Russia is historically destined to maintain the dominant role over these historic regions of Russian control that define the very character of Russia; they are its sine qua non. Russia must therefore employ all means to reconstitute the empire, particularly by encouraging those elements in the republics sympathetic to the imperial order—albeit on a more rational basis this time—to gain power in the republics. A democratic order is not a prerequisite, and relations with the West take a backseat to preservation of the empire.

Distinct domestic and foreign policy implications inevitably flow from these three positions toward Russia's relations with the former Soviet republics. A new Russian nation-state that has realistically come to terms with its diminished boundaries is the most likely to continue to pursue and maintain democratic governance and a tolerant and flexible stance toward all its neighbors. It would therefore probably seek close association with other democratic nation-states, and pursue the economic benefits that flow from those relationships as well. It would look to international instruments for the resolution of most international conflict, and would be inclined to use negotiation, rather than force, against the former republics. It would have little inclination to provoke problems within the former republics as a pretext for military intervention. It would probably devote limited attention to the republics beyond a concern for a few basic interests, discussed below.

The future politics of Russia cannot, of course, be that simple: while democratic forces may dominate, they are likely to be engaged in constant struggle with nondemocratic or nationalistic-chauvinistic forces within Russia that are far less generously inclined toward the former republics. These political elements may in fact nurture an agenda that calls for constant increase of Russian power over those regions, even if they are never formally integrated into a Russian state. At the very least, the existence of these groups, regardless of their actual power, would create suspicions among already paranoid non-Russian peoples that Moscow seeks to manipulate them and is behind local ethnic or other troubles. The gradual slippage of nearly every Central Asian state (except Kyrgyzstan) and Azerbaijan back into the neocommunist orbit can only lend substance to these fears. Furthermore, any democratic government in Moscow must keep a weather eye upon potential accusations from the neoimperialists that they are betraying the Russian national interest if they "allow" excessive independence to emerge in the former republics.

The third option, a commonwealth or confederation, presents a more complicated picture of relations with the former republics. The present form of such a commonwealth is the CIS, an almost meaningless institution with no legal status in international terms. Its real value has been to serve as a forum to facilitate the orderly dissolution of empire, the adjudication of interrepublic problems, the search for common approaches to certain kinds of economic and security problems, and evolution toward new confederal relations. But the CIS is more likely to grow weaker than stronger over time, given the disparate interests of its members. More to the point, as its members develop new political and economic identities on the world scene, their interests are in a state of flux. The

Central Asian republics in particular, ill prepared for independence, are only beginning to establish their own identities and to determine their new places and relationships in the world. Their domestic politics are still deeply in thrall to elements of the former communist nomenklatura and its mechanisms. As domestic politics evolve and new leaderships emerge, these states are likely to develop differing perspectives on their relationships with both Moscow and their immediate neighbors who were so long outside the Iron Curtain.

For Moscow, however, the CIS represents the most effective means of reestablishing paramount influence in the region. A zone of significant economic cooperation could in fact evolve, but it is more likely to require construction from scratch among new, more mature consenting nations than it is to be put together on an ad hoc basis out of bits and pieces of decaying imperial institutions and arrangements. Despite its uncertain evolution, the CIS still presents a useful vehicle for an indefinite period of time for adjudication of relations in a variety of contentious areas. Its existence, and the requirements it places upon Moscow to treat its members as sovereign states possessing their own legitimate interests, may in many ways hinder the emergence of darker, more imperialist forces within the Russian body politic. While the CIS could conceivably become the quasi-legal vehicle for the reassertion of Russian imperial control over the former republics, the member states will be wary of any such process and will likely loosen ties if that threat seems real.

The CIS still poses many problems to its members, particularly in the economic field. The republics' economies remain highly dependent upon Russia's reform process and its general economic health. If that association proves too burdensome, certain republics will choose to keep their distance. That is already the case. Turkmenistan, with its major oil and gas reserves, finds little market benefit from close association with Moscow. Kyrgyzstan has broken out of the "ruble zone" to establish its own currency, and Uzbekistan and Kazakhstan will likely follow suit, because of the nearly intolerable problem of allowing a foreign state (Russia) to determine their monetary policies.

The security aspect of the CIS also poses special problems. The newly independent states do not yet even know what all their security problems and needs will be. These security concerns fall into at least three areas: protection of the old external borders of the former Soviet Union from foreign attack; peacekeeping in any interrepublic warfare; and prevention of armed rebellion or ethnic conflict within any member republic. A fourth, unwritten role is the preservation of the security order within the republics—that is, protection of existing regimes. These security functions are not always clearly separable.

External security represents the simplest conceptual task: acts of aggression from external border states can be jointly rebuffed. Such threats in Central Asia can potentially emanate only from Turkey, Iran, Afghanistan, and China. In fact, turmoil in Afghanistan—which originated in the Soviet invasion of Afghanistan in 1979—has already spilled over in the form of Afghan guerrilla assistance to Tajik antiregime insurgents within Tajikistan.

Nor can other future problems be excluded anywhere along this border:

- between Turkey and Armenia in the event of adverse developments in the conflict between Armenia and Azerbaijan

- between Iran and Azerbaijan over potential separatism in Iranian Azerbaijan

- between Iran and Turkmenistan over ethnic issues

- between Afghanistan and Turkmenistan, Uzbekistan, or Tajikistan in the event of the breakup of Afghanistan and the reordering of ethnic groups and borders in the region

- between China and Kazakhstan, Kyrgyzstan, Tajikistan, or Russia over potential breakaway movements among the Turkic population of Xinjiang.

Some CIS security role in these eventualities is hardly beyond the realm of likelihood; nearly all of the above scenarios have quite realistic elements to them. But the precedent established in Tajikistan against Afghan irregular forces had other, more political overtones to it. While guarding the Tajikistan-Afghanistan border, CIS troops in the 1992–1993 intervention were also on the side of neocommunist forces in Tajikistan's civil war. CIS—mainly Russian—troops were augmented by larger forces from Uzbekistan dedicated specifically to supporting the neocommunists against more democratic elements, mixed with Islamists. This was justified in the name of preventing the expansion of Tajikistan's ethnic conflict into Uzbekistan. While the process was tailor-made to meet the internal security needs of President Islam Karimov's authoritarian regime in Uzbekistan, this kind of internal political intervention will likely be viewed as very unwelcome by any future democratic forces that may emerge.

CIS troops in principle can also help keep the peace in confrontational situations between ethnic groups, much as the United Nations might do. Here again, however, in a more sinister mode, suppression of ethnic conflict can be a code word for support of unpopular regimes against broader publics, in which case democratic forces within the republics will clearly see the CIS mechanism as an instrument of repression and intolerable in a future order. The introduction of CIS forces becomes completely ambiguous when it involves the (always undiscussed) confrontation between the interests of Russia and the other republics, a high likelihood sometime in the future in Kazakhstan. Russia could not be counted on to provide "peacekeeping forces" when Russians themselves are a party to conflict.

Thus the role of CIS forces remains an ambiguous and open question for the foreseeable future. At best the CIS can provide a useful, mobile peacekeeping force; at worst it can serve as a vehicle for cruder and perhaps more chauvinistically inclined unilateral intervention by Russia on behalf of its own interests. Many republics in the CIS were discomfited by Russian President Boris Yeltsin's February 1993 remarks to the Civic Union parliamentary group in which he stated that "the time has come for distinguished international organizations, including the UN, to grant Russia special powers of a guarantor of peace and stability in regions of the former USSR." These thoughts clearly serve a variety of Russian actions, ranging from benign and constructive peacekeeping to threatening neoimperialism. The ambiguous and murky role of Russian forces in ethnic separatist movements in Georgia and in the downfall of the first truly nationalist government of Azerbaijan, led by President Ebulfez Ali Elçibey, in July 1993 provide further grounds for caution. In this writer's view, however, the evidence is still far from conclusive that Russia's role in the southern republics is clearly designed to support reconstitution of empire. The situation will bear close watching.

A true neo-Russian empire—the goal of a small number of avowed imperialists in Russia—can be reconstructed only through force. Even the neocommunist leaderships in power in Central Asia and Azerbaijan are sufficiently nationalist in orientation that they would be unwilling to deliver their states over to Russian control. Their first allegiance is unquestionably to their own republics, regardless of their willingness to cooperate with Moscow when doing so is useful and appropriate in their view. One could nonetheless imagine a situation of creeping restoration of empire based on a number of factors:

- the continuation in power of neocommunists who require support from Moscow to retain a firm hold on authority

- leaders who seek to suppress strong nationalist forces within their countries

- continuing deterioration of the economies of the republics that are ill equipped to trade successfully outside the ruble zone, creating continued dependence on Moscow to stay afloat.

While it is quite possible to imagine such situations, whereby large elements of independence are bartered away, one might equally well ask how willing Moscow would be to play this game. The Yeltsin regime would clearly seem to have more important priorities. Other nationalist regimes in Moscow could have a different order of priorities. Thus, over time, the resuscitation of empire seems a decreasingly likely scenario. Indeed, serious attempts by Moscow to reimpose it, or frictions with Moscow over the status and situation of Russians in the republics, will likely lead to serious long-term confrontation and alienation of relations between Russia and the Central Asian republics.

CONCRETE RUSSIAN INTERESTS IN CENTRAL ASIA

Whatever its overall foreign policy vision, Russia maintains several clear-cut interests in Central Asia. Key among them are preservation of economic and political relationships through CIS institutions, the Russian diaspora in the "near abroad," border security, nuclear proliferation, and protection of the Russian Federation itself from fissiparous ethnic tendencies that abound in the region.

Preservation of the CIS

The Soviet economy was by definition highly—and artificially—interdependent; the collapse of the USSR and the newly won sovereignty of the republics has severely dislocated long-established economic relationships that cannot be readily restored. Indeed, perhaps they should not be restored. Many of the economic relationships were "artificial" in the sense that they were created by fiat by central planning and not founded on organic market relations. As the entire system moves over to a market economy, many of these relationships will by definition atrophy to the extent that they are no longer "natural." While in principle all trading partners have a stake in maintaining the old trading patterns, in fact nearly all republics, including Russia, now look to sell much of their resources abroad for hard currency rather than on the ruble market or on a barter basis internally. Russia will supply oil to the former republics only at market prices, for example. On the same basis, much of the oil of Kazakhstan and Azerbaijan has been lost to Russia as an asset, since it will be produced by Western oil companies and marketed abroad. For Russia these were only potential resources, of course, as yet unrealized, and Russia has much oil of its own. But Russia has lost much of the cotton crop from Uzbekistan that feeds Russia's textile mills. The refusal of Uzbekistan to maintain its full cotton quota to Russia at the old nonmarket prices has forced Russia to turn to the international market to maintain its textile mills in Ivanovo, for example. The Central Asian states are nonetheless losing more than Russia is, for they have been totally dependent upon it for consumer goods and industrial products. The old trading relationships are still important where the member states cannot afford to meet their economic needs by hard currency purchases. But these same economic relationships are also undergoing severe restructuring with as yet uncertain outcomes.

Maintenance of the ruble zone is another important goal for Russia. But the structures of the CIS continue to deteriorate, and many of the basic requisite economic institutions are still lacking, such as shared control of monetary issuance, enforceability mechanisms in trade relations, and an economic court. Bilateral trading patterns are gaining ascendancy over multilateral arrangements. Along whatever lines CIS economic relations may evolve, the Central Asian republics almost certainly will continue to expand their trade ties with the outside world, particularly when it comes to the sale of raw materials—in which local processing is of such low quality that it often creates only a negative value added, in comparison with the price of the raw materials themselves on the open market. Russia's own natural resources are extensive enough, however, that over time Moscow's main interest will be more to find markets for its industrial products than to purchase raw materials in the republics.

The CIS also retains value to Russia as a structure for rebuilding a commonwealth—and, in the eyes of some, potentially even the empire. The existence of the CIS suggests that Russia has not been definitively reduced to a "small Russia" and that it remains a great power. CIS structures may serve a useful regional security function if Moscow can refrain from using them as instruments for rebuilding imperial connections, and instead relies on them to meet genuine peacekeeping needs in the republics. Distrust of Russian motivation, especially by future democratic, nationalist, anticommunist leaderships in the republics, may well hinder the full development of this role by Russia.

Russians in the "Near Abroad"

The status of Russians living in the newly independent republics will be a permanent Russian interest as long as they remain there in great numbers, as noted above. This issue is highly political in character: the actual status and problems of the Russian population per se in the near abroad are less important than how the issue is perceived politically in Russia. Few issues play as readily into the politics of the nationalist right, forcing even the liberal-internationalist Yeltsin government into a defensive position. While Russians in Russia may exhibit some degree of apatl.y about the fate of their brethren at a time when they have enough to worry about at home, the issue is always ripe for exploitation by nationalist demagogues. No Russian government will be able to ignore this issue, and some Russian governments could actively seek to exploit the issue as a means of exerting influence or pressure on neighboring governments or, worse, as justification for armed intervention. Russia's internal security would also be severely affected by a deterioration of the conditions of millions of Russians in the republics that forced them back into the Russian Federation, where shortages of jobs and housing are already severe.

Although all Central Asian republics have Russian minorities, the numbers vary widely. Nearly ten million Russians live in Central Asia overall. The Russians in the southern states—Tajikistan, Turkmenistan, Uzbekistan, and Kyrgyzstan—have no meaningful future in the area. They are relatively small in both absolute and relative numbers: 300,000 in Turkmenistan (representing 13 percent of the population), 400,000 in Tajikistan (10 percent), 900,000 in Kyrgyzstan (22 percent), and 1.7 million in Uzbekistan (11 percent). These figures compare dramatically with the 6.4 million who live in Kazakhstan, making up 40 percent of the population.

The Russians in the southern republics began an exodus from the region several years ago—especially from war-torn Tajikistan, where the Russian presence has drastically shrunk from its preindependence levels. This departure stems from concern that the Russians are vulnerable as a community—specifically, that the titular nationalities in charge of the state in each case subtly discriminate against them via language laws (the legal but not fully enforced requirement to use the native "state" language) and by other forms of preferential treatment and affirmative action that make their position more difficult and life increasingly uncongenial, if not tense. The situation is especially sad for many Russians who were born in these republics and whose families may go back several generations. But the handwriting is on the wall: the future belongs to the native titular nationality.

But the new governments of Central Asia are not endorsing any policies of outright discrimination against the Russians; in fact they often seem ambivalent about the precise tactical handling of the problem. On the one hand, they recognize that overt mistreatment or gross discrimination could spark pressure tactics from Russia, or potentially even intervention. A high proportion of the Russians resident in Central Asia are skilled technicians, and many play important roles in the operation of the industrial or administrative economy. If they depart en masse, the economy will function less capably without them—at least for a decade. The actual degree of dependence differs widely from republic to republic and the specific type of job involved. The Russian role in Kazakhstan is the most salient in terms of skills that are largely absent among that country's population. On the other hand, Russians occupy housing, jobs, and higher educational facilities that the titular nationalities covet, and the republican governments are under pressure to find new ones for their titular populations. The state is under pressure furthermore to "nativize" the local culture through new stress on the local language in all walks of life. The state in overall terms seeks to be as independent as possible from Russia. The long-term trend, then, is clearly in favor of the gradual departure of the Russians.

The most serious demographic problem of all in Central Asia is in Kazakhstan, where Russians represent some 40 percent of the population, about the same proportion as Kazakhs themselves. In Kazakhstan's advanced industrial economy, the Russians occupy key roles from which they cannot be readily removed. Even more significantly, the northern counties (oblasts) are heavily Russian in population and are home to few Kazakhs. These regions, lying just south of the Russian border, are thus part of a Russian cultural continuum, and their demographic character is not easily changed. The Russians there, unlike their kinsmen in the southern republics, do not live in a "foreign cultural environment" and are not likely to leave, especially since life is significantly better in Kazakhstan right now than in Russia. They are numerous enough to defend themselves, even without the potentially unlimited help from Russia just over the border. Indeed, the central issue in Kazakhstan's politics is the possibility that these counties might just decide to secede at some point and join the Russian Federation. This fear dominates politicians in Kazakhstan and engenders intense emotion among them.

To some extent the problem of the "overseas" Russians is a diminishing one. Russians will continue to leave all the southern republics, and probably most of southern Kazakhstan as well. Any democratic government in Russia would probably just as soon not have to deal with the politically sensitive problem of external Russians, since it is an issue tailor-made for the nationalist right and the neoimperialists. Time will reduce the salience of the problem, and Russia can do little to prevent the gradual exodus of Russians from there under nonviolent, nonemergency conditions. Kazakhstan remains highly sensitive for reasons already stated, however, and a confrontation with Russia would have the severest consequences for Russian interests in the region.

Russia's Border Security

The problem of Russia's border security possesses a vastly changed character after the breakup of the empire simply because the new republics themselves now function as buffer states between Russia and the former external states—Turkey, Iran, Afghanistan, and large sections of the Chinese border, as well as Romania, Slovakia, and Poland. In fact, for Russia itself, only one old external border remains: China. China does, however, represent a potentially highly unstable border because of the Uighur population of Xinjiang, which will surely seek to separate from Beijing upon the demise of Chinese communist power—possibly to join their Turkic brethren in Central Asia. At that time Russia will need to calculate whether its interests dictate support of breakaway Chinese provinces. In this writer's opinion, Russia will at least tacitly welcome the breakup of China's Inner Asian empire of Tibet, Xinjiang and parts of Inner Mongolia as a reduction of power of this long-time Asian rival and the creation of buffer states there.

Nuclear Security

Kazakhstan's formal possession of strategic nuclear weapons located on its soil must remain a potential concern to Moscow. These weapons are under firm Russian command and control, however, and Moscow will place the highest priority on ensuring that their control never passes over to Kazakhstan, which would present a serious threat to Russia. Nonetheless Kazakhstan may well attempt to gain some voice over their disposition and will be able to use their existence on its soil as a bargaining chip on security issues with Moscow and even the outside world. The chances are good that Moscow will seek their withdrawal to Russian soil as soon as this is financially and technically feasible.

The nuclear issue contains the broader issue of the former Soviet nuclear test sites at Semipalatinsk in Kazakhstan. While the continued use of these sites is theoretically important to Russia, Kazakhstan's government and intellectual circles are strongly anti-nuclear. They trumpet the fact that the Soviet Union had used these sites in blatant disregard for the health of the people who live in the region; a permanent exhibition in Almaty exposes the horrors of radiation and mutations produced by indiscriminate testing. The government is extremely unlikely to accede to any further use of these facilities for nuclear testing.

Preservation of the Russian Federation from Breakup

Apart from ethnic conflict within the former republics, the more serious issue of ethnic and religious "contagion" is spreading into the Russian Federation's own multiethnic and multireligious makeup. This contagion could take several forms. First is the "demonstration effect" of breakaway separatism. The Russian Federation is vulnerable to separatism not only on an ethnic basis, but potentially even on the basis of Russian regionalism, whereby local regional governments object to the centralizing political and economic policies of Moscow and themselves seek greater autonomy or independence. These drives for autonomy are based primarily on the unwillingness to share with Moscow large revenues from local natural resources. The claims of smaller ethnic groups in the region can often serve as a partial pretext for claims by Russians themselves in the same region of autonomous status. Yakutia is one such separatist possibility: The native Yakut population is indeed only a small proportion of the predominantly Russian population, but could facilitate separatism from Moscow. In this case, the local region—including both Russians and Yakuts— could profit enormously from the freedom not to share with the central government profits from the immense natural riches of the region.

Ethnic and religious contagion from Central Asia can also be serious for Russia, especially in the Federation's Turkic areas of Tatarstan and Bashkortistan. Tatarstan is already negotiating the terms of its "independence" from Moscow, even when Tatars represent only a demographic plurality in the region. A serious flare-up of ethnic trouble between Russians in the near abroad and the native Turkic populations (especially in almost neighboring Kazakhstan) could have serious impact on the psychological relationship between the Muslim Turkic Tatars and Bashkirs on the one hand, and the Russians within the Russian Federation, on the other. Indeed, one might argue that Russia might actually promote the secession of Russian-dominated northern Kazakhstan precisely to eliminate the possibility of a geographic contiguity or linkage between the Tatars and Kazakhstan that could give Tatarstan an "external" border, as opposed to being an enclave landlocked inside Russia.

The religious factor of Islam reinforces the ethnic distinction between Turkic and Slavic peoples, although a few other Muslim non-Turkic peoples live within Russia, especially in the Caucasus. The spread of Islamic fundamentalist ideas in the regions south of Russia thus threatens the exacerbation of ethno-religious differences within Russia and in the Central Asian republics, leading to the potential formation of a broader "Christian-Muslim fault line" along Russia's borders and on into Russia proper. Such a fault line would augur poorly for everyone's interests.

KEY TRENDS IN CENTRAL ASIAN POLITICS AFFECTING RUSSIA

Whatever foreign policy choices Russia may make for itself, its relations in Central Asia will of course be affected by developments within Central Asia as well. What are the key factors that will directly affect Russia?

Authoritarianism and Nationalism

A distinct and growing tension exists between Moscow's interests and the forces of nationalism and democracy in Central Asia. The Central Asian republics, with the exception of Kyrgyzstan, are still ruled by neocommunist officials. Without doubt most of them are "nationalist" in the sense that they seek what is best for their own republics and reject the exploitative character of the imperial past. None of them would hesitate to play the "nationalist card" against Russia if doing so would strengthen their positions of power. But most of them are wedded to old communist techniques of the security state and intrusive controls—albeit diminished from the Soviet period—such as control of the press, major state control over the economy, avoidance of serious privatization, and an absence of genuine political opposition or democratic procedure and marginal regard for human rights.

Many of these rulers still regard ties with Moscow as serving to provide general support to their positions of power. Old Soviet economic institutions and their supporters still exist in Russia that help provide comforting moral support to the neocommunists of Central Asia. The Central Asian republics (with the exception of Turkmenistan) support the CIS more seriously than do most other republics of the former USSR, and they see cooperation with Moscow as being in their long-term interest. This is particularly the case since Moscow at this point must view stability in Central Asia as the highest political virtue. Even Yeltsin, who may have no particular brief for the kind of neoauthoritarian rule reemerging there, understands that these rulers are committed to protecting the security of the Russian minorities, thereby protecting Yeltsin's own right flank from strong nationalist groups. Central Asia's rulers have equal incentive to avoid trouble with the local Russians in order to obviate any conflict or potential intervention from Russia. These rulers will also prevent strongly nationalist leaders from emerging in their own republics who could create greater friction with Moscow in the region.

In short, the neocommunist leaders of Central Asia (and now Azerbaijan's leader, Haydar Aliev) perpetuate the old values of multiethnic societies as much as possible within the new nationalist context. This kind of stability is in the Russian interest. Thus, a kind of symbiosis exists between Russia and the authoritarianism in Central Asia, in which the interests of both are preserved. Indeed, the Russian right views these new authoritarian rulers as the potential instruments for future resuscitation of the empire. It does not expect that local rulers will betray their own states out of loyalty to Moscow, but sees them as offering the best hope for preservation of some kind of neoimperial structure in the region.

The other side of this relationship, however, suggests that as these states move toward greater democratic practice, they will become more nationalist, more ornery, more sensitive, and potentially more anti-Moscow as the seat of the old imperial oppression. Azerbaijan, the only Turkic republic that was for nearly two years in the hands of a genuine anticommunist leader, Elçibey, and a relatively democratic nationalist party, is a good example of a state that had grown exceptionally cool toward Russia and was determined to limit its relationship with Moscow, including refusing to join the CIS structure. This example may suggest the character of future strong nationalist leadership elsewhere in Central Asia. Nonetheless, a quite authoritarian and neocommunist Turkmenistan also rejects deep involvement in the CIS structure; thus a strongly nationalist regime does not necessarily have to be democratic to be anti-Moscow.

A key hypothesis of this analysis, however, is that any move away from neocommunism or authoritarianism increases the republics' independence from Moscow. Aspirations for maximum independence by no means exclude membership in some kind of mutually beneficial confederation, but confederation will have to be far more attractive and rational in structure than the CIS if it is to win permanent adherents. Overall, the drift of the republics away from Moscow is ongoing. Temporary closeness to Moscow, born of the shock of suddenness of independence, for the moment belies a longer-range tendency to broad ethnic and cultural distinctiveness and separateness. Time therefore plays against strong Russian influence in the republics. By this logic, most Russian regimes are therefore likely to lend at least limited support to present authoritarian trends in Central Asia, out of longer-term self-interest.

The Nature of the Nationalist Threat to Moscow

Nationalism in the republics not only will lead in most cases to a distancing from Moscow, it also will seek a weakening of the position of Russian minorities in all the republics and will encourage their departure. Nationalists see the Russian presence as a permanent potential fifth column that could one day spark Russian political or military intervention, threatening the sovereignty of the republics—a threat perhaps more theoretical than real.

Apart from withholding support to Russia and discriminating against its citizens, the Turkic countries of Central Asia (and Azerbaijan) are a threat to assist separatism within the Russian Federation itself, a high proportion of whose non-Russian elements are Turkic (most notably Tatars, Bashkirs, and Yakuts). A growth of pan-Turkic and anti-Moscow sentiment will lead Central Asian nationalists to lend at least moral support to their Turkic brothers within Russia, a serious problem for Moscow, especially if it does not handle its own internal ethnic problems skillfully. It is worth noting that the Tatars played the key role in bringing the Muslim nationalist message to the other Turkic peoples in the nineteenth century. Are they destined to repeat this role in some way as they cling fiercely to their Muslim Turkic identity?

The Case of Kazakhstan. If the nationalist movement in Central Asia is concerned about the Russian presence in general, Kazakhstan from the nationalist point of view is in the greatest peril of all. The territorial integrity of the state is in thrall to the Russians who overwhelmingly dominate northern Kazakhstan and could readily secede. Indeed, this eventuality would seem more likely over time as Kazakhstan grows more nationalist and less hospitable to Russians.

The Kazakhstan challenge is of far greater importance to Russia than any other relationship in Central Asia. Kazakhstan's size, its economic importance, and its integration into the Russian economy as almost an extension of Russia place it almost on a par with Ukraine, although it lacks the Russian cultural and historical ties of Ukraine. Russia finds it hard to imagine the longer-range future without Kazakhstan as an integral part of its economic and social space.

From Kazakhstan's point of view, however, the situation looks very different. A small but important and growing Kazakh nationalist elite has as its first goal the preservation of the very fragile Kazakh culture, whose expression and very language have been extraordinarily weakened over the past century under strong Russification. The new elite is determined to reverse this trend. While Kazakhstan's Nursultan Nazarbaev is probably the most astute postcommunist leader anywhere in the new republics of the former USSR, he represents a careful compromise between Russian power and resurgent Kazakh nationalism. All Kazakh nationalists know that if they misplay the nationalist card at this stage with Russia, they will be the losers, with the northern Kazakh territories probably seceding to Russia. The nationalist task, then, is very cautiously to build up the Kazakh presence within the state from its current 40 percent to well above 50 percent in order to gain a major and firm hold over the state's own policies.[1]

Over the short term Kazakhstan is likely to be a constructive and progressive ally of Russia and of Yeltsin. As Kazakhstan grows increasingly independent with time, and more nationalist cadres move into positions of leadership, the state will likely develop closer ties with the other Turkic states to the south and perhaps with Turkey and the Muslim world as a whole. Like Tatarstan, it will always retain intimate ties with Russia, lending it distinctiveness vis-à-vis the southern republics, but its intense nationalist character beneath the surface should not be underestimated. Kazakhstan will play a key role of bridge for Russia to the south, but that bridge may be more or less cool to Moscow, depending on Russian policies. In the end it is hard to imagine Russia's going to war to maintain control of Kazakhstan, but the northern industrialized and agricultural territories are very vulnerable to Russian power. Indeed, Russia has been highly tolerant of the Russian Cossack movement, which is active in the northern and western border regions and which sees these northern regions as an integral part of Russia.

The Islamic Challenge

Russia also shares a concern about the resurgence of Islamic fundamentalism, or Islamism, in the region. Islam ranked high, of course, on the Soviet list of bogeymen, as a challenge to the atheist state, and as a constant rallying point of nationalism against state power even during the tsarist period. With the end of Soviet power and communist policies, we now witness a resurgence of Islamic practice in the region, nearly all of it an entirely understandable reaction to Islam's long oppression under communism. Mosques are springing up all over the place, reflecting the conditions of Islamic practice elsewhere in the Muslim world. In historical terms, Islam arrived very late in nomadic Kazakhstan and Kyrgyzstan, and only weakly impressed itself upon those societies. Islam is also viewed as historically very moderate in its expression throughout most of Turkic Central Asia. The conventional prognosis, then, has been that Islam is not likely to be a strong factor in Central Asian politics, especially in Kazakhstan and Kyrgyzstan. This judgment requires further examination.

The Islamic factor may yet be a challenge in at least two areas, both of which have considerable importance for Russia. First, Islam is an increasingly important facet of Central Asian identity, in a region that is searching desperately for a modern identity. While Islam is not an important factor in the politics among Central Asian states, it will be significant in dealing with Russia, since Islam, along with Turkishness, is what distinguishes the republics from Russia. Islam becomes, in short, an element of nationalism itself. Whoever is Turkic is Muslim, and vice versa (except for Persian-speaking Tajikistan). It is likely, therefore, that as nationalist movements build identity and grow vis-à-vis Russia in the decade ahead, the Islamist factor will increasingly play a part in any confrontation. Islam and nationalism, rather than being opposing forces, are likely to grow in tandem and feed each other. To the extent that Russian and Turkic nationalism are confrontational, Islam will play in that same equation. This factor must be of concern to Moscow, although there is not a lot the latter can do about the problem other than exercise sensitivity in dealing with growing nationalist sentiment in the republics.

Islam is also likely to grow as a vehicle of protest against Central Asian regimes when they are oppressive, incapable of meeting economic and social needs, or otherwise seen as "illegitimate." While Islam in Central Asia during the past seventy-five years has been deprived of any political role, there is no reason that Central Asia should be immune from the pattern of Islamic political trends and movements that we see in other Muslim states of the world, where the Islamists have often become the primary vehicle of organized opposition against the illegitimate or failing state. As noted above, we are likely to witness growing opposition to repressive states over the next decade.

The existence of Islamic political trends today serves as a pretext to authoritarian regimes all over the Muslim world to justify further repression and absence of political participation in the name of stemming the "fundamentalist tide." Uzbekistan in particular emphasizes this point with Washington in an effort to get dispensation for violation of democratic norms. The more these repressive regimes are linked with Moscow, the greater their loss of legitimacy in Islamist eyes. And as elsewhere in the Muslim world, the combination of cultural factors and government policies usually ends up inadvertently leaving the entire field of opposition almost exclusively to Islamic forces. Only toleration for the emergence of other legitimate opposition parties and forces will diminish Islamic monopoly of opposition politics.

Just as Turkic nationalism can operate as a threat to the territorial integrity of the Russian Federation, with its large Turkic minorities, Islam can function in the same way, since these peoples are also Muslims. Islam is a powerful unifying factor among all these peoples, linking their national outlooks against a non-Muslim great Slavic power. Islam need not be the sole linking factor, but can become so if other political outlets are not available.

In general, resurgent nationalist and Islamic impulses of an anti-Russian nature—whether directed against Russia itself or against Russian populations resident in Central Asia—should also be of some concern to the West. These confrontations play into the hands of Russian extreme nationalists and xenophobes who in the worst case could find justification to intervene in Central Asia—even with force. Cultural confrontation will also exacerbate an overall sense of Russian paranoia, isolation, and xenophobia, none of which is in the Western interest.

The West needs to be discriminate in viewing the Islamic resurgence in Central Asia. Islam will surely play a growing role in politics, but it need not automatically become radical or threatening to Western interests. To the extent that social and economic trends in the region are negative, Islamic radicalism will serve as the vehicle for discontent, but is not the cause of that discontent. Central Asian Islamic movements are also unlikely to fall captive to Iran, although connections between them are certain. Iran, too, has interests to pursue in the region other than the propagation of its form of Islamic vision.

Integration of Central Asia into the Muslim World

The final major trend affecting Russia in Central Asia is the region's inevitable reintegration into the external world around it. These relationships are indeed entirely natural and were broken artificially by the tsarist and Bolshevik empires. They are now being restored and will to some extent weaken the monopolistic character of Russian ties with the republics in the economic and security realms. States whose influence will grow in the region, at Russian expense, are China, India, Pakistan, Afghanistan, Iran, Turkey, and selected Arab countries. Farther afield, Western Europe, Japan, and the United States will also find some measure of growing influence there. The Central Asian states in any case are unlikely to link their futures with any one state in the region; they are interested in getting whatever benefits possible from all states from East to West.

CENTRAL ASIA AND RUSSIAN FOREIGN POLICY

Russia not only is casting about for approaches to the near abroad, but also is actively debating questions about its broader orientation to the world. The Atlanticists, largely flowing from the Shevardnadze tradition and continued by Foreign Minister Andrei Kozyrev, are committed to a firm break with the communist past and to a future relationship linking Russia integrally with the "Atlantic"—that is, Western—democratic tradition and its international institutions, possibly even with an American orientation. An alternative orientation over time will be the social-democratic movements of Western Europe.

The other main Russian foreign policy school, embracing a broad diversity among its constituents, is often referred to as the "Eurasianist." This group posits that Russia is not simply a European power, but rather a Eurasian power whose interests and worldview do not neatly dovetail with Western positions. The operative factors driving the "Eurasianists" are diverse, but the numbers and influence of this school are growing as Russia expresses frustration with its truncated post–Cold War world role. The first challenge arises in economics, for the Atlanticist orientation posits a need to move forcefully ahead with radical reforms and privatization in order to advance and integrate Russia more closely into European and global economic institutions. Many of the Eurasianists are linked to the former military-industrialist complex, which is most threatened by privatization and elimination of state subsidies to failing mega-industries; they are wary of the strongly re-formist Atlanticist approach, which will weaken their elitist position within the economy.

In the ideological realm, however, the two schools differ even more sharply. As a diverse group, the Eurasianists might roughly be divided into "mystical" and more pragmatic orientations. A nearly mystical vision of the "special role" and mission of Russia in history—which draws in part on the nineteenth-century Slavophile vision—leads some Eurasianists to see Russia in a special moral light that is different from the "materialism" of the West. The more pragmatic elements eschew any particular religious or moral tone to policy, but speak more simply of the need for Russia to propagate its "own" foreign policy rather than simply linking itself to erstwhile American and European rivals, whose interests they perceive as different by definition and possibly hostile to Russia. At times it seems that the Eurasianists seek to be different for the very sake of being different, to differentiate Russia in any way possible from the West. Indeed, after the Soviet loss of its "superpower" role, many Russians seem psychologically discomfited by any suggestion of "me-tooism," in which Russia would subscribe to an Americo-centric order in post-Soviet foreign policy. If the Russian state is to be a great power, the reasoning goes, it must have its own distinctive foreign policy role in the world.

Much of this differentiation may almost be formalistic in character, designed for domestic consumption. The Eurasian school does not adduce convincing evidence of genuinely differing interests between Western and Russian international interests—except as it relates to the hardships of *perestroika* and the damage the democratization and reform process has done to the once powerful Soviet state. The Eurasianists pose no serious, substantive ideological alternative except to be "different."

There is, obviously, no question that Russia is a Eurasian power; not to recognize this would be absurd, given Russia's sweeping geographic location right across the Asian continent. But what does a "Eurasian" policy imply? That Russia should take its Asian relationships and interests as seriously as its European connections? Such a position seems so obvious as to be beyond debate. Of course Russia must devote considerable attention to its relations with Japan, China, Korea, and India, among others. Russia is a Pacific power as well as Western power. But one senses that many of the Eurasianists read something deeper and more mystical into the term. Should Russia be "Asian" in terms of its style and character of government? Indeed, Russia has been accused for centuries of maintaining "Asiatic despotisms," right on through the communist period. Surely this is not the mystical implication the Eurasianists seek to impart today.

Yet other Russian foreign policy specialists suggest that Russia must carve out a special arena in which it can play a significant role, where its influence will be felt. By this reasoning Russia calculates that it cannot seriously play in European politics where it lacks the economic clout or the tradition of involvement. East Asia is largely beyond consideration as well, again because of Russia's weak economic position in an already well-defined Asian game dominated by China, Japan, and a growing Korea. Russia is thus "left" with the Middle East as an arena for action, a region where it has traditionally exercised major influence and still can "make a difference." The Middle East furthermore contains numerous states that used to be close to the old Soviet Union and in principle could still be close to Russia today—although there is no inherent reason that Russia should be limited strictly to the old client states. Indeed, it would seem to be self-defeating for Russia to seek to restore its privileged position in such radical states as Syria, Iraq, and Libya, where it would instantly win the enmity not only of the West, but of the moderate Arab states (including oil-producing states) as well. Additionally, Russia has little to offer the old radicals except more weapons and some limited diplomatic support. A decision by Russia to relink itself with Middle Eastern radicals would be tantamount to a return to a broad ideological confrontation with the West as a whole. Therefore, any kind of "distinctive" Middle Eastern role would have to be broad and nonideological in order to avoid an explicit and ruinous anti-Western character.

Nonetheless, Russian "distinctiveness" can already be seen in some contexts in Russian extreme right-wing nationalist circles that have sent volunteers to Serbia and supported Iraq rhetorically. These ultranationalist positions seem to be driven by a groundless desire to oppose the West almost for the sake of doing so. There are few logical correlations to any realistic gains for Russia of any kind. Still, Russia has good reasons to consider maintaining a serious role in the Middle East, on historical as well as economic grounds. But what, then, are the implications of a strong and independent Russian role in the Middle East? How does it relate to Russian policies and interests in Central Asia?

Basically a deep contradiction exists between a major Russian role in the Middle East and a simultaneous, parallel position of confrontation, conflict, or neoimperialism in Central Asia. Central Asian regimes, whose own ties with the rest of the Muslim world are improving, would be quick to denounce Russia in Islamic circles in ways that could damage Russia's credibility. They would seek alliances in the Muslim world against Russia, and in principle could conduct their own subversive operations within Russia itself to support Muslim separatism there.

Furthermore, a policy of confrontation in Central Asia would affect Turkey's role in the region. The Central Asian states would inevitably seek some kind of Turkish support, and Turkey would find it difficult to remain outside the conflict—at least on the political level. Under these circumstances Russian pressure would inadvertently serve to consolidate pan-Turkic feelings and intensify opposing Slavic vs. pan-Turkic cultural belts across Asia. Confronted with resurgent Turkish and Muslim influence in Central Asia, Russia might then turn to back Iran against Turkish power, strengthening a "Persian belt" running from Iran, across northern Afghanistan into Tajikistan, just south of the Turkic belt. Such a Russian posture would only hasten broader Turkish-Iranian confrontation that already may develop out of conflicting interests in Azerbaijan. If Russia seeks to weaken Turkey, the Iranian card will inevitably be an element of that strategy, with perhaps other, unintended anti-Western overtones as well.

Another possible "special" role for Russia would be as champion of Third World causes, even if not in a purely confrontational fashion against the West. Russia, as a country facing severe problems with the transition to capitalism, dependent in many ways upon the export of raw materials in a fickle international commodities market, concerned about domination of the international market systems by the more advanced West, in debt to Western financial institutions, could surely find many common causes with the Third World in which to seek to redress grievances, disparities, and inequities in the international economic order. It could press for the strengthening of UN mechanisms as a means of weakening the unilateral power of Western states. The international political spectrum offers room for some country to perform this function as spokesman and advocate for Third World causes, even if not in a revolutionary or confrontational fashion. Many Third World states are uncomfortable with a unipolar world in which they feel they have less room for maneuver and political play than during the bipolar Cold War, which offered the opportunity to play off opposing camps in order to maximize their own freedom of maneuver. This kind of Russian role might find significant resonance among many Third World states. But even this role would seem difficult to square with one in which Russia was engaged in ethnic and religious conflict with the Central Asian and Caucasian states along lines that smacked of Russian/European chauvinism.

A Russian nationalist-chauvinist government in Moscow could take the opposite position and actively work against the Turkish/Muslim threat to the south, but such a position might be tantamount to declaring war against Islam as a whole. The only natural ally for such a policy in the region would be India, which already views with dismay the resurgence of Islam in Central Asia, long an area under firm Russian control with no meaningful Islamic content. It is important to note that it was Central Asian Turkic conquerors who conquered northern India six centuries ago and established the Mughal Empire, one of the glories of high Islamic civilization. Today the emergence of Central Asia marks the first time in many hundreds of years—since the competing British and Russian empires closed off Central Asia from the subcontinent—that the Muslims of the subcontinent are once again directly joined with their coreligionists in Central Asia, via Afghanistan. The huge new "Islamic strategic depth" that Pakistan has acquired has greatly excited Pakistan and upset India.

How will Russia react to these events? Could it turn to India, to squeeze Central Asian–Muslim power from north as well as south? Such a bold confrontational position toward Islam would likely carry a high cost for Russia in the Islamic world. Here, too, then, Russia's Central Asian policies strongly affect its broader external options. Settlement of its Central Asian policy would seem to be prerequisite to Russia's playing any number of other significant roles in the Middle East.

China, likewise, cannot be left out of this equation. As communism collapses in China, resurgent nationalist-separatist forces there will immediately arise, threatening the Chinese empire. Uighur Turks in Xianjing and Tibetans have had long claim to independence. The Mongols of Inner Mongolia seek relief from Chinese ethnic cleansing along the borders of Outer Mongolia, which they would like to join. These three nationalities already are in contact with each other about their future options of independence from Chinese control. What position will Russia take on this potential separatism in China? On the one hand, Russia would almost surely rejoice at the diminution of the size and influence of its largest land rival on the Asian continent. But a strengthening of the Turkish belt could also run counter to Russian interests if Russia has chosen the path of confrontation with the Turks. In short, future events in China will also pose serious strategic questions to Moscow that will require resolution—the most basic being the character of its relations with the Turkic belt.

Implications for the United States

American interests in Central Asia are primarily two: economic and geopolitical. In economic terms the region has nothing at all of vital importance to the United States. We depend on no vital commodities, nor is there a pattern of trade that we wish to preserve from the past, as there is between Russia and Central Asia. The main U.S. economic interest lies in investment opportunities, primarily in the energy resources (oil and gas) of Azerbaijan, Turkmenistan, Kazakhstan, and Uzbekistan, as well as in some of the mineral resources, such as the gold reserves of Uzbekistan and Kyrgyzstan. These are valuable opportunities for U.S. firms, but do not represent crucial economic interests for the United States as a whole or affect its oil supply. Given U.S. capital and energy expertise, the United States in fact does have significant competitive advantages in investing in these energy projects.

Geopolitically, the character of U.S. interests is primarily negative—that is, to prevent negative developments in the region that could directly or indirectly affect other, more critical American interests. These interests are prevention of nuclear proliferation or conflict in Central Asia, the emergence of radical anti-Western Islamic governments, and Russian-Islamic confrontations in Central Asia that could have negative impact on the course of Russian political evolution and foreign policy.

Nuclear proliferation is particularly a concern because Greater Central Asia is already to some extent nuclearized. Many of the larger regional players—Russia, China, India, Pakistan, and Kazakhstan—possess nuclear capabilities. Central Asia as a cockpit for future geopolitical struggle could involve nuclear powers, although, one would hope, not at any level of basic national survival that might invoke the use of nuclear weapons. Anticipation of ethnic fault lines and nationalists' aspirations there is an important first step in handling the inevitable destabilization inherent in the breakup and geopolitical change of western China after the fall of communism.

As elsewhere in the world, the United States has an interest in preventing the spread of Islamic radicalism in the region. In reality, however, the United States can do little about this problem, since such a phenomenon will have indigenous roots almost exclusively beyond U.S. influence or control. The Russian reaction is of greater importance to the United States, if it leads to either a resurgence of genuine Russian imperialist intervention in the region or a strengthening of anti-Western chauvinist Russian nationalism. Either of these developments would have negative impact on international politics in Eurasia. One must take care, however, to distinguish between Russian great-power interest and influence in the region— even as the first source of external intervention in cases of turmoil ("Monroeski Doctrine")—and resurgent imperialism aiming at recreation of a Russian Empire with imperial ambitions and an expansionist ideology to go with it. The difference is profound in terms of the interests of the international community at large.

American interests in the future of Russia are obviously far more intense than any possible American interest in Central Asia. This does not mean that the United States will invariably sacrifice the interests of the Central Asian states to the interests of Russia.

To a considerable extent, American geopolitical interests in Central Asia should in fact not be markedly at odds with a *liberal-democratic* Russia's interests there as well. If Russia withdraws from membership in the liberal-democratic community, then American interests become vastly less congruent with any aspects of Russian interests. In short, serious contradiction need not exist between Russian and American interests in Central Asia as long as basic shared political values exist.

ARE GEOPOLITICS INEXORABLE?

This study has focused on fundamental geopolitical forces at work in the Eurasian region. It posits basic elements of potential confrontation and clash between the grander forces of Russia, China, Central Asia, and Turkish and Iranian nationalism. Yet it would be a mistake to assume that we are somehow talking about inexorable, inchoate forces that are destined to clash in the dark night of geopolitics. These forces are not necessarily foreordained to clash. Much depends not only on the *location* of these states and their political culture, but also on the *character* of governance in each. If they are highly authoritarian, the chances of conflict expand considerably. Ambitious unconstrained rulers can operate largely at will against each other.

On the other hand, if these states are committed to some kind of democratic governance and participatory politics, the chances of conflict are significantly reduced. Liberal-democratic governments are much more likely to face constraints on both their ideological zeal and their ability to commit their peoples and countries to conflict. If the major states are fortunate enough to be managed by moderate forces, the geopolitical future of the region can witness a period of cooperative and mutually beneficial relations. Nationalist and geopolitical rivalries can be reduced from a state of zero-sum game to one of "normal" ajudicable frictions. The character of the governments in the region thus takes on critical importance for the stability and calm of the region and for the interests of its various players.

The importance of Central Asia to Russia thus varies considerably with the ideological vision of the government in power. To a moderate democratic Russia, the primary interest would seem to focus on a stability in Central Asia designed to reduce risk to the welfare of the large number of Russians living there, to avoid the possibility of conflict and war that might drag Russia into the fray, and to avoid the emergence of regimes and ideologies hostile to Russia and its interests. Russia would naturally prefer mutually beneficial relations with the republics and maintenance of a modicum of influence in the region. To a democratic Russia, a more "Atlanticist" policy would come more naturally, in which the value of economic and political relations with the West would outweigh the importance of Central Asia. But if Russia is ruled by more radical nationalists, the goals might differ substantially. That kind of a Russia would seek to maximize its influence in the region and possibly to restore some kind of neoimperial control over the states there. Such policies would inevitably call for far more interventionist politics from Moscow, and would enhance the prospects for friction and clash. It might also involve Russia in rivalries with neighboring and regional states for influence as well. Central Asia would loom larger as part of a neoimperial design, partially overshadowing Russia's ties with the West. It would likely be accompanied by a policy of emphasis on an ill-defined "special role" for Russia, mainly for the sake of seeming to demonstrate the characteristics of a great power—even if the goals of that power were not carefully defined.

Central Asia thus varies in its importance to Russia, depending on the specific geopolitical goals of any given regime. Even with modest geopolitical goals, Russia must come to terms with its policies for the "near abroad" before it can chart a more comprehensive foreign policy for the external world. Its policies for the near abroad will inevitably affect the character of its wider external relations. In short, Russia's approach to the loss of empire will have the most decisive impact on its future handling of the region. Other exogenous factors include the actions and policies of neighboring strong states, such as Turkey, Iran, Pakistan, India, and China.

Whatever set of policies emerge from the various regional states, one point is clear: Central Asia is aptly named. It lies at the heart of the vast Eurasian region, potentially the cockpit of the conflicting forces of Asia as a whole. The situation in the region is only beginning to unfold in the new world environment. If Russia has begun a process of accommodating to its dramatic new circumstances, China has not even initiated the process of imperial collapse, potential breakup, and ideological reorientation. The Central Asian states themselves have not yet attained their new identities, which may be fully revealed only when the neocommunist leaderships currently at the helm bite the dust and cede power to more nationalist, nativist forces. It will thus be many years before all of the basic new geopolitical forces of the region emerge and solidify. In the meantime, Russia will continue to evolve its new policies in the region, which will in turn sharply affect the character and behavior of other states and regimes. Stability is not likely to mark the decade ahead as this Asian heartland establishes itself on the new geopolitical map of the world.

NOTES

1. Indeed, Nazarbaev should not be viewed as antinationalist or a Russian toady. But he represents the tie of continuity with the past, a leader who has the confidence of both the Russians and the Kazakhs for the moment, as well as great competence as a leader. Kazakhstan is fortunate to have him, but he is essentially transitional in character. He can preserve stability as the country and its more nationalist elite build the foundations for a future Kazakh-dominated Kazakhstan that is not at risk of losing the northern territories. That implies a delicate process of gradual Kazakh takeover throughout the country, including the north, but done so imperceptibly as not to spark secession there.

Chapter 4

Central Asia and the West

Robert Cullen

Western contact with Central Asia is at a peak not seen since the year 1241, when Batu Khan and his horsemen rode out of the East, laid waste to Hungary, and then disappeared back into the steppe. In the post-Batu era, Central Asia receded rapidly from the Western field of vision. Remote and landlocked, it was ignored by Westerners exploring the world by sea. Hostile or indifferent empires controlled its peoples. No cultural or religious links facilitated contact. For Westerners, Central Asia was part of the world's outback, a region slightly more accessible than, say, the North Pole, but hardly as interesting.[1]

With the collapse of the Soviet Union and the emergence of five new Central Asian states, one of which contains nuclear weapons, a reassessment is obviously required. And some analysts have begun to make the case that Central Asia is now an area of strategic concern to the West, a region whose importance is "difficult to overestimate."[2] International oil executives have rushed to the scene and pronounced it "a new Kuwait."[3] Spinners of scenarios wonder what would happen if Murphy's Law ran amok and Kazakhstan became a radical Islamic state, took control of its portion of the old Soviet nuclear arsenal, and shared it with Iran. In fact, the West has significant interests in Central Asia. Deciding whether they rise to the level of vital and strategic concerns requires, first, a brief look at the history of the region.

THE PAST

The eponymous peoples of Kazakhstan, Uzbekistan, Turkmenistan, and Kyrgyzstan are descendants of nomadic Turkic and
Mongol tribes that have migrated and jostled one another over the
high Central Asian plateaus and river valleys from the time before
the age of written history. (Tajiks are of Persian origin.) For almost
fifteen hundred years, beginning in the second century B.C., Central
Asia produced the fiercest armies in the world. Their military su-
premacy began roughly when the invention of the stirrup gave a
mounted warrior the ability to ride and fight at the same time;
Central Asian nomads did this better than anyone. Their su-
premacy ended when the invention of explosives and firearms
tipped the military balance in favor of settled cultures better able
to absorb and develop technology.

For reasons rooted in their nomadic culture, the Central
Asians lagged behind the West in the development of urban centers, technology, and industry. When the European powers began
subjugating the pastoral and nomadic peoples of the world in the
sixteenth and seventeenth centuries, the Central Asians had no effective defense. The population was largely rural and illiterate. The
average man's loyalty lay with his clan, rather than with a state. He
moved with the clan and its herds from summer to winter pastures,
living in a yurt. In a loose way, the territory was governed by
khans, who were the weak heirs of Attila, Chingis, Batu, and
Tamerlane. One by one, beginning in the time of Peter the Great,
these khanates fell under the domination of an expanding Russia.
By the middle of the nineteenth century, virtually all of Central
Asia had been colonized. Although groups of intellectuals were
slowly stirring in the towns of the region, colonization occurred
before any of the Central Asian societies developed the attributes
of a modern nation.

As elsewhere in the world, colonization was at best a mixed
blessing. It brought the region railroads, more settled agriculture,
and more education. But neither the tsars nor the Bolsheviks dis-
played much understanding of the region or any desire to help it
toward political and economic modernity. Boundaries were drawn
arbitrarily, and territories were misnamed. Kazakhstan, for exam-

ple, entered the Soviet Union under the name Kyrgyz Autonomous Soviet Socialist Republic, because the authorities in Moscow were not sure of the difference between a Kazakh and a Kyrgyz. In other instances, the Stalin regime followed a policy of drawing borders that divided clans and tribes into different subdivisions, putting many Tajiks in Uzbekistan, for example, and many ethnic Uzbeks in Kyrgyzstan. It left Uzbekistan with claims to parts of Kyrgyzstan, and Tajikistan with claims to the traditionally Persian-speaking cities of Samarkand and Bukhara, which are in Uzbekistan. The Soviet republics were themselves artificial distinctions. Prior to their creation, the region was most commonly called Turkestan, since its peoples (with the exception of the Tajiks) spoke Turkic languages. The notion of an Uzbek nation or a Kazakh nation was created largely in the Soviet period.

In these respects, then, the new nations of Central Asia, though they are often thought of as former components of a global superpower, bear a great resemblance to the countries of Africa when they emerged from colonial status in the 1960s. And they can be expected to go through many of the nation-building problems and border conflicts that have plagued Africa in the past thirty years.

THE SOVIET LEGACY

Central Asia's Soviet patrimony includes other daunting problems. The political elites of each new state have grown up in a one-party, winner-takes-everything system. (Four of the republics are led by former Communist Party first secretaries; in the fifth, Kyrgyzstan, President Askar Akayev's authority is under challenge from ex-Communists in the parliament.) These men are accustomed to central control of agriculture and industry. The political competition that has existed among them tends to revolve around regional or clan rivalries rather than parties representing class interests or other ideologies. In Kazakhstan, for instance, Kazakh political patronage must be balanced among the descendants of three tribal military coalitions, the Great Horde, the Middle Horde, and the Small Horde. (Dinmukhamed Kunaev, the Kazakh leader under Leonid Brezhnev, came from the Great Horde. So does President Nursultan Nazarbaev.) In Tajikistan, power struggles tend to revolve around regional rivalries, with the politicians from the north generally emerging on top.

Soviet economic and environmental policies left a calamitous legacy. The demands of Moscow's central planners for ever more cotton led to the creation of a ruinous monoculture in much of the region's fertile area. Rivers were siphoned off to irrigate cotton fields; as a result, the Aral Sea has been partially destroyed, the salinity of the water supply has tripled, fishing has been wiped out. Winters in the Aral region are now longer and colder; summers are shorter and drier. In Uzbekistan, forests and orchards have all but disappeared to make room for more cotton fields. The population shows increased rates of typhoid, cancer, and hepatitis, apparently because of the vile mix of bad water and chemicals placed in the fields to raise cotton yields. Near the Aral, mothers sometimes immolate themselves after discovering that their breast milk, polluted by the surrounding environment, has brought disease to their children. Each year, over 1,500 people in Kyrgyzstan die from digestive illness, and more than 300,000 (in a population of 4.6 million) contract typhus, viral hepatitis, and other diseases caused by water pollution. Soviet rule amounted, said two observers, to a "sixty-year pattern of ecocide by deliberate design,"[4] and it will take Central Asians generations to recover.

The Soviet system accelerated the migration of Slavs to Central Asia, particularly in the areas of northern Kazakhstan, contiguous with Russia, that were the subjects of Nikita Khrushchev's Virgin Lands campaign. Slavs (Russians and Ukrainians) now outnumber Kazakhs in Kazakhstan. The other republics have Russian minorities ranging from 3 percent to about 20 percent. These minorities tend to live in cities and to occupy skilled and managerial positions in industry, while the indigenous populations engage in agriculture. Since independence, thousands of them have decided to return to Russia. This leaves the Central Asian governments with the delicate challenge of appeasing nationalist sentiment among the indigenous population without alienating Russians, who are vital to the local economies. If they fail, the consequences could be worse than merely more economic inefficiency. The Central Asians run the risk of upsetting relations with a Russia worried about absorbing refugees from the erstwhile Soviet republics.

These legacies suggest still more difficulties for the Central Asian states in their first years of independence. The region faces staggering environmental cleanup costs at the same time it attempts to develop a diversified economy. It seems fated to an extended struggle with the type of poverty endemic in the developing world; it will not be a consumer products market of importance for many years. The potential for political instability, violations of human rights, ethnic clashes, and border conflict is high. Western investment in the region, whether of political or financial capital, will almost certainly be a risky venture.

WESTERN INTERESTS

The foreign policy interests of a nation or group of nations fall roughly into three categories. Vital national interests encompass those bearing directly and forcefully on a country's physical security or standard of living. A second tier of interests involve the physical security and prosperity of a nation's key friends and trading partners. From the point of view of the United States, this list might include the North Atlantic Treaty Organization (NATO) allies, Japan, Israel, the oil-producing states of the Persian Gulf, and a handful of others; a stable and pluralist Russia falls into this second category. The third category includes a broad range of strategic, economic, and humanitarian interests that, though significant in many cases, never justify major expenditures of blood or treasure.

What might elevate Western interests in Central Asia beyond the third category? The area appears to be no more vital to Western interests than any other remote and potentially turbulent region of the developing world—and perhaps less so, since the West bears no moral responsibility for helping to overcome the problems created by colonialism there. Of the three major non-Slavic regions of the former Soviet Union, Central Asia is geopolitically the least important. The newly independent states of the Baltic region are an integral part of Europe; war or instability there could lead to a direct threat to American interests of the second category. The Trans-Caucasus is more distant, but still the turmoil there has a limited potential to engage Turkey, an important part of the

Western alliance, or to spill over into the Persian Gulf. Central Asia is so far removed that it presents, at first glance, almost no vital concerns for the West, save, perhaps, for its potential to affect the stability of Russia.

But four questions peculiar to the region require a closer look before Central Asia can be dismissed to the rear burners of Western policy. Will Central Asia add significant momentum to the radical Islamic movement that threatens Western interests in the Middle East? Might the exploitation of Central Asian oil and gas resources reduce Western dependence on the volatile Persian Gulf region? Might the nuclear weapons and weapons components remaining in Kazakhstan fall into the hands of a rogue government or terrorists? And should the attempts by regional powers—Russia, Iran, Turkey, and China—to extend their spheres of influence cause serious concern in the West?

ISLAM

According to U.S. government sources,[5] as many as fifteen thousand new mosques (many no grander than huts) have opened in the five Central Asian states since *perestroika* freed religion from the shackles of traditional Soviet policy. A smaller number of Islamic schools have opened, offering both general education and clerical training. The old, discredited clergy of the Soviet period are being replaced by younger men, many of them trained in Egypt, Libya, and other Middle Eastern nations. Support for these developments comes from a variety of sources: the regional governments; private benefactors; and foreign powers, including Saudi Arabia and Iran. It seems safe to predict that within a few more years, Islam will be well established as the dominant religion in a region once officially classified as atheistic. But will it be a radical, revolutionary Islam, adding strength to a movement that promises to struggle against Western interests and influence throughout the Middle East?

Several factors suggest that it will not. First, 98 percent of Central Asia's Muslims are Sunni, not Shi'ite. Obviously, this works to the disadvantage of the most radical Islamic clergy in the region, in Iran, and to the advantage of more conservative elements. According to U.S. government sources, the growth in the ranks and strength of Islam in Central Asia has roughly followed the traditional proportion—that is, overwhelmingly Sunni. Sunnis have their radicals. But no evidence suggests that radical Sunni elements like the Muslim Brotherhood are attracting converts in most of Central Asia.

Second, Islam never occupied as prominent a place in pre-Soviet Central Asian societies as it did in neighboring regions. "The pastoral nomads (the Kazakh masses and most of the Kazakh nobility) had only the sketchiest knowledge of Muslim tenets and practices," Martha Brill Olcott of Colgate University observed in her survey of the Kazakhs.[6] This was true as well of the equally nomadic Kyrgyz and Turkmen. The Uzbeks and Tajiks, whose societies had produced the major cities of the region, had a more formal adherence to Islam, but never a theocratic state.

The Soviet period did nothing to deepen Islam's roots in Central Asia. Soviet religious authorities grudgingly permitted a small number of mosques and clerics. The approved clerics had a deserved reputation for being under the thumb of the state. Foreigners traveling in Central Asia in the last two decades of Soviet power generally found that religion occupied a minor place in people's lives.

Third, the political elites in the Central Asian states have been thoroughly indoctrinated in the concept of a secular state. Their own self-interest dictates that they not confront, but rather carefully circumscribe, the role of religion. If an Islamic party came to power in Central Asia, the job security of former Soviet officials would be rather dramatically diminished. In conversations since independence, Central Asian leaders have suggested they want a church-state relationship like that in Turkey. The wiser of them will seek an accommodation with Islam and strive not to let it become a vehicle for expressing dissent and resistance.

This, unfortunately, appears already to have happened in Tajikistan. The civil conflict raging there is sometimes described as a battle between old-guard communists and Islamic rebels. But in fact it began as a more complex situation than that, with both regional and ethnic dimensions. The government leaders who returned to power in November 1992 are communists or former communists, generally from the area around Khujand, in northern

Tajikistan. The Khujand area has a significant Uzbek population; its politicians tend to promote Uzbeks and to favor less nationalistic policies than those from predominantly Tajik areas. The factions now in revolt originally included an amalgam of Tajik nationalists, particularly from the impoverished southern region; democratic intellectuals; separatists from the Gorno Badakhshan region of the Pamir Mountains; and the Islamic Renaissance Party (IRP).

But as the conflict grew more violent and government repression grew more severe,[7] the role of Islamic militants within the rebel factions grew as well, and so did the role of foreigners. According to reports from the scene,[8] *mujahedeen* factions in the Tajik-populated region of neighboring Afghanistan and from Arab states have been training, arming, and otherwise assisting the IRP's guerrillas. The party appears to have become the dominant faction within the rebel camp.

The war in Tajikistan now involves Russia, which supplies border troops to Tajikistan under the nominal command of the Commonwealth of Independent States (CIS). Uzbekistan, which also has a government of ex-communists worried about religious militants, has also supplied troops to fight the Islamic rebels. On April 5, 1993, the Islamic rebels captured ten Russian border guards.[9] As long as the war continues, such incidents are likely to multiply.

But unfortunate as the war is, several improbable events would have to take place for it to rise to the level of a serious threat to Western interests. First, Russia would have to make a major force commitment to defend the ex-communists now in power in Dushanbe, Tajikistan's capital. Given the present Russian government, this is all but impossible. Memories of Afghanistan are too fresh, and sympathy for ex-communists in too short supply. A more nationalist government might replace the Yeltsin government and show more interest in restoring the former Soviet Union. But the nationalists now on the scene in Moscow seem likely to focus their attention on the Slavic, European parts of the former empire than on the Muslim areas of Central Asia, which most Russians look upon as a collection of dependent states that take more from Russia than they contribute. Aleksandr Solzhenitsyn, in his July 1990 essays in the Moscow newspaper *Komsomolskaya Pravda*, suggested that Russia had no real claims or interests in any of Central Asia except for northern Kazakhstan, where the population is largely Russian. Boris Yeltsin implied as much when he proceeded without the Central Asian presidents at the meeting that established the CIS in December 1991. Subsequent assertions of a unilateral Russian right to intervene as a "peacekeeper" in the old Soviet territory do not alter Central Asia's secondary rank on Moscow's list of priorities.

Even if Russia does take a more active role in the Tajik war, the West will have cause for major concern only if the fighting destabilizes the government in Moscow or if, less probably, it provokes an Islamic alliance that includes Iran, Afghanistan, Pakistan, and perhaps several Central Asian states, ready to take Russia on in a major war. Given the ethnic, religious, and political rivalries within those states, this has to be considered an extremely unlikely chain of misfortune.

And the formation of such an alliance is not an event the West has much leverage to prevent. Certainly there is no conceivable direct intervention by the United States or by a Western coalition that could affect the growth of Islam in Central Asia. At best, the West can encourage as much contact as possible between Central Asian Muslims and their coreligionists in moderate states like Turkey and Egypt. They, rather than Iran, should be the countries that sponsor and train the next generation of Islamic clerics and intellectuals in Central Asia. The West can also encourage the existing governments in Central Asia to recognize that a commitment to pluralist political institutions is one way to prevent the emergence of an opposition movement under the Islamic banner.

OIL AND GAS

Belief in Central Asia as a latter-day El Dorado for Western oil and gas companies requires an almost deliberate suspension of judgment. The existence of oil in the basin of the Caspian Sea has been known for more than a century. Baku, on the Caspian's western shore, was an oil boomtown in the 1890s, and its oil fields were a strategic objective for the German Wehrmacht in 1941. Moreover, Soviet geologists were not incompetent; they managed to find oil and other minerals in some of the most remote and inhospitable regions of Siberia. The idea that they would have overlooked vast Central Asian deposits that now await ready exploitation by more canny Western firms smacks, at best, of hubris and, at worst, of a desire to extract some fat commissions and consulting fees from gullible investors.

According to the unpublished and presumably disinterested estimates of experts at the U.S. Geological Survey, the proven and potential reserves in Central Asia suggest that it will become a significant petroleum source, on the order of Alaska's North Slope—but hardly a new Kuwait.[10] The most important Central Asian field, in the Tengiz Basin of western Kazakhstan, is already the subject of a reported $20 billion deal between the government of Kazakhstan and Chevron Corporation.[11] Its identified reserves are estimated at sixteen billion barrels, about one-sixth the proven reserves of Kuwait. Estimates of this field's undiscovered reserves range from ten billion to one hundred billion barrels, with the safest guess being around thirty billion barrels. An additional twelve billion barrels of identified reserves lie under the Caspian Sea, in fields shared by Russia, Azerbaijan, Kazakhstan, and Turkmenistan. Only one other field, the North Ustiert, shared by Kazakhstan and Uzbekistan, has identified reserves of more than a billion barrels.

Moreover, two problems will hinder the exploitation of these fields. First, the oil tends to have a high sulfur content and therefore requires a more expensive and complex refining process than the sweet crude oil of Saudi Arabia. More important, there is no easy way to export oil from Central Asia. A long, transnational pipeline will have to be built to get the oil from the fields to a seaport. One potential route, the favored choice of Kazakhstan and the oil companies as of this writing, is across southern Russia to the port of Novorossisk on the Black Sea. An alternative route would go through the Trans-Caucasus and across Turkey to the Mediterranean. The shortest route would be south, through Iran, to the Persian Gulf. For obvious reasons, Turkey, Russia, and Iran each has a favorite route, and each is pressing hard to be selected. Turkey has suggested that it might not permit the passage of oil tankers through the Bosporus if the Russian route via Novorossisk is selected. But the Turkish route would require crossing the Trans-Caucasus, a region that does not appear likely to be a safe place for pipelines in the foreseeable future.

The West has several interests in all this. The first is that Central Asian oil be added to the world's supply. The second is that Western companies get a fair opportunity to sell the technology and expertise that would be required to exploit the Central Asian fields. The market seems to be doing nicely in these regards. Given their lack of capital, marketing experience, and technical expertise, Kazakhstan and the other Central Asian governments have little choice but to export oil and to seek partners among Western firms.

The third Western interest is to minimize the participation of Iran. This would require encouraging Russia and Turkey to reach an equitable agreement that splits the revenues to be gained from transporting the oil out of the region. And it would require letting the Central Asian governments know that their access to financial and other assistance from the West will be affected if they permit Iran to play a significant role in their oil business—by selecting Iran as the pipeline route, for example.

NUCLEAR WEAPONS

Kazakhstan was the only Central Asian republic integrated into the Soviet Union's strategic weapons program. One of the two Soviet underground nuclear testing sites was in the republic, in the Semipalatinsk region; Kazakhstan's government has announced the termination of testing there and stated that the facility will be converted to other uses. A plant in Ust-Kamenogorsk produces nuclear fuel for electricity generating stations and beryllium products used in nuclear weapons. A plant at Aqtau, on the Caspian, processes uranium ore, and a breeder reactor there produces an estimated 110 kilograms of plutonium per year.[12] A plant in Petropavlovsk produced the nuclear-capable SS-21 short-range ballistic missile. Intercontinental ballistic missiles (ICBMs) were tested from the launch pads at Tyuratam.[13] Finally, the Soviets stationed 104 SS-18 ICBMs in Kazakhstan with a presumed total of 1,040 nuclear warheads, as well as 40 Bear-H long-range bombers carrying an estimated 370 nuclear warheads mounted on air-launched cruise missiles.[14] On paper, this gives Kazakhstan a formidable nuclear capability.

On the ground, however, Kazakhstan's arsenal is rather less formidable. The missiles remain firmly in the control of the CIS, which effectively means Russia. Even if Kazakhstan were to obtain control, its ability to maintain the missiles in a ready condition is dubious. The bombers, too, are under CIS control; according to some sources, the air-launched cruise missiles no longer have the computerized targeting information they need to be fired accurately.

Moreover, Kazakhstan has agreed, in the Lisbon Protocol to START I, to destroy these missiles and bombers within seven years. It has also acceded to the Nuclear Non-Proliferation Treaty (NPT). This, obviously, is a subject that requires the closest monitoring.

Assuming Kazakhstan does follow through on its commitments, the potential problem of leakage of fissionable material, bomb components, and scientific expertise will remain. U.S. government sources who have studied the situation point out that Kazakhstan produced only components and never had anything approaching an independent capability to manufacture nuclear weapons.

Nevertheless, the West has a clear interest in Kazakhstan's compliance with the Lisbon Protocol; and the NPT; and the establishment of monitoring systems adequate to verify that nothing leaves the country that might be useful in an attempt by Iran, North Korea, or some other state to develop a nuclear weapon. Congress has appropriated funds to promote these goals under legislation sponsored by Sens. Sam Nunn and Richard Lugar. As of late 1993, the Clinton administration is continuing to negotiate with Kazakhstan over the disbursement of the first $14.5 million of this money. It is to be spent on communications links, emergency response equipment, an export control system, and a system for monitoring civilian nuclear material. The success of these efforts is, perhaps, the only truly vital Western interest in the region.

REGIONAL POWERS

For much of modern history, Central Asia has fallen under the influence of Russia, Arabia, or, to a lesser degree, Iran. Its people, except for the Tajiks, speak Turkic languages and look to Turkey as a cultural center. It is not surprising, therefore, that with the collapse of Soviet power, all four of these nations have tried to expand or, in Russia's case, maintain, their influence in the region. These efforts are dealt with elsewhere is this volume. The question here is whether the West should be concerned or enthusiastic about them and whether it can do anything to influence their outcome.

An expansion of Turkish influence causes the fewest concerns for the West. A (roughly) common language, a common history, common religious and cultural traditions, and reasonable geographic proximity give it unique entrée in the region. And Turkey offers the most pro-Western developmental model to the Central Asian states, one that is relatively moderate, democratic, and secular. Turkey can promote a brand of Islam that acknowledges the separation of state and religion. It can demonstrate respect for human rights and private enterprise in a context more persuasive than Western countries can offer. Ten thousand Central Asian students are studying in Turkey, according to U.S. government sources. Turkey could be the West's ideal surrogate in the region.

But the case for Western promotion of Turkish influence has flaws. One is Turkey's limited economic reach. Another is the specter of pan-Turkism. On occasion, there are warnings that Turkey sees a dominant position in Central Asia as the first step toward the restoration in a new form of its old empire, based this time on a pan-Turkic philosophy. These fears seem badly overdrawn. Pan-Turkism remains the interest of only a thin layer of intellectuals in most Central Asian countries. The governing elites seem inclined to guard against the accumulation of too much influence by any one of the regional powers. Turkey has shown no inclination to impose itself on unwilling partners, and it is hardly a military threat. It does not possess the reach or resources to sustain the role of security guarantor or imperial power. This, of course, makes it a more attractive partner for the insecure governments of the region.

A third flaw is Turkey's relations with Armenia. Encouraging the Turks to play an active role in the region will not please the Armenians or their many defenders in the West. To the extent that the West feels compelled to defend Armenia, it may be compelled to oppose Turkey's desire to aid Azerbaijan. This, however, appears to be one of the complications of life in the region, like the enmity between NATO allies Greece and Turkey, that the West will simply have to cope with.

Similarly, the West should encourage Russia to remain involved in the region. The Central Asian leaders have suggested they wish this to happen, particularly in the security sphere. They know that Russia is the only regional power remotely capable of protecting them from guerrillas based in Afghanistan or Iran. It is the only power that can enforce their avowed desire to live with the borders bequeathed to them by the Soviet Union.

For understandable reasons, trepidation surrounds any Western policy that encourages Russia, even tacitly, to play the role of security guarantor in any part of the old Soviet Union. But for a long time, Russia will be the only market for much of what the Central Asian economies produce. Millions of ethnic Russians live in the Central Asian countries and can become refugees very quickly if their status deteriorates. Russia has to cope with whatever turmoil and instability disrupt its southern flank. Clearly, Russia has major interests in the region that the nations of the West do not. It has reason to feel entitled to protect them. The West has nothing to fear, and much to gain, if Russia does so in a moderate, restrained fashion. The alternative would be a vacuum, and a major opportunity for Iran.

Iran is the regional power the West should strive to isolate and contain. As long as the regime in Tehran remains implacably hostile to the United States and to Western values, the West has an interest in diminishing its influence, in Central Asia and elsewhere in the Middle East. The desire to contain Iranian influence must not, of course, be exaggerated, or provoke heavy-handed pressure on the Central Asian governments. They have stated their intention to develop relations with all interested countries, including Iran. They realize that to some degree, they can play the West and Iran off against one another in their quest for development aid. So they are going to have connections to Iran, and the more they feel the West is ignoring their problems, the more ostentatious those connections are likely to be.

The best way to combat Iranian influence is by encouraging Russia, Turkey, and Saudi Arabia to leave no vacuums for Iran to exploit. Continuing economic and military links suggest Russia's role. Turkey's cultural and religious links suggest its role. Saudi Arabia can contribute investment funds, oil and gas expertise, and religious exchanges. The West's interests will be best served if all three of them are active and engaged in Central Asia, balancing one another's influence and leaving little room for Iran.

Even if this strategy failed and Iran were to extend its influence in the region, it would be hard to make a case that this would threaten vital Western interests. The West survived seventy-four years of Soviet control over Central Asia without severe difficulties. It could survive a period of Iranian influence over, say, Tajikistan. In fact, there could be worse things for the West than to see Iran distracted from adventures in the Persian Gulf and the Middle East by the burden of involvement with a dependent Central Asian state.

CONCLUSION

Apart from the fate of Kazakhstan's nuclear potential and the stability of Russian democracy, then, the West has only tertiary interests in Central Asia. Some of them, such as participation in the development of oil reserves, have already been enumerated. But there are others.

The West must be concerned with the observance of human rights in the region. More is at stake here than merely the normal humanitarian concern for the fate of political or religious dissidents. Each of the new Central Asian states became a member of the Conference on Security and Cooperation in Europe (CSCE). The adoption of CSCE human rights standards in 1975, and Western insistence on their observance, contributed significantly to the undermining of Soviet domination of Russia and Eastern Europe. Those same standards, if observed, could contribute significantly to the maintenance of peace in post–Cold War Europe. Obviously, the CSCE's ignominious failure to enforce its standards in Bosnia or in the Trans-Caucasus has drastically diminished its credibility. If they are widely flouted in Central Asia, their usefulness could well end. This cannot, of course, mean that the West insists that the Central Asian nations become models of multiparty democracy overnight. But the West can insist that the governments in the region refrain from jailing and torturing their opponents, that they respect religious and ethnic minorities, and that they afford their people the right to travel and a free press. If they fail to meet these standards, the consequences ought to include international opprobrium, the cessation of high-level visits, and, in extreme cases, economic sanctions.

These kinds of interests suggest the necessity of an active, if modest, American presence in each Central Asian nation. This would include embassies staffed by professionals who speak the local language, an intelligence apparatus, and a Drug Enforcement Administration presence to discourage the growth of narcotics trafficking. It would include Voice of America broadcasts, cultural exchanges, and technical and Peace Corps advisors where the host government requests them. The West should rely on multilateral institutions, rather than bilateral contributions, to supply financial aid. And it should leave security guarantees and arrangements to Russia or the CIS.

It is not hard to describe the kind of Central Asia that would best serve Western interests. It would be a region of peaceful, democratic, and secular governments, committed to pluralism and respect for human rights. They would adopt economic policies that would foster a steady climb from the poverty and pollution the Soviet Union bequeathed to them. They would be open to reasonable investment offers from the West and would protect the property rights of investors. They would balance their relations with the various regional powers. They would eliminate their nuclear weapons and adopt a control regime designed to prevent the proliferation of components and expertise.

Nor is it hard to predict that, given all their problems, one or more Central Asian nations will fall short on nearly all these counts. But only the threat that Kazakhstan's nuclear weapons, or important nuclear components, might fall into the hands of a rogue state like Iran would justify forceful Western intervention, assuming that a situation developed where intervention might be effective. The rest of the turmoil that likely lies ahead for the Central Asian nations will be unpleasant to witness and saddening. But it will involve only tertiary Western interests. Limiting such problems, and coping with those that do arise, is work the West would best leave to informal partners—Turkey, Russia, and Saudi Arabia.

NOTES

1. Some mountainous areas of the region were not fully mapped until the 1930s and 1940s.
2. Boris Z. Rumer, "The Gathering Storm in Central Asia," *Orbis*, vol. 37, no. 1 (Winter 1993), pp. 89–105.
3. Steve Coll, "Central Asia's High Stakes Oil Game," *Washington Post*, May 9, 1993, p. 1.
4. Murray Feshbach and Alfred Friendly, Jr., *Ecocide in the USSR*, 1991 (New York: Basic Books).
5. These sources asked not to be identified by name or organizational affiliation.
6. Martha Brill Olcott, *The Kazakhs* (Stanford, Calif.: Hoover Institution Press, 1987).
7. One source, Dovlat Khudonazarov, a government opponent, said in a speech at the U.S. Institute of Peace on April 29, 1993, that one hundred thousand people have died and five hundred thousand have been displaced.
8. Steve LeVine, "Afghan, Arab Muslim Militants Back Rebels in Ex-Soviet State," *Washington Post*, April 27, 1993, p.1.
9. Foreign Broadcast Information Service, *Central Eurasia*, April 7, 1993, p. 78.
10. Kuwait's proven reserves, according to the American Petroleum Institute, are 94 billion barrels. The North Slope had proven reserves of 9.6 billion barrels when production began.
11. Nick Moore, "Chevron Sets Big Deal to Develop Oil Field in Kazakhstan," *Washington Post*, April 7, 1993, p. C1.
12. William C. Potter et al., "Nuclear Profiles of the Soviet Successor States" (Monterey, Calif.: Center for Russian and Eurasian Studies, Monterey Institute of International Studies, 1993).
13. Central Intelligence Agency, *The Defense Industries of the Newly Independent States of Eurasia* (Washington, D.C., 1993).
14. Figures supplied by the Arms Control Association, Washington, D.C.

Chapter 5

Capitalism on the Silk Route?

Shafiqul Islam

L IKE THE OTHER REPUBLICS OF THE FORMER SOVIET UNION, THE five post-Soviet states of Central Asia confront the challenge of carrying out four separate, but related, transitions. The first transition involves a move from the status of a cog in the wheel of a command and highly interdependent Union economy to building a national economy. The others involve moves from a centrally planned economy to a market economy; from a semicolony of an empire to a sovereign nation-state; and from a totalitarian society to one based on individual freedom and democracy.

This chapter focuses on the second transition—developing capitalism within the national boundary of each Central Asian state out of a rigidly structured command economy. That task is, however, much complicated by the interactive strains and stresses of the other three transitions. Indeed, it is not possible to adequately describe, let alone analyze, the dynamics of the transition from a command economy of a newly independent state to capitalism without referring to the aggregate fallout of the interplay of all four transitions.

The transition to a market economy of the Central Asian countries is further burdened by two other factors. These newly independent states are among the least developed former Soviet republics, and are the most isolated from market-based economies. Consequently, their managerial, technical, and institutional capacities to carry out market reforms are relatively weak. They are also among the most specialized and interdependent economies, with a relatively greater degree of dependence on Russia. Thus the breakup of the Union economy and the economic weaning from Russia have caused them greater dislocations, complicating the task of initiating and sustaining a coherent program of market reforms.

Finally, two methodological points need spelling out at the start. First, most basic data on these economies essential for standard economic analysis are either highly unreliable or simply not available. Therefore, all economic data presented in this chapter should be viewed as providing orders of magnitudes, and not taken at face value. For example, little distinction should be made between output decline of 10 percent in one economy and of 8 percent in another. Second, transition toward a market economy has not even begun in Tajikistan because of the civil war that has engulfed the country since 1992. This chapter therefore has little to say on economic reforms in Tajikistan. Also, virtually no macroeconomic data are available for Turkmenistan. As the government until recently has shown little interest in moving to a market economy, it has not been particularly cooperative in providing the necessary statistics to economists from the International Monetary Fund (IMF) and the World Bank, making it difficult for them to create a preliminary base of the most basic data. This chapter thus focuses mainly on the other three economies of Central Asia—Kazakhstan, Uzbekistan, and Kyrgyzstan.

STAGE OF DEVELOPMENT, ECONOMIC STRUCTURE, AND RESOURCE ENDOWMENT

The five economies of Central Asia are typically described as landlocked, backward, and victims of "cotton monoculture," sitting on massive reserves of oil, gas, gold, and other precious natural resources. Like all stereotypes, this collective image is only partly true. What it ignores is that great diversity characterizes Central Asia: the five former republics exhibit important differences—in terms of stage of development, economic structure, and resource endowment.

As is true for virtually all economic data from the newly independent states, estimates of per capita incomes are not very reliable. The difficulties in measuring the sharp drops in each country's national income during 1991–1992 compound the problem. Precise comparisons of national incomes within and across the regional boundary are thus next to impossible. The estimates, however, provide orders of magnitudes and thereby permit rough comparisons. With these caveats in mind, the standard practice of using per capita income as a crude measure of stage of development can shed some light on how the Central Asian countries compare with each other and with some major developing countries, including some of their powerful neighbors.

With respect to *stage of development* (with 1991 per capita income used as a proxy measure), Kazakhstan leads the region (see Table 5.1). Kazakhstan's per capita income in 1991 was perhaps not much lower than that of Malaysia—a country already in the upper echelon of the so-called Third World. Despite the continuing plunge in output, Kazakhstan may still be richer than Iran and Turkey—the two Muslim neighbors vying for the role of the big brother in the region. Even more important, Kazakhstan is a nuclear power with advanced space and satellite technology.

By contrast, Tajikistan is the region's poorest country, with a per capita income of no more than half that of Kazakhstan. A $1,000 gap in per capita income within the developing world is a huge difference. Thus from the standpoint of national income alone, Kazakhstan is as different from Tajikistan as Chile is from Jordan. Indiscriminately applying generalities to these two post-Soviet states just because they are part of the same geographic region is like lumping Jordan and Chile together and labeling both poor and backward.

Uzbekistan—Central Asia's most populous and politically dominant state, with a rich cultural heritage—is the region's second-poorest country. It is clearly poorer than Iran and Turkey. Thus even a simple comparison of per capita incomes—the most commonly used measure of living standards and economic development—points to great economic diversity within Central Asia. The most populous country, Uzbekistan, is poorer and less developed than Iran and Turkey, whereas the second-most populous state, Kazakhstan, turns out to be richer and more developed than these two influential neighbors.

TABLE 5.1.—SELECTED ECONOMIC INDICATORS, CENTRAL ASIAN AND COMPARISON COUNTRIES, 1991*

Sectoral Composition of Output and Employment‡
(% of total)

Country	Per Capita Income (U.S.$)	Output			Employment			Population (millions)
		Agriculture	Industry	Services‡	Agriculture	Industry	Services‡	
Kazakhstan§	2,470	34	37	29	16	18	66	17
Turkmenistan**	1,700	48	16	36	42	11	47	4
Kyrgyzstan	1,550	28	38	34	22	19	59	5
Uzbekistan	1,350	36	28	36	45	14	43	21
Tajikistan**	1,050	38	29	33	43	13	44	6
Malaysia	2,520	17	44	39	31	27	42	18
Iran	2,170	21	21	58	25	28	47	58
Turkey	1,780	18	34	49	46	22	32	57
Indonesia	610	19	41	40	54	8	38	181
China	370	27	42	32	73	14	13	1,150

Sources: World Bank, *World Development Report 1993* (Washington, D.C. 1993); World Bank, *Statistical Handbook: States of the Former USSR, 1992* (Washington, D.C., 1992); International Monetary Fund, *Economic Reviews: Kazakhstan 1992* (Washington, D.C., 1993); and Asian Development Bank, *Asian Development Outlook 1992* (Manila, 1992).

*Data reflect more than usual range of uncertainty and should be viewed as preliminary.
†The employment shares for the reference countries are annual averages for 1989–1991.
‡Services include all unallocated items, including construction.
§Estimates of employment shares involve only the state sector, which accounts for 90 percent of total employment.
**The composition of output calculations are based on 1990 data on net material product, and not gross domestic product. Because of significant sectoral variations in output declines, the sectoral composition of aggregate domestic production and unemployment have changed substantially since 1990.

The diversity is no less pronounced in the economic structure. Kazakhstan and Kyrgyzstan are the two most industrialized economies of the region, with industrial output accounting for more than 35 percent of gross domestic product (GDP) in 1991 (see Table 5.1). The degree of industrialization is no lower than that in Turkey (34 percent) and higher than that in Iran (21 percent). Data on industrial employment, however, reverse that ranking. Share of employment devoted to industries is higher in Turkey (22 percent) and Iran (28 percent) than in Kazakhstan and Kyrgyzstan (less than 20 percent). This apparent contradiction may result partly from unreliable data. But it may also reflect the fact that in these two Central Asian economies, industrial labor is more productive relative to labor in other sectors than is the case in Turkey and Iran.

Turkmenistan—the region's second-richest country—is Central Asia's industrial laggard, with industrial output accounting for about 15 percent of net material product (NMP). Interestingly, it is also the only Central Asian country—indeed, the only republic of the former Soviet Union—to have a hard-currency trade surplus. Uzbekistan and Tajikistan are in the middle, with industry producing nearly 30 percent of aggregate output.[1]

Data on the share of national output produced by the agricultural sector are consistent with the above observations. Kazakhstan and Kyrgyzstan, the region's more industrialized economies, are also the least agricultural ones. By contrast, farming dominates Turkmenistan's economy, contributing nearly half of the national output. Interestingly, in terms of shares of agricultural output, Uzbekistan and Kazakhstan differ little. But in terms of agricultural employment, they differ markedly: with 45 percent of employment devoted to farming, Uzbekistan can be characterized as an agricultural economy, whereas the same cannot be said about Kazakhstan (agriculture absorbs only around 15 percent of the employed work force).

Comparisons with Iran and Turkey put the regional diversity with respect to dominance of farming in a new light. In terms of jobs—and therefore—life-style, Kazakhstan and Kyrgyzstan appear to be less of an agrarian society than Iran. The picture is more striking when the reference country is Turkey: each of the five Central Asian countries is no more an agrarian society than Turkey, and most are less so. These comparisons once again confirm that Central Asia is not a monolithic regional economy that can be described with sweeping generalizations, and some countries in the region are in many ways more advanced than Turkey and Iran— the two Muslim neighbors widely seen as competing for the role of the region's hegemon.

The intraregional distribution of resource endowment only reinforces the above conclusion (see Table 5.2). The image of Central Asia, portrayed by the Western Sovietologists, as a region impoverished from one corner to another by an all-encompassing "cotton monoculture," imposed and perpetuated by the Kremlin's Soviet colonialists, is an overblown one. Cotton monoculture— agriculture dominated by cotton production, and industry dominated by cotton processing—does pervade the economy of the subregion that extends from Turkmenistan to Tajikistan, with Uzbekistan constituting the core. But the tyranny of "cotton colonialism" is perhaps as palpable in Kazakhstan and Kyrgyzstan as in Florida: cotton simply does not figure prominently in the output and employment of these two countries, where 40 percent of the region's population live.

The natural resource that has most attracted the attention of American, Japanese, and other foreign investors to Central Asia is energy—oil and natural gas. But here again the cross-country differences are striking. Kyrgyzstan and Tajikistan are the unlucky neighbors of energy-rich Kazakhstan, Turkmenistan, and Uzbekistan. Furthermore, the three energy-rich countries differ from each other when it comes to specifics of their endowments. Kazakhstan's principal underground wealth is oil. By contrast, Turkmenistan, while rich in oil deposits, is the proud possessor of the world's third-largest reserves of natural gas. Uzbekistan's known oil and gas reserves are modest in comparison: even with greater exploitation than now, the most it can expect in the foreseeable future is to become a modest net energy exporter.

Gold is another resource Central Asia has plenty of. The regional distribution of this natural wealth, however, is even more inequitable. Uzbekistan tops the list—it has the world's fourth-largest reserves. Next is Kazakhstan, and Kyrgyzstan is a distant third. Turkmenistan and Tajikistan have no known deposits of gold. This summary reveals a cruel truth: If oil, gas, and gold are what make foreign investors salivate over this region, then the "Central Asia" that most experts write about excludes Tajikistan, and perhaps even Kyrgyzstan. As far as natural resources are concerned, these two economies have only one—water. Thus the only bounty they can extract from nature is hydroelectric power by extracting energy from water rushing through the mountains.

To sum up, geography—not economics—underpins the characterization of Central Asia as a region. Beyond geography, economic diversity—not homogeneity—is the hallmark of Central Asia. The level of national income and economic development, the relative dominance of agriculture and the degree of industrialization, and the pattern of resource endowments all point to this conclusion.

The other conventional wisdom that deserves critical scrutiny is that Central Asia is part of the Third World. To begin with, the Third World as an easily definable group of countries with similar features is under challenge. As East Asian countries rapidly catch up with the advanced industrialized countries, and South Asia and Africa fall behind, development experts are increasingly wondering about how to define the Third World, which countries belong there, and whether the concept is more confusing than illuminating. A consensus is emerging that the Third World encompasses countries that have more differences than similarities in economic as well as demographic terms, and thus is not a very meaningful concept.

But even if one could define the Third World, the five Central Asian economies—embodying many features of the Soviet system—still constitute a category by itself. In some ways, they possess attributes of a "typical Third World country." But in other ways, they are more advanced (see Table 5.3). Their advances in certain areas reflect several positive achievements of the Soviet regime—a high degree of industrialization; strong emphasis on high school education for all; an excellent public transportation system; a high premium on higher education and research in engineering, sciences, and mathematics; and a comprehensive social safety net with universal access to health care.

TABLE 5.2.—RESOURCES AND TRADE PATTERNS, CENTRAL ASIA, 1990–1991

Country	Principal Natural Resources	Major Farm Products and Industrial Activities	Major Exports	Major Imports	Major Trading Partners	
					Former Soviet Union	Others
Kazakhstan	Oil and gas, chrome, iron ore, coal, gold, copper, lead-zinc ore, wolfram	Wheat, barley, meat, wool, metallurgy, textiles, machine building, petrochemicals, agroprocessing	Oil and gas, coal, nonferrous metallurgy, grain, garments, footwear	Machinery, oil and gas, processed food and beverage, ferrous metallurgy	Russia, Ukraine, Uzbekistan, Kyrgyzstan	China, Germany, Sweden, Switzerland
Turkmenistan	Natural gas, oil, iodine-bromine, mineral salts	Cotton, textiles, oil and gas production	Natural gas, oil products, ginned cotton, hand-made carpets	Machinery and metalworks, light industrial products, processed food	Russia, Ukraine, Uzbekistan, Kazakhstan	Germany, Bulgaria, Czech & Slovak Republics, Poland
Kyrgyzstan	Hydroelectricity, gold, mercury, uranium, coal, cesium, antimony, natural gas (not confirmed)	Tobacco, livestock, wool, metallurgy, agro-processing, electronics, textiles, sugar refining	Agro-machinery, wool, tobacco products	Oil and gas, wheat, processed food, machinery, chemicals, light industrial products	Russia, Ukraine, Kazakhstan, Uzbekistan	Germany, Bulgaria, Czech & Slovak Republics, China

Uzbekistan	Oil and gas, gold, coal, silver, copper, lead-zinc ore, wolfram	Cotton, fruits and vegetables, textiles, cotton harvesters, textile machinery, metallurgy	Cotton, gold, gas, fertilizers, light industrial goods	Machinery, oil and gas, chemicals	Russia, Ukraine, Kazakhstan, Kyrgyzstan	Switzerland, South Korea, Turkey, China
Tajikistan	Hydroelectricity, radium, uranium	Cotton, metallurgy, machine building, agro-processing, light industry	Cotton, machinery and metalworks, aluminum, fertilizers, refrigerators, and washing machines	Oil and gas, ferrous metallurgy, chemicals	Russia, Kazakhstan, Uzbekistan, Turkmenistan	Austria, Germany, Sweden, Afghanistan

Sources: World Bank, *Statistical Handbook 1993: States of the Former USSR* (Washington, D.C., 1993); and other published sources from the World Bank and International Monetary Fund.

TABLE 5.3.—SELECTED DEMOGRAPHIC AND HUMAN DEVELOPMENT INDICATORS, CENTRAL ASIAN AND COMPARISON COUNTRIES, 1990–1991

Country	Population Growth, 1990–1991	Total Fertility Rate (births per woman),* 1991	Infant Mortality Rate (per 1,000 live births), 1991	Life Expectancy at Birth (years), 1991	Human Development Ranking,[†] 1990
Kazakhstan	0.6	2.7	27	69	54
Turkmenistan	2.6	3.9	53‡	66	66
Kyrgyzstan	1.3	3.6	30	69	83
Uzbekistan	1.9	3.9	36	70	80
Tajikistan	2.1	4.9	43‡	70	88
Malaysia	2.8	3.7	15	70	57
Iran	1.5	6.2	44	66	103
Turkey	2.5	3.4	60	65	73
Indonesia	2.4	3.0	68	62	108
China	1.5	2.4	29	70	101

Sources: UNDP, *Human Development Report 1993* (New York, 1993); World Bank, *World Development Report 1993* (Washington, D.C., 1993); World Bank, *The World Bank Atlas, 25th Anniversary Edition* (Washington, D.C., 1992); World Bank, *Statistical Handbook 1993: States of the Former USSR* (Washington, D.C., 1993); and International Monetary Fund, *International Financial Statistics,* September 1993 (Washington, D.C., 1993).

* The number of children that would be born alive to a woman during her reproductive lifetime, if she were to bear children at each age in accordance with prevailing age-specific fertility rates.

[†] These figures rank each country in terms of a human development index (HDI) developed by the United Nations Development Programme (UNDP), with the top performer assigned a score of 1. These indices are estimated as weighted averages of three indicators: life expectancy at birth; a measure of human capital; and per capita income. The figures are based on 1990 data and taken from the UNDP's *Human Development Report 1993.*

‡1990 data.

Consequently, the system has achieved strong pockets of heavy and high-technology industries in economies that are otherwise relatively underdeveloped and dominated by extraction of natural resources, animal husbandry, and farming. While deteriorating with deepening economic crisis, the transportation systems—both local and long-distance—in all five countries are more advanced than those in Third World countries at similar stages of development. In education and health, the achievements remain much below the level attained by the advanced capitalist countries, and yet are impressive when judged against developing countries with comparable per capita incomes.

Perhaps the most important feature that sets Central Asian states apart from Third World countries of comparable (or often higher) levels of per capita income is their quality and stock of human capital. Thanks to mandatory secondary education under the Soviet regime, the region boasts a highly educated and skilled labor force. The extent of adult literacy and high school education equals that in East Asia's newly industrialized economies. The Academies of Sciences—especially those in Uzbekistan, Kazakhstan, and Kyrgyzstan—host some of the world's best scientists, mathematicians, and engineers. The defense, high-technology, and heavy industries employ thousands of engineers, technicians, and professional and skilled workers. The majority of this work force are local people, though ethnic Russians—most born and brought up in Central Asia—account for a substantial minority. While many of them are leaving because of fear of future ethnic discrimination and in search of a materially better life, and have already caused some difficulties in certain industries in Kazakhstan, Kyrgyzstan, and Tajikistan, most are likely to stay unless prolonged economic hardship, virulent anti-Russian nationalism, or sudden eruption of ethnic violence drives them out.

The threat to Central Asia's most valuable asset is coming from the continuing economic crisis. The resulting scarcity of essential resources accompanied by disorder since Mikhail Gorbachev launched *perestroika* has been gradually eroding the quality of formal education, the environment for research and innovation at the Academies of Sciences, and the technical infrastructure at the plants and factories. Ironically, as this trend accompanies the move toward the transition to markets, the Central Asian economies are losing the asset that is of most value in helping them make this transition. But even with this adverse trend, the region's superiority over the developing countries in human capital is likely to remain in the foreseeable future.

FROM CENTRAL PLAN TO MARKETS: STATED GOALS AND ACTUAL STRATEGY

A full-scale civil war since 1992 has ravaged the economy of Tajikistan, slamming the door on the country's initial steps toward market reforms. Therefore, any regionwide generalization through the rest of the chapter refers to the other four countries. Several common features characterize the articulation and implementation of the overall reform strategy in the region.

First, at least in the initial phase, the pace of political reforms has been positively correlated with the pace of economic reforms—the former seems to have determined the latter. For example, Kyrgyzstan—the region's most committed political reformer—has gone the furthest in implementing market reforms. The 1992 U.S. Department of State survey on human rights gave Kyrgyzstan one of the best evaluations among all republics of the former Soviet Union, including the "Westernized" Baltics.[2] In May 1993 Kyrgyzstan adopted a constitution that embraces the principle of separation of power between the three branches of government (executive, legislative, and judiciary) and incorporates strong support for human and minority rights. The country that exemplifies the same linkage between politics and economics from the other end of the spectrum is Turkmenistan: it is run by a dictatorial president with no open opposition who so far has largely protected the old command economy from the wave of market reforms.

Second, democratic or not, a single man charts the course of each country's polity and economy. The personal philosophy and statesmanship of the principal political leader—the head of state—largely determines the scope and pace of both political and economic reforms. Kyrgyzstan has been most successful in dismantling the totalitarian regime precisely because the country's president, Askar Akaev (an internationally recognized physicist and the only head of government among the fifteen post-Soviet states not to have been a Communist Party apparatchik), is most committed to the principles of liberalism and democracy among his peers. Thus, paradoxically, the democratic reforms of Kyrgyzstan are being spearheaded by one man. With Akaev's popularity dwindling in 1993, it is not clear that a new president will move in the same direction, let alone with the same commitment.

In a similar vein, Turkmenistan continues to be ruled by a totalitarian regime because its president, Supramurad Niyazov—the former first secretary of the Turkmen Communist Party—is a man who cares little about political liberalism. He simply renamed the Communist Party of Turkmenistan the Democratic Party and won the presidential election held in June 1992, in which he was the only candidate. Uzbekistan's economic and political changes are being largely dictated by its authoritarian president, Islam Karimov. This one-man rule implies great uncertainty for the prospects of market reforms in each country. With the change of one man at the top, a country's economic program can take a completely new turn.

Third, the region's heads of state seem to have the same *stated* goal on the economic front. They all want to build a "socially oriented market economy." The differences arise on the actual "social/market" split. For example, "socially oriented" for Kazakhstan's President Nursultan Nazarbaev means "the people's right to free medical service, education and pensions."[3] President Niyazov of Turkmenistan uses the same phrase to mean free water, electricity, and gas for every citizen of the country, at least for 1993. On one feature of a market economy, however, the degree of convergence is striking: all four governments are desperately seeking foreign direct investment and trading partners outside the former Soviet Union to sell their exports. That is, while the philosophy of how to build a domestic market economy diverges greatly, the desire for integrating into the world economy is strong throughout the region.

Fourth, all four governments are pursuing "gradualism" with varying scope, stress, and speed. For example, Kyrgyzstan has gone further in macroeconomic stabilization and liberalization than others, but has made little progress in privatization, development of new start-ups and entrepreneurship. By contrast, Uzbekistan, while hesitant in liberalizing prices and trade, has gone far in privatization of dwellings—almost all housing in Tashkent has been privatized.

These differences, however, have not affected the governments' highly positive attitudes toward the international financial and development institutions. All five are members of the IMF, the World Bank, and the European Bank for Reconstruction and Development. They are all also preparing for membership in the Multilateral Investment Guarantee Agency—an affiliate of the World Bank. In August 1993 Kazakhstan, Uzbekistan, and Kyrgyzstan were approved for membership in the Asian Development Bank.

Finally, no country's strategy is set in stone; indeed, each one is in a state of flux. Thus the last word on how one country's market reforms—in terms of intention and accomplishment—compare with those of another will not be in for quite some time. Already faced with popular backlash resulting from declines in living standards, Kyrgyzstan has backslid in some areas. By contrast, Turkmenistan is thinking the unthinkable: it appears to be getting ready for a major step toward price liberalization in preparation for introducing its national currency, the menat.

FROM CENTRALLY PLANNED INTERDEPENDENCE TO MARKET-ORIENTED INTERDEPENDENCE

Macroeconomic dislocations that have ravaged Central Asia's five economies are largely the consequences of the breakup of the Soviet Union, and not domestic market reforms. Like the rest of the former Soviet Union, Central Asia's five newborn states are simultaneously suffering from three separate—though related—painful developments: the collapse of the Union-wide command economy, with its highly *interdependent* system of production, trade, and payments; the *sudden independence* from Russia, the giant core of the system; and the *continued dependence* on Russia, which itself is gripped by economic and political crisis.

Plunging output, runaway inflation, and declining living standards in the region have so far resulted largely from this painful coexistence of independence from and dependence on the core of a rigidly interdependent economy that fragmented in a chaotic way (see Table 5.4). Macroeconomic stabilization and liberalization measures—to the extent they have been implemented—have only compounded the economic crisis. They have not been the main driving force behind the macroeconomic dislocations.

The adverse economic and social fallout of this three-way friction between the forces of interdependence, independence, and dependence define the limits within which the ruling elites of each Central Asian state are operating. While the overall approach to market reforms diverges considerably among the five, the overarching economic strategy and the actual policy measures embraced by the political leadership of each state are being continually shaped by unpredictable—and often explosive—shifts in this triangular linkage characterizing the disintegrating Union economy.

One such fundamental economic strategy concerns the exit from the "ruble zone." This decision has divided the region, with profound implications for all aspects of economic reforms. Kyrgyzstan left the ruble zone in May 1993 and introduced its own national currency, the som. Turkmenistan has publicly declared its intention to introduce a new national currency, the menat, in November 1993.

After many declarations and statements on the introduction of a national currency, the other three have so far decided to remain in the ruble zone. The motivation is political and economic. By remaining in the ruble zone, they wish to avoid total cessation of subsidies and transfers from Russia, and importing oil at world prices. Politically, these states want close relations with Moscow to prevent the erosion of the pool of the managers, engineers, and professionals by mass migration of the local ethnic-Russian population, and to obtain the security umbrella from Russia.

On September 7, 1993, along with Belarus and Armenia, the Central Asian-3 (CA-3) signed an agreement to use the Russian ruble as their common currency. The accord calls on the members to "Russify" their customs, taxation, banking, and hard-currency regulations, as well as to coordinate with Russia monetary growth, interest rates, and budget deficits. In essence, Russia is to take charge of their fiscal and monetary policies. The accord also provides for a transition period, as these measures will require legislative changes (bringing the economic laws of ruble-5 [R-5]

TABLE 5.4.—BASIC MACROECONOMIC DATA, CENTRAL ASIAN AND COMPARISON COUNTRIES, 1990–1992*

Country	GDP Growth (%)			Industrial Production (%)			Retail Price Index Inflation (%)†			General Government Budget Deficit‡ (% of GDP), 1992	Current Account Deficit§ (% of GDP,) 1992
	1990	1991	1992	1990	1991	1992	1990	1991	1992		
Kazakhstan	-4	-13	-14	-1	-1	-15	4	150	2,670	7	2
Turkmenistan	-3	-5	-5	3	4	-20	na	150	650	(surplus)**	(surplus)**
Kyrgyzstan	3	-4	-26	-1	0	-27	3	180	1,260	15	10
Uzbekistan	-3	-1	-10	2	2	-6	5	170	790	13	15
Tajikistan	-1	-4	-34	2	-2	-24	na	na	380	na	na
Russia	-2	-9	-19	0	-8	-19	6	145	2,320	20	8
Ukraine	-2	-10	-14	0	-5	-9	4	140	2,740	15	na

Sources: World Bank and International Monetary Fund, various published sources; and PlanEcon, *Review and Outlook 1993* (Washington, D.C., 1993).

na = not available.
*Data reflect more than usual range of uncertainty and should be viewed as preliminary.
†December-to-December percentage change in retail price index for 1991 and 1992; year-to-year change for 1990; for Russia and Ukraine, 1992 inflation is measured in terms of consumer price index.
‡Extrabudgetary funds, including credits to public enterprises, are excluded for all but Russia. Includes unbudgeted import subsidies for Russia.
§Very crude estimates.
**Estimates are not available, but balance had substantial surplus in 1992.

countries in line with Russian laws) to be approved by national parliaments. During this period, the R-5 can continue to use pre-1993 rubles or specially marked Russian bank notes.

In all likelihood, the transition period may last for a very long time or for a very short time. In other words, this agreement is unlikely to survive. The R-5 are likely to find it politically impossible to embrace Russian laws as their own. With Russia's political and economic turmoil continuing and possibly deepening in the near future, by surrendering national fiscal and monetary policies to the Kremlin, the R-5 may succeed only in importing macroeconomic instability and sky-high inflation. With macroeconomic policies controlled by an unstable Moscow, which itself cannot qualify for an IMF standby loan, the R-5 countries are likely to learn the hard way that the confidence of foreign investors and businesses gained by the IMF's seal of approval is worth a lot more in the long run than dribs and drabs of subsidies and transfers from Russia. The IMF cannot monitor a country's monetary policy if the national central bank has no control over it. And without a national currency, the country's monetary authorities cannot create the domestic stock of money and credit, and control their growth. This is why the IMF is unable to approve a standby program for a country unless it makes a clean break from the ruble, introduces a new national currency, and conducts its own monetary and budget policies.

To be sure, political considerations are, in some cases, more important than pure economic ones. For example, President Nazarbaev of Kazakhstan understands the economic arguments. But he continues to resist the IMF pressure to delink from the ruble because he fears it may provoke a negative reaction from the country's already resentful vast Russian population and may even jeopardize his close personal relationship with President Boris Yeltsin, and thus damage Almaty's close defense, space, and nuclear collaboration with Moscow. Clearly, these political, ethnic, and security risks are critical and must be managed with great care and finesse before Kazakhstan can break out of the ruble zone. If left unresolved—as they are now—the risks will only grow over time, nourished by deepening economic crisis. That will make the exit from the ruble zone more disruptive, with the potential for dealing a crushing blow to the whole program of economic reforms.

So far, however, Kazakhstan, Uzbekistan, and Tajikistan are clinging to the option of postponing the day of reckoning. The latest testament to this tendency is an accord to form a new economic union agreed upon by nine Commonwealth of Independent States (CIS) countries on September 24, 1993, in Moscow. Along with Moldova, Azerbaijan (which earlier left the CIS but rejoined it by signing this accord), and Kyrgyzstan (which has found living without the ruble even more difficult than living with it), the R-5 members signed the framework agreement. They pledged to coordinate monetary and fiscal policies, to establish a free trade zone and a currency union, and to promote ties among enterprises across member states.

This accord is not likely to survive either. A clue to its ultimate fate can be found in a statement made by Russian Prime Minister Viktor Chernomyrdin as he hailed the accord: more than thirty documents would have to be drafted and signed before the economic union could fully take effect. The credibility of this accord is also clouded by the fact that it includes Kyrgyzstan—which introduced a new national currency just a few months before signing the document essentially agreeing to reenter the ruble zone. While a free trade agreement is desirable and feasible, sustaining an effective currency union is a much tougher enterprise, because it requires a single central bank, a single monetary policy, and close coordination of fiscal policy.

The R-5 agreement to create a new ruble zone and the CIS accord to create a new economic union are two concrete (and confused) responses to the conundrum that the Central Asian and other non-Russian republics of the former Soviet Union face: efforts to speed up the cessation of the economic *dependence* on Mother Russia and the dismantling of the Union economy's centrally planned economic *interdependence* greatly compound the macroeconomic and social costs of building a national economy where economic interdependence is determined largely by market forces.

AN OVERVIEW OF COUNTRY STRATEGIES

Kyrgyzstan is one of the first countries of the former Soviet Union to launch an ambitious program of market reforms. In 1992 President Akaev and his followers enacted a plethora of laws and decrees, created new market institutions, and developed a set of ambitious privatization targets. Unfortunately, Kyrgyzstan also happens to be the Central Asian state with the greatest "ambition-capacity gap." This resource-poor country simply has too many odds working against it. The economy is characterized by excessive specialization and heavy dependence on trade with the republics of the former Soviet Union; it also depended on massive transfers and subsidies from the Union (11 percent of GDP during 1990–1991); imports from outside the former Soviet Union are twenty times higher than exports, which account for only 2 percent of total exports; and it is a net importer of food and highly dependent on imported oil and gas. Given its location, the country has been relatively isolated from exposure to market economies, and it suffers from limited technical and management capacity, which constrains the operational capability of newly created institutions needed for adequate economic and political governance. With so many formidable roadblocks on the path toward capitalism, even the most committed leadership will be unable to move fast. Thus it is no surprise that with the deepening economic crisis, the government has been forced to periodically reverse gear as it has confronted growing political opposition to the economic program.

Even in such an adverse environment, President Akaev and his reformist government have taken some bold steps. With prices liberalized in April 1991, January 1992, and again later in 1992, nearly all prices are free; the exceptions involve bread, milk, poultry products, vodka, rent, and transportation. To narrow the budget deficit—which soared because of the end of Union transfers, collapse of revenues resulting from declining production and shrinking tax base, and relief outlays for damage caused by earthquakes and mudslides in the spring and summer of 1992—the government reduced real wages of government employees, food subsidies, and transfers of child allowances.

The authorities have also reformed the state order system. That may help Kyrgyzstan gradually wean itself from a Byzantine Union-wide system of export licensing, bilateral protocols including strong elements of barter arrangement, and artificial pricing for long lists of specific commodities. However, unless a system of multilateral payments settlement allowing direct enterprise-to-enterprise trade to expand is established among the newly independent states, the elimination of Kyrgyzstan's state order system may in fact precipitate a further decline in the country's trade within the former Soviet Union.

In addition, the government has revamped the old Soviet monobank system. The country's's banking sector now consists of a central bank, the National Bank of Kyrgyzstan; three large commercial banks, which are joint-stock companies with shares held mostly by enterprises; nine small commercial banks; and one large savings bank, which almost exclusively serves the household sector.

Kyrgyzstan has earned the distinction of being the first non-Baltic former Soviet republic to accomplish three tasks simultaneously: introduce a new currency, the som; obtain the IMF seal of approval, with a $38.5 million loan under a standby program; and receive an additional $23 million soft-conditionality loan from the IMF's newly created systemic transformation facility (STF). Furthermore, Kyrgyzstan has won approval for a $62 million import rehabilitation credit from the International Development Association, an affiliate of the World Bank, and a concessional Japanese loan of $60 million, pledged at the first consultative group meeting for Kyrgyzstan, held in December 1992 in Paris. All this came together in May 1993. In September the IMF approved another $23 million STF loan.

With its own national currency backed by IMF money, Bishkek—and not Moscow—is in charge of the country's monetary policy, the critical instrument in controlling inflation. This independence, however, has so far failed to achieve the desired macroeconomic stabilization. While the authorities seem to be meeting the IMF targets, taking monetary control away from the proinflation Russian Central Bank has not enabled them to get inflation under control. In fact, the som so far appears to have created more problems than it has solved. Fearing a flood of unwanted rubles will raise their inflation rates even higher, neighboring Kazakhstan and Uzbekistan responded to the introduction of the som by demanding hard currency from Kyrgyzstan's citizens and confiscating goods from its traders crossing the border in either direction. In addition, an angry President Islam Karimov ordered an immediate cutoff of gas and telephone lines serving southern Kyrgyzstan as he declared the introduction of the som "political subversion" directed against Uzbekistan.

Uzbekistan lifted the economic blockade at the end of May, after Akaev went to Tashkent to "apologize" to Karimov. Cross-border travel and trade have also been normalized, with the Russian ruble performing the role of interstate currency. These initial som shocks have, however, left a lingering corrosive effect. Output has dropped further with disruptions of trade and supply of energy. But the biggest victim has been the som itself: many people in Kyrgyzstan appear to view the som more as a source of national insult than of national pride. The som has brought the country much-needed foreign money; but to an average citizen, the som has meant nothing but trouble.

Several nationalist and democratic parties are convinced that the som has plunged the economy into a serious crisis, and in August 1993, for the first time, they called for early presidential elections. It appears that the IMF staff who pressured Kyrgyzstan's financially bankrupt government to introduce the som to gain monetary control from Russia have been partially responsible for these adverse turns of events. The top authorities, including the heads of states, of the neighboring countries were not briefed in advance on the exact date of the som's introduction and steps that Bishkek was taking to prevent any negative spillover effects across the border. The IMF should have organized a meeting of the heads of state, involving at least Uzbekistan, Kazakhstan, and Russia, just before the som was introduced, to explain why Kyrgyzstan needed the som and how the logistics will be handled, and to allay misconceived concerns and suspicions.

If *Kazakhstan* is more "gradualist" than Kyrgyzstan in intention, its greater institutional and governing capacity has taken this country furthest along the road toward a market economy. President Nursultan Nazarbaev—perhaps the most pro-Western and popular national leader in the region—wants to transform Kazakhstan from a supplier of materials to a diversified economy with a competitive manufacturing sector. Kazakhstan has made a big stride in price liberalization. With deregulation implemented in

January and May 1992, prices are essentially free except for a few items, such as some types of bread and flour, passenger fares, basic communication services, and several petroleum products.

During 1992 enterprises in Kazakhstan had to operate within a complex state-controlled structure involving the interstate trade agreements, the state order system, and export quota and licensing arrangements. These agreements covered nearly two hundred products and specified over one thousand bilateral import and export arrangements with the other fourteen former Soviet republics. Under the state order (*goszakaz*) system, the state determined allocation of around 70 percent of output between the domestic market, interstate markets, and foreign markets.

In 1993 the state order system was abolished, and was replaced by a system of state purchases. Under the new system, one-fifth of the products covered and one-third of the separate interstate export and import arrangements have been eliminated. Even more remarkable, the coverage on trade with Russia in industrial machinery, consumer foodstuffs, and nonfood products has been completely eliminated.

Kazakhstan's parliament also approved a budget with major tax reforms. The measures include the unification of corporate income tax rates at 35 percent, the introduction of a minimum corporate income tax, a value-added tax rate of 20 percent, and an increase in excise tax rates. The government, however, failed to persuade the parliament to eliminate a variety of consumer, sectoral, and industrial subsidies.

Uzbekistan is pursuing a gradualist path of building state capitalism. President Karimov has repeatedly declared since late 1991 that he is committed to gradual introduction of a market economy. After price liberalization in January 1992 resulted in student demonstrations in Tashkent and two deaths, "gradualism" and "stability" became the guiding principles for his reform program. Since then, the growing domestic opposition and the fear of a negative fallout from the war in Tajikistan on Uzbekistan's Tajik population made an increasingly authoritarian Karimov shift his focus from economic reforms to consolidation of his power. He has identified five principles of the "Uzbek road to capitalism": the de-ideologization of the economy; the maintenance of the state as the main reformer; the primacy of the law of the land; a strong social policy to protect the vulnerable segments of the population; and a "stages approach" to building a market economy.

But since the summer of 1993, Karimov has seemed to be looking more favorably toward speeding up the transition and establishing a greater role for market forces. He has summed up the economic program's main task as the creation of a mixed multisector economy, a competitive environment, and gradual price liberalization. In a speech in July 1993, Karimov called on the people to drop their free-ride mentality, "whose prisoners they became during the empire of the Soviets."[4] He also praised the "Swedish model" because "the prices there are not restrained on the whole, not controlled and are free. The needy are getting aid." In the same speech, he stated that the forces behind the absence of unemployment in Uzbekistan are "enterprises that spend state credits to maintain a superfluous workforce," and disparaged "the wrong idea that if part of the people lose their jobs, we would have many beggars."

President Niyazov of *Turkmenistan* sums up his economic program with two words: "open doors." The strategy calls for foreign investment to finance the exploitation of the country's oil, gas, and natural resources, and thus obviate the need for market reforms. All natural resources will remain state property, but foreign investors will not have to pay taxes until their projects become fully operative and profitable. His strategy until late 1993 was to create two parallel economies: the natural-resource sector, integrated with the world markets; and the rest of economy, controlled by the state. The program also aimed at buying social peace with subsidies: during 1993 all citizens enjoyed gas, water, and electricity services free of charge.

In late 1993 President Niyazov seemed to be changing his mind in favor of a gradual move toward a market economy. In preparation for introducing the national currency, the menat, he reportedly has agreed to liberalize most prices. If Turkmenistan can successfully introduce its national currency, thanks to its hard-currency earnings and the resulting budget surplus, it may become the first Central Asian country to achieve macroeconomic stabilization.

PRIVATIZATION AND PRIVATE-SECTOR DEVELOPMENT

Kazakhstan and Kyrgyzstan are Central Asia's leaders in privatization and developing a private sector. Their accomplishments, however, remain modest. And yet, except for Russia and Lithuania, they may be the former Soviet Union's top two achievers.

Kazakhstan launched its enterprise privatization program in August 1991. The pace picked up in 1992 when six thousand enterprises—mostly small—out of a total of roughly thirty-one thousand state-owned enterprises (SOEs) went private. About four thousand privatized enterprises are engaged in trade, catering, and consumer services. Most were sold to worker collectives, and some were sold through auctions or by direct tender. In addition, four hundred firms were transformed into joint-stock companies. By the end of 1992, enterprises holding about 15 percent of total fixed assets of the enterprise sector had been corporatized (converted into joint-stock companies). These enterprises employed about seven hundred thousand workers.

Kazakhstan has also made visible progress in privatizing the agricultural sector. In 1992 private farms and private plots of land leased by state farm workers produced 70 percent of the country's output of potatoes, 40 percent of vegetables, 40 percent of meat, 55 percent of milk, and 35 percent of wool. Some 30 percent of the total stock of cattle, horses, and poultry belonged to these private farms. Almost half of the country's dwellings are estimated to be in private hands. As is true elsewhere in the former Soviet Union, land cannot be privately owned, but can be leased for up to ninety-nine years; the leases can be inherited and transferred, but cannot be used as collateral.

Kyrgyzstan's approach to privatization has gone through major shifts since the Law on Privatization and Entrepreneurship was passed on December 20, 1991. These shifts have substantially slowed down the implementation of a highly ambitious program. By December 1992, nearly two thousand small enterprises—shops and trade and service establishments—had been privatized. About one-fifth of them were sold to labor collectives, and over half were sold through auction or tender. Some 140 of Kyrgyzstan's one thousand large SOEs have been corporatized (transformed into joint-stock companies). Housing privatization has proceeded most rapidly. Almost fifteen thousand apartments had been sold or transferred to their occupants in 1992 alone. Ten thousand farms have also been "privatized," though the state is still not ready to recognize private ownership of land.

Uzbekistan has adopted a cautious and gradual approach to privatization of SOEs. By March 1993, two thousand small and thirty medium-size enterprises had been leased or sold to labor collectives. Individual ownership remains restricted. About 250 enterprises have become joint-stock companies, with the state maintaining a controlling, 51 percent ownership in large SOEs. Foreign investors can acquire state property subject to a priori approval and quotas. Once again, privatization has moved at the fastest pace in the housing sector. As mentioned before, housing in Tashkent is now privately owned.

Not surprisingly, *Turkmenistan* has so far moved little toward developing a private sector. The Ministry of State Property and Business Support drafted a privatization program in 1992 for consideration by the cabinet, but the final outlines of that draft were still being debated in early 1993. Under various schemes, part of the housing stock has been privatized. In March 1993 a positive development occurred: President Niyazov signed a decree on state support for entrepreneurship to develop the private sector and a class of property owners. A joint-stock bank for the development of entrepreneurship was to be established to finance investment projects of Turkmen business enterprises. The government also approved a law that gives every citizen the right to *own* a plot of land up to fifty hectares, or to lease up to five hundred hectares on a long-term basis. Additionally, the government announced its decision to create seven free enterprise economic zones. Little information is available, however, on how much progress the government has made in implementing these programs.

FOREIGN ECONOMIC RELATIONS

A close look at the shifting pattern of trade of the Central Asian countries, and their economic relations with the rest of the world involving direct investment, private loans, and official assistance, reveals a number of regionwide phenomena. First, the Central Asian states have placed the greatest priority on attracting private direct investment, typically in the form of joint ventures. Unlike their counterparts in the Third World, the governments of these poor countries are much less eager to receive official aid. They are also wary of taking private loans from foreign commercial banks and other nonbank institutions.

Second, with the possible exception of Turkmenistan, which boasts a hard-currency current account surplus, the governments are eager to maintain good relations with multilateral agencies. They want standby programs and loans from the IMF, largely to earn policy credibility and thus gain confidence of foreign investors. They are also seeking project finance, rehabilitation loans (foreign exchange to buy critical imported inputs), and technical assistance from multilateral development agencies, in particular the World Bank.

Third, with respect to trade, the Central Asian economies have inherited a peculiar Soviet attribute: they are unusually *open* within the former Soviet Union, and to a lesser extent to countries belonging to the Council on Mutual Economic Assistance (CMEA), but virtually *closed* to the outside world. The Soviet command system imposed a highly interdependent structure of production and trade among the republics while keeping the Union economy—and with it each republic—behind an "economic iron curtain." A principal challenge facing each Central Asian republic is to move from this politically determined, highly skewed trade structure to one determined by global market forces. This transformation requires each economy to become more closed to other former Soviet economies while opening up to the rest of the world. Disruptions from the breakup of the Soviet Union have already initiated a disorderly restructuring of production and reorientation of trade. Collapsing trade within the former Soviet Union and within the CMEA has already forced rapid progress toward making the Central Asian economies more closed to their former Soviet and CMEA trading partners. The macroeconomic dislocations and social pain resulting from this process of "trade destruction," however, have not been remotely compensated by progress in "trade creation" with the rest of the world. Available evidence suggests that Kazakhstan and Uzbekistan have expanded trade with countries outside the former Soviet Union and the CMEA, but the expansion and the resulting increase in "openness" remain marginal.[5]

Fourth, with regard to their share of the foreign debt of the former Soviet Union, the Central Asian countries (like most other former republics) have chosen the so-called zero option proposed by Russia. According to this scheme, each country will relinquish its claims on the assets of the former Soviet Union to Russia in exchange for Moscow's assuming the liability for that country's share of the Union's foreign debts.

Finally, the Central Asian states are pursuing a multitrack approach to developing and managing their foreign economic relations. Toward the former Soviet republics, they are following a three-track approach—bilateral, regional, and cooperation through the framework of the CIS. The bilateral track appears to be yielding the most useful and concrete results. This is specially true in dealings with Russia. On promoting economic and security cooperation within the framework of the CIS, Kazakhstan's President Nazarbaev and Kyrgyzstan's President Akaev are the region's—and perhaps the former Soviet Union's—most ardent proponents. By contrast, President Niyazov of Turkmenistan cares little about building up the CIS; he strongly prefers to go the bilateral route in developing and maintaining close relations with Russia, and with other newly independent states.

Efforts at regional cooperation began in June 1990 at Almaty, with a meeting among the Central Asian heads of state at the initiative of Nazarbaev. Since then, many summits and a plethora of declarations, proposals, and accords have been aimed at regional economic and security cooperation. President Karimov—with support from Nazarbaev and Akaev—has been the main driving force behind these initiatives, ranging from an agreement to coordinate economic policies to the creation of an Aral Sea Fund, to the establishment of a Central Asian common market. Once again, Turkmenistan's leader, Niyazov, has been openly cool toward the idea of regional cooperation. His preferred approach remains nonregional bilateralism; it matters little to him whether the partner is from Central Asia or from somewhere else. On this subject, Niyazov has proved himself to be more in touch with the reality than his counterparts. Regional initiatives have yielded few concrete results. Consequently, even President Karimov has moved gradually toward embracing bilateralism and toward joining hands with Nazarbaev and Akaev in efforts at transforming the CIS into an operational entity capable of yielding practical results.

On developing economic relations with countries outside the former Soviet Union, the Central Asian states are also pursuing a multitrack approach, with greatest emphasis placed on developing close bilateral ties. The common motto seems to be "Open door for all," but "No big brothers are allowed." Economics—not geography, culture, or religion—is the primary philosophy guiding Central Asia's foreign economic policy. All five states are vigorously courting the major economic powers from the West and from the East, as they continue to establish trade and investment links with others that show interest.

In this context, it is worth noting that Israel has been more active and successful in developing economic ties than have Saudi Arabia, Kuwait, and other rich Muslim Gulf states. Israel has assisted Uzbekistan in improving its irrigation system. A delegation of Israeli businessmen, headed by the minister of science and economics, visited Almaty in March 1993 and discussed specific projects in Kazakhstan's agricultural sector and food processing and pharmaceutical industries. The Israeli parliament has approved a huge specific-purpose credit for Kazakhstan, the first time the Israeli government has taken such a step for another country.

The Central Asian states have joined the Economic Cooperation Organization—a regional organization with Turkey, Iran, Afghanistan, and Pakistan as members—and routinely participate in its meetings. But by now, it is clear that the organization does not have the political coherence and financial resources to help Central Asia build its market economy. On a bilateral basis, Turkey is expanding its trade and investment ties with Kazakhstan, Uzbekistan, and Turkmenistan. But the money involved pales in comparison with that committed to Kazakhstan from the United States, Britain, and Germany, mainly in the form of direct investment. Turkmenistan has developed the closest *economic* relations with Iran, and has signed a number of contracts, including one to upgrade and extend rail links from the Caspian Sea to the Persian Gulf. But little has followed in terms of action on the ground.

Recognizing the limited financial capacity of Turkey and Iran—not to mention financially bankrupt Pakistan—Central Asia has begun to nurture relationships with countries and multilateral institutions where the big money is. The United States, major European countries, Japan, China, and South Korea are on their way to becoming the region's major trading partners and investors. Several countries from Southeast Asia—in particular, Malaysia and Indonesia—are likely to find the Central Asian countries to be natural economic partners and political allies, and they have the money and the institutional capacity to play the role of mentors with an attractive development model. The IMF and the World Bank have begun to supply much-needed foreign exchange to the region. Having accepted three countries as members, the Asian Development Bank also will soon be active. With new management, the European Bank for Reconstruction and Development is gearing up to accelerate its involvement in the region.

Thus, contrary to conventional wisdom, the capital-constrained Muslim countries of the Near and Middle East are likely to play the least important economic role in the capital-hungry Muslim countries of the former Soviet Union, at least in the foreseeable future. Much more significant actors in Central Asia's struggles to build market economies are going to be the capital-rich West, Japan, the Far East, and Southeast Asia.

Within the next few years, South Korea and several members of the Association of Southeast Asian Nations—with Japan at the core—may begin to play the most active role in Central Asia. Of course, this assumes no eruption of regionwide ethnic violence. Japan has vital economic and security interests in this resource-rich area: Central Asia offers Japan the most effective opportunity to diversify its reliance out of the volatile Middle East. The region also allows Japan to find a way—and a commercially lucrative one—to partially decouple itself from U.S. foreign policy interests in the Gulf. Japan has officially announced its strong commitment to the economic development of Central Asia. Since Yeltsin's sudden cancellation of his Tokyo trip in 1992, the number of official and private missions to the region has increased sharply. The United States wants Japan to give more development aid and take more global responsibilities. Japan will find Central Asia a perfect place to do just that.

NOTES

1. The degree of industrialization in Turkmenistan cannot be adequately compared with that of Uzbekistan, as Turkmenistan's share of industrial output is calculated by taking NMP as aggregate output because estimates of GDP are not available. The same is also true for Tajikistan.
2. U.S. Department of State, *Country Reports on Human Rights Practices for 1992* (Washington, D.C.: 1993).
3. ITAR-TASS, September 29, 1993, reprinted in Foreign Broadcast Information Service (FBIS), *Central Eurasia,* FBIS-SOV-93-188, September 30, 1993.
4. Arkadiy Dubnov, "Uzbek Reforms Promise to Be 'Special.' People Asked to Drop Dependence Mentality Engendered by 'Empire of Soviets,'" *Segodnya,* July 20, 1993, p.5, reprinted in FBIS-SOV-93-138, July 21, 1993, pp. 55–56.
5. The exclusion of many traded items in the official compilation of a rapid rise in barter transactions and smuggling, as well as the failure of authorities to monitor transactions by new private enterprises, has sharply reduced the reliability of the merchandise trade data since the collapse of the Soviet Union. For example, the IMF estimates the official data on Kazakhstan's trade may capture no more than two-thirds of all transactions. It is therefore difficult to draw conclusions with any degree of confidence on the changes in the composition and destination of trade data. The data on other components of the balance of payments—services; interest, profits, and dividends; foreign direct investment; and other forms of capital flows—are simply not collected. The lack of such basic data rules out a systematic review of various dimensions of the emerging foreign economic relations of the Central Asian states, let alone an intraregional comparative analysis. See International Monetary Fund, *Kazakhstan,* IMF Economic Reviews, no. 5 (Washington, D.C.: 1993), p. 35.

Chapter 6

The Central Asian States: Defining Security Priorities and Developing Military Forces

Susan Clark

WITH THE DEMISE OF THE SOVIET UNION, THE SUCCESSOR STATES essentially split into two camps on the question of the future of the Soviet armed forces—one advocating the formation of new national armies in each state and the other seeking to maintain some type of unified force, still largely run by Moscow. The five Central Asian states generally favored the latter approach until it became clear that the other successor states were increasingly moving toward the creation of their own national armies. The reluctance of the Central Asian states to undertake the creation of their own militaries is not surprising, given their lack of a significant ethnic officer corps on which to draw, their interest in dedicating scarce economic resources to more pressing needs, and their general appreciation that they cannot effectively ensure their security independently.

An independent military must obtain equipment and receive training for its nascent officer corps, and as in other ex-imperial situations, this raises political problems and uncertainties. This chapter explores each Central Asian state's decisions to create a national military force, some of the possible security threats each will face in the coming years, and the countries to which they are turning to meet their perceived security requirements. The relationship of each with Russia clearly remains a central one for many of these considerations. Of additional importance to some of these states in the context of broadening their security contacts is the development of ties with Turkey, certain other North Atlantic Treaty Organization (NATO) countries, and international institutions. Within the region itself, the competition between Kazakhstan and Uzbekistan to be the leader in Central Asia is also a factor shaping the others' security considerations.

The five Central Asian states are examined individually in the sections that follow. A table outlining the main structures of each state's military development is supplied in appendix A, page 206.

KAZAKHSTAN

Of all the leaders of the newly independent states, President Nursultan Nazarbaev was arguably the strongest proponent of retaining unified forces. Thus, even though Kazakhstan took the Fortieth Combined Arms Army under its jurisdiction in April 1992, Nazarbaev stressed that it would continue to be within the framework of the Commonwealth of Independent States (CIS) forces as long as other states did not begin creating their own forces. Only after Russia had declared its intention of establishing separate, Russian forces did Kazakhstan follow suit. In doing so, Nazarbaev decreed that the Kazakh State Defense Committee be transformed into the Ministry of Defense in May 1992, and the committee's former chairman, Col. Gen. Sagadat Nurmagambetov, was appointed minister of defense.[1] In addition to the considerable conventional forces on its territory—including an army headquarters, four army divisions, an air force division, and two regiments of air defense forces—Kazakhstan has inherited 104 SS-18 intercontinental ballistic missiles and forty strategic bombers from the former Soviet armed forces.

As regards control over these nuclear forces, Kazakhstan has leaned more toward Ukraine's position than that of Belarus, favoring the right to some administrative (though not operational) control over the nuclear weapons as long as they remain stationed on its territory. While all four of the new nuclear states initially supported control of all ex-Soviet nuclear forces by the CIS command, Belarus, Kazakhstan, and Ukraine began to diverge in their policies as Russia increasingly moved to claim unilateral authority over these weapons regardless of where they were located. Belarus has reached agreement with Russia that all strategic forces on its soil do, indeed, belong to Russia and is seeking to have them removed even more quickly than called for under the START treaty. In contrast, Ukraine has entered into a bitter and highly visible dispute with Russia over this issue, which Kazakhstan has closely watched. Despite several Russian statements—spanning almost a year—that an agreement with Kazakhstan, similar to the one with Belarus, was "imminent," to date they have managed to agree that 50 percent of Kazakhstan's nuclear arsenal will be destroyed within seven years.[2] Also like Ukraine, Kazakhstan has pushed for security guarantees from the nuclear states and for compensation for the enriched uranium from the missiles.

The abolition of the CIS joint command in July 1993 effectively removed any notion of unified control and placed nuclear control squarely in the hands of the Russian leaders, although the other three states theoretically retain veto power over the use of these weapons. While Kazakhstan has not proved as accommodating as Belarus, this is not to imply that relations between Kazakhstan and Russia on the nuclear question have been as strained as those between Ukraine and Russia. Nazarbaev above all realizes the vital importance of maintaining a good working relationship with Russia for the sake of his country's stability (above all because of the high concentration of ethnic Russians living in Kazakhstan).[3] At the military-security level, Nazarbaev has argued that his country must receive security guarantees from the United States, China, and Russia before nuclear weapons on Kazakhstan's soil can be relinquished.[4]

Perhaps even more important are the political and economic considerations: Kazakhstan's leadership has realized the international prestige and attention that come with the possession of nuclear weapons, and this attention can translate into various forms of international economic and technical assistance for Kazakhstan. Having used this leverage and gained what it apparently considered adequate security guarantees, the parliament (in July 1992) was the first of the four states to ratify START I and the Lisbon Protocol; the following month Chief of the Russian General Staff Viktor Dubynin reported that Russia and Kazakhstan had reached agreement on keeping nuclear weapons in Kazakhstan for another seven years.[5]

In creating its own armed forces, Kazakhstan plans to incorporate both conscripts and contract personnel. Draftees with higher education will serve twelve months; those without higher education, eighteen months; and those entering the navy, twenty-four months. Initial contract service (for men and women) is for two or three years; there is no provision for alternative service. Like the other Central Asian states, Kazakhstan has a notable lack of officers of the indigenous nationality: only some two thousand to three thousand Kazakh officers served in the entire Soviet officer corps, and almost 70 percent of all officers serving in Kazakhstan today are Russian citizens.[6] More officers from other states of the former Soviet Union, especially Ukrainians and especially junior officers, have been leaving Kazakhstan (partly because there is no provision for dual citizenship) than have returned, leading to a shortfall in the overall officer corps as well.[7]

In terms of force structure, plans call for ground, air, air defense, and naval forces, as well as internal troops, a presidential guard (subordinate to the president), and border forces (subordinate to the National Security Committee, made up of former KGB officials). Kazakhstan's desire for a naval force is perhaps surprising, given that the state is largely landlocked, with access only to the Caspian Sea. The modest naval force it plans to develop will be dedicated largely to coastal and border protection, as well as cooperative efforts with Russia, Turkmenistan, and Azerbaijan (perhaps on drug interdiction, for example). A maritime capability is also useful for shipment of Kazakhstan's considerable oil reserves. The mission of the border forces is to guard the land borders—namely, those with China and Kazakhstan's southern neighbors, since the border with Russia remains transparent on both sides. Border protection is an important effort in several respects, including controlling migration, illegal trading, and drug trafficking. The eventual size of Kazakhstan's overall military forces is as yet unclear; fifty thousand troops appears to be the minimum acceptable level, but the total will probably be about eighty-five thousand.[8] It will, in any case, be smaller than the number of forces inherited from the USSR (on the order of two hundred thousand);

the quantity of weapons and military equipment will likewise be smaller. Kazakhstan plans to sell the excess.

Kazakhstan, unlike the other Central Asian countries, has facilities, industries, and raw materials that were essential to the Soviet military effort. Defense industrial facilities in Kazakhstan are the most significant after those in the Slavic states (Russia, Ukraine, and Belarus), numbering some fifty defense enterprises, although they lack repair facilities.[9] Assuming continued close cooperation with Russia, both bilaterally and within the context of CIS collective security arrangements, Kazakhstan should be fairly well placed to provide for its defense needs—so long as its future security threats do not emanate from Russia itself. As for future purchases of defense equipment, Defense Minister Nurmagambetov has indicated that the republic has no intention of looking for suppliers outside the former Soviet Union. More generally, Kazakhstan has reached agreements with Russia on several points, namely: Russian assistance in Kazakhstan's development of its military, training for Kazakhstan's military personnel in Russia, cooperation between their border guards (including on manning these forces and training the officers), the use of the Emba and Sary-Shagan test sites by the Russian military for air defense and antiballistic missile activities, and the creation of a common defense zone. At the same time, Kazakhstan has asserted its independence by banning further military testing on at least four of the test sites within its territory, and reducing the number of hectares of land dedicated to military uses in the state from seventeen million to five million. In the first of these efforts in 1991, Kazakhstan placed a ban on future nuclear weapons tests at the Semipalatinsk site; that site has since been converted to a national nuclear physics research center.

Although Russia's close relations with Kazakhstan are second only to its relations with Belarus, Russia and Kazakhstan have had some serious areas of dispute, most significantly over the future of the Baikonur space facility.[10] Thus far, their only apparent agreement is on staffing: Baikonur's military facilities are to be jointly staffed, except for its military construction units, which are under the Kazakh Ministry of Defense and staffed entirely with citizens of Kazakhstan.[11] On the issue of ownership and control, however, Russia—notably Minister of Defense Pavel Grachev—seeks to maintain Baikonur as a Russian military facility, arguing that only with Russian expertise and financing can the facility continue to function.[12] Kazakhstan rejects the idea of unilateral Russian control, insists that Baikonur belongs to Kazakhstan, and proposes joint command over the facility and its forces. It also wishes to convert the facility from a military enterprise to a civilian space research center and a (semi)commercial launch facility. To this end, officials of Kazakhstan have made proposals to Indian officials and U.S. firms to help set up an international space company. As of early 1994, Kazakhstan and Russia had signed an agreement that will allow Russia to lease the facility, but the terms of this agreement (such as the duration of the lease, the amount to be paid, etc.) have yet to be established. It cannot, therefore, be ruled out that Baikonur may remain a serious point of contention between the two states for the foreseeable future. Tensions over Baikonur could fuel possible future disputes between Kazakhstan and Russia, as outlined below.

Kazakhstan's heavy emphasis on security relations with Russia has not precluded it from reaching bilateral agreements with other states. It has signed plans for cooperative efforts on intelligence sharing and on combating terrorism, drug trafficking, organized crime, and corruption with Uzbekistan, Belarus, Kyrgyzstan, and Ukraine, as well as Russia. Among Western countries, Kazakhstan has established contacts in the defense sphere with Germany and the United States, and has expressed an interest in NATO assistance as it tries to develop its armed forces. Thus, Kazakhstan's leadership seeks to establish quite a broad range of contacts, although at the same time it realizes that current Western receptivity to playing an active role in security cooperation with Kazakhstan (or any of the Central Asian states) is fairly limited, and a good relationship with Russia is paramount to its internal stability and to meeting any external security challenges (and avoiding any such challenges from Russia itself).

One way in which President Nazarbaev has sought to establish a more visible role for himself and his country on the international stage and among the Central Asian states has been through his proposal to create an Asian counterpart to the Conference on Security and Cooperation in Europe (CSCE). He officially presented this idea at the fall 1992 United Nations General Assembly meeting, and in March 1993 representatives from eleven Asian states, the secretariats of the UN and CSCE, and observers from Japan, Indonesia, and Thailand convened in Almaty (Kazakhstan's capital) to further explore this idea. Nazarbaev views this initiative of a "CSCA" not as an alternative to the CSCE, but as a stepping-stone to cooperation between the two regions, perhaps eventually in the form of a security and cooperation organization covering all of Eurasia.

The security threats Kazakhstan may face will be determined by both domestic policies and events beyond its borders. President Nazarbaev's very carefully balanced policies focus on keeping peace between the heavily Russified northern part of Kazakhstan and Kazakhs in the south; Nazarbaev has not tolerated manifestations of nationalism from either Russians or Kazakhs living within the republic. His ability, and that of any eventual successor, to maintain such a balanced policy will be crucial to the well-being of the state.[13] The greatest domestic threat to upsetting Kazakh-Russian relations is probably a serious deterioration in the state's economy, although disputes between Russia and Kazakhstan over the Baikonur space facility, for example, could also lead to heightened domestic tensions. An inability to control border traffic—involving both people and goods, such as drugs and military equipment—is a potential domestic threat, the response to which could involve collective actions with other states in the region.

Among the external developments that could affect Kazakhstan's security are the following: increased Russian nationalism (which could lead to attempts to redefine the country's northern border, incorporating the Russified north into Russia); instability to the south (in the form of either Islamic movements,[14] other expressions of political or socioeconomic instability, or Uzbekistan's determination to assert a leading role in the region); general buildups of military forces and bases located near Kazakhstan's borders (including in China); and the possible disintegration of the Russian Federation (which not only would create instability on the northern border, but also would raise serious questions about any Russian ability—or willingness—to offer security guarantees, including nuclear ones, to Kazakhstan). In short, a change of leadership in either Russia or Kazakhstan that ceased to recognize the importance of accommodation in their relations could raise serious questions about a north-south divide and the future of nuclear weapons in Kazakhstan (assuming they are still located there).

The military's role in such scenarios could frequently prove difficult to define. For example, its main task is considered to be defending the country's territorial integrity and independence. But how will it react should the threat to these ideas emanate from the Russian Federation, particularly if a significant number of ethnic Russians are still serving in Kazakhstan's forces? (This seems likely, given their bilateral agreement allowing Russian officers to serve in Kazakhstan until 1999.) Ensuring security through collective efforts also receives priority. Collective participation in peacekeeping missions poses similar questions about the Russian dimension of such efforts and additional uncertainties. While the national law on military structure adopted in December 1992 allows Kazakhstan's military forces to participate in peacekeeping operations, both the president and the Supreme Soviet must authorize their use in this capacity. In the case of peacekeepers being sent to Tajikistan, the Supreme Soviet proved quite reluctant to grant this authorization for several months, finally doing so only in April 1993. A general reluctance to send troops outside national borders (especially into dangerous situations) and a steadily expanding fear throughout the former Soviet Union that the Tajikistan conflict will turn into another Afghanistan were at least two of the concerns in becoming involved in this peacekeeping mission.

KYRGYZSTAN

Kyrgyzstan played only a peripheral role in the former Soviet military complex, yet it has become caught up in the violent politics of Tajikistan and Uzbekistan, and is beset with economic crisis as President Askar Akaev tries to move it toward a market economy and democracy. To date, Kyrgyzstan has shown the least interest of any of the Central Asian states in forming its own military.[15] In fact, the leadership has consistently stated that it does not have, or plan to have, either a national army or a ministry of defense. In August 1993, however, it did establish a general staff, under Vice President Feliks Kulov, to coordinate all state defense activities and policies.[16] The State Committee on Defense (which in other former

Soviet states has been the precursor to the ministry of defense), chaired by Maj. Gen. Myrzakan Subanov, now falls under the authority of this general staff.[17] In contrast to the other successor states, Kyrgyzstan demonstrated marked reluctance even to assume jurisdiction over those military forces located on its territory: about fifteen thousand men in the 8th Motorized Infantry Division, an air force training center, and some air defense surface-to-air missiles. It was apparently only after Marshal Yevgeny Shaposhnikov, commander in chief of the CIS joint armed forces, applied pressure on Kyrgyzstan's leadership to take on this responsibility that it did so in May 1992.[18]

Kyrgyzstan continues to conduct drafts in the spring and fall each year, with a term of service of eighteen months. Since the spring of 1992—when Chairman of the State Committee on Defense Maj. Gen. Dzhanibek Umetaliev indicated that about 65 percent of Kyrgyzstan's draftees would be required to serve outside the country's borders—conscripts have gradually acquired a greater say in where they will be sent to serve. Thus, in March 1993 President Akaev decreed that conscripts have the right to choose between serving in units within Kyrgyzstan or outside it (in the border guards or CIS strategic forces) and between military and alternative service (although parliament still has not passed the law on alternative service). Within the country, Kyrgyzstan is creating its own national guard (established in August 1992) of about nine hundred men and a border guard force of some four thousand. Vice President Kulov has stated that the number of forces currently located in Kyrgyzstan could be cut in half without jeopardizing the country's security. Significantly, President Akaev has embraced the notion of "armed neutrality," which asserts that Kyrgyzstan will aspire to a policy similar to that of Switzerland: it will not belong to any military blocs, it will adhere to a policy of internationally recognized neutrality, and the small number of military forces within the country will be used for emergencies such as rescues in natural disasters.

Kyrgyzstan's lack of interest in establishing a national army can be attributed primarily to two factors: its especially difficult economic situation (even by standards of the former Soviet states) and its recognized inability to ensure its security independently. The fact that Russia provides the bulk of officers in the country reinforces Kyrgyz attitudes that accommodation with Russia, under the rubric of collective security, is its most likely guarantee of national security. From the standpoint of internal unrest, the most likely source of tension that could erupt into armed conflict is a confrontation between different ethnic groups due to further deterioration in socioeconomic conditions. Akaev has noted that the Chuy region, with a large portion of the country's one million Slavs, and the Osh region, with a significant share of its half-million Uzbeks, would be particularly susceptible to this scenario. A violent confrontation already erupted between Kyrgyz and Uzbeks in Osh in 1990. In addition, Kyrgyzstan is concerned about having an adequate border protection capability to prevent the flow of weapons, drugs, and refugees across its borders; the unchecked flow of any or all of these elements would pose serious threats to Kyrgyzstan's internal security.

In terms of foreign relations, Kyrgyzstan hopes to be able to find a balanced role for itself between East and West, and between Russia and China. For the moment, the greatest external threat emanates from potential spillover from the Tajikistan conflict, which Kyrgyzstan would hope to prevent—or at least quickly contain—through cooperation with Russia and other CIS states. This threat could be compounded by a Kyrgyzstan-Tajikistan border dispute over the use of water and arable land that has affected relations between the two countries since the late 1980s. Kyrgyzstan has proposed a treaty affirming the inviolability of existing borders, but representatives of Tajikistan have rejected this idea.[19] In the context of the Tajikistan conflict, the question of whether to participate in CIS peacekeeping efforts there has sparked considerable debate within Kyrgyzstan. In the fall of 1992, Kulov sought to play a mediating role in this conflict and offered to send a peacekeeping force, only to have this idea soundly rejected by Kyrgyzstan's parliament, which argued that such efforts should be undertaken collectively by the CIS. Subsequently, in March–April 1993, Kyrgyzstan deployed a battalion of forces on the Tajikistan-Afghanistan border, but withdrew it almost as soon as it was deployed.[20] Then, in August 1993, Kyrgyzstan sent about three hundred troops to this border again, joining up with Russian border guard forces already stationed there. Among other potential threats to its security, Kyrgyzstan must be concerned about neighboring China and Uzbekistan (especially given the large Uzbek population in Osh oblast), and possible border disputes with them.

Top priority in Kyrgyzstan's security relationships certainly belongs to Russia. The two countries have signed several bilateral agreements pertaining to military issues, including on procedures for the use of Russian military installations in Kyrgyzstan; the status of servicemen from the Russian armed forces serving in Kyrgyzstan, and vice versa; the supplying of troops in Kyrgyzstan with weapons, equipment, and basic living necessities; and the training of Kyrgyz officers.[21] More generally, Subanov has noted that the republic's military doctrine has been developed (although not yet adopted by parliament) and that it focuses on close cooperation with Russia and other CIS states.

A fairly close bilateral security relationship with Russia has not, however, prevented the establishment of security contacts with others as well. Kyrgyzstan has signed the collective security treaty, which is seen as somewhat of a two-edged sword: it can strengthen the prospects for defense cooperation among the signatories, but it also can contribute to the fostering of Russian imperialism. As for other bilateral security arrangements, a 1992 agreement with Uzbekistan provides for closer military cooperation and contacts, extending to the use of training grounds in Kyrgyzstan by Uzbekistan's troops—another two-edged sword. The use of these facilities already has generated outcries of indignation in the media, while government officials in Kyrgyzstan have seemed more concerned about how the actions would be perceived in Tajikistan.[22] For its part, the government of Kyrgyzstan may have been motivated to conclude this bilateral arrangement as a means of keeping a check on one of its potential security threats. In addition to Uzbekistan's aspirations to play a dominant role in the region (raising concerns in other states, including Kyrgyzstan, about how much it would wish to "dominate") and long-standing tensions between the two states, Kyrgyzstan must be concerned about the Uzbek population within its boundaries. Kyrgyzstan has also reached other, less significant military cooperative arrangements with Turkey and Ukraine. In the case of officer training, a majority of candidates from Kyrgyzstan are being trained in Russia, while Uzbekistan and Turkey are each training a smaller number.

TAJIKISTAN

Military-security issues in Tajikistan are obviously dominated by its ongoing civil war, which has taken the lives of anywhere from twenty thousand to seventy thousand people and has created hundreds of thousands of Tajik refugees.[23] Although a detailed examination of this conflict is beyond the scope of this chapter,[24] a brief overview is in order to set the context for the range of problems facing Tajikistan today and for the foreseeable future.

The fighting in Tajikistan began in late May 1992, after President Rakhmon Nabiev, a former communist, agreed to turn over one-third of his government's ministerial posts to a coalition of democratic, nationalist, and Islamic groups. Nabiev's supporters in southern Tajikistan did not approve of this compromise and began actions to bring his government down. At the risk of oversimplification, the two opposing sides can be broken down as follows: One side consists of anticommunist, prodemocratic, and pro-Islamic supporters, including the Democratic Party of Tajikistan; the Tajik nationalist movement Rastakhiz; the Islamic Renaissance Party; and another nationalist movement, La'l-i Badakhshan. The other side is made up of procommunist forces, many of whom were united into the Popular Front of Tajikistan, which opposes fundamentalism and the democratic opposition.[25]

In September 1992 President Nabiev was forced to resign (at least in part because of a planned bilateral military agreement with Russia and Boris Yeltsin's decree in August that placed CIS border troops in Tajikistan under Russian jurisdiction, raising the democratic opposition's concerns that Russia was seeking to reestablish control over Tajikistan;[26] as a result, the opposition (prodemocratic, pro-Islamic) forces gained greater control. In October 1992 the procommunists who were in the process of taking parts of the capital, Dushanbe, were temporarily thwarted in their efforts, partly because of the actions of the Russian 201st Motorized Rifle Division, protecting what it then regarded as Tajikistan's legal government.[27] Nevertheless, by November, the procommunists controlled most of southern Tajikistan, and the coalition government resigned on November 10. By the end of 1992, the procommunist elements were back in "control," although it cannot be said that they control all of Tajikistan; the country remains fiercely divided.

Fighting both within the country and on the Tajikistan-Afghanistan border continues apace; especially, government troops have frequently been accused by organizations such as Amnesty International of gross brutality against segments of the opposition and local population.[28] In this fighting, both sides have sought out allies who have supplied military equipment, forces, and economic assistance. The present procommunist government, headed by Imomali Rakhmonov, is supported above all by forces from Russia and Uzbekistan, while the opposition has received support from the Afghan *mujahedeen* and Iran.

In terms of the formation of a national military, the government issued a decree in mid-December 1992 to create its own armed forces based on forces subordinate to the People's Front (led by Sangak Safarov until he was killed in March 1993) and other progovernment armed formations.[29] In January 1993, an ethnic Russian who had previously served in Uzbekistan's Ministry of Defense, Aleksandr Shishlyannikov, was appointed to head Tajikistan's Ministry of Defense, with the personal approval of President Islam Karimov of Uzbekistan. Conscripts were drafted in the first two months of 1993, and during that time Defense Minister Shishlyannikov and other officials noted that priority was being given to the formation of ground, air, and air defense forces; the border guards are under the jurisdiction of the Russian Federation and staffed with conscripts from Tajikistan. By the year 2000, the plan is for Tajikistan to have an army corps of three or four brigades, an air force, air defense, and special purpose (*spetsnaz*) forces.[30] For the foreseeable future, close cooperation with Russian forces clearly is receiving priority.

In addition to the government's official development of a military force based on previously existing unofficial paramilitary forces, other paramilitary organizations favoring the opposition (especially those in Gorno Badakhshan), largely supported and trained by Afghanistan, are playing an important role in Tajikistan's internal security situation today. These opposition forces have also reportedly received weapons supplies from Iran and CIS forces (including through Tajikistan's conscripts). The size and number of these unofficial military organizations is unclear, but a *Financial Times* article in November 1992 cited foreign diplomats and Tajik officials who estimated the existence of about fifty private armies, and Uzbekistan's President Karimov (who would admittedly seek to inflate the number) stated there were fifteen thousand Islamic opposition forces.[31] More recently, Prime Minister Abdumalik Abdulladzhanov has suggested that it will take three years to disarm all the illegal paramilitary formations in the country, including in Dushanbe itself.[32]

In both economic and military respects, Tajikistan's leadership sees its relations with Russia as paramount. For example, on the economic front Russia postponed Tajikistan's full repayment of its 1992 debt until 2000 and extended it additional credits for 1993. In the military sphere, the most significant factor has been Russia's protection of Tajikistan's borders with Afghanistan and China (the border forces in Tajikistan were placed under Russian jurisdiction in August 1992) and the support rendered by the 201st Motorized Rifle Division, headquartered in Dushanbe. All told, at least fifteen thousand Russian troops are stationed in Tajikistan, with more being sent. While official Russian military policy has been to remain neutral in the conflict (and simply to protect important facilities and the borders), these Russian forces have been increasingly drawn into the civil war and border conflict, both in terms of supplying government forces with equipment and in terms of sending additional troops to the region. Many of the Russian volunteer troops going to Tajikistan had previously fought in Afghanistan. Russian policy has been to have other CIS states (notably the other Central Asian states that have signed the Collective Security treaty) also provide forces for guarding the 870-mile border between Tajikistan and Afghanistan. In other words, Russia has sought quite consistently to place the effort within a multilateral, rather than bilateral, context. Aside from Uzbekistan, however, these other states have so far taken quite limited action.[33]

Tajikkistan's government is well aware of its inability to field a military force on its own, even under ideal circumstances, let alone in today's conditions of a civil war, when it has neither the time nor the money to do so; Russia is its main source of protection. Current agreements provide for the following: The 201st Division is to be stationed in Tajikistan as a Russian unit until 1999 (with Russian soldiers serving in it only on a voluntary basis). Russia is to help train its officer corps and is to supply military equipment and weapons. Russia's air defense system is to protect Tajikistan against attacks from Afghanistan. And Russian troops engaged in combat operations in Tajikistan are to be legally protected and are authorized to use aircraft and missiles. Russia also furnishes virtually all the financial support for the forces located in Tajikistan (the Russian Ministry of Defense has indicated that maintaining the 201st Division and offering border protection cost 3 billion rubles in 1992).

It should be noted that Russian involvement in Tajikistan has certainly not been universally supported. Debates in both the Russian press and parliament have raised concerns about Russia's being dragged into another Afghan-like quagmire, and Russian military officers stationed there (and those given orders to be transferred there) have expressed doubts about their mission: Whose interests are they supposed to protect? From the perspective of Tajikistan's government (let alone that of opposition forces), there appears to be dissension on whether Russian forces will—and should—remain in the country beyond 1999, at which point it is planned that Tajikistan will have established its own military.[34]

Uzbekistan's military support for Tajikistan's government, while arguably not as extensive as that supplied by Russia, has nevertheless been absolutely vital and no less visible. To a question during an interview in June 1993 about whether aid from Uzbekistan has been commensurate with the scale of Russian aid, Prime Minister Abdulladzhanov responded: "Our relations with both Russia and Uzbekistan are equally important to us. It would be political shortsightedness to give preference to one at the expense of the other. Both Russia and Uzbekistan stood by us in the republic's hour of need."[35]

Uzbekistan and Tajikistan have concluded a treaty on cooperation, which includes the stipulation that Uzbekistan will defend Tajikistan's airspace; Uzbekistan has also furnished weapons and military equipment (such as helicopters and armored equipment), some ground forces, and training for Tajikistan's internal troops.[36] Indeed, many of Tajikistan's forces are controlled directly by Uzbekistan, as is, for all intents and purposes, the northern portion of Tajikistan (Khujand), where many Uzbeks live.[37] Another factor sure to influence this bilateral relationship is that Tajikistan's defense minister previously served in Uzbekistan's Ministry of Defense and received Karimov's approval to serve in Tajikistan.

The way in which the civil war is eventually resolved will obviously have a fundamental impact on the security concerns Tajikistan will face in the future: What will be its relationship with Afghanistan? Will a Russian military presence still be welcome in the country?[38] Will Tajiks living in Afghanistan merge with (parts of) Tajikistan itself, such as the southern (Dushanbe) region? Might such an alliance then find itself in opposition to a northern Tajikistan (Khujand)-Uzbekistan alliance? Or will relations between the two countries become more confrontational? In this connection, new forms of internal unrest are a distinct possibility, given that the majority of Uzbeks, who constitute almost one-fourth of the total population in Tajikistan, live in the north and that many of them have shown some interest in federating with Uzbekistan. Because of the heavy degree of Tashkent's involvement in this region of Tajikistan already, it is not difficult to envisage the exacerbation of ethnic tensions here. If such unrest does erupt, it could spread beyond Tajikistan proper, with Uzbeks laying claim to parts of Khujand oblast and Tajiks vying for Samarkand and Bukhara. Either for these ethnic reasons or for others (such as regional economic differences), the divide between the more industrialized and urbanized north and the more agricultural south could become a source of domestic tension. Finally, the potential for renewed (or new) border disputes, such as the one between villages in Tajikistan and Kyrgyzstan over water rights and arable land, has been noted in the section on Kyrgyzstan.

TURKMENISTAN

President Supramurad Niyazov has demonstrated a distinct lack of interest in collective CIS security efforts (or the joining of any other form of military bloc) and, instead, has pursued bilateral arrangements with Russia to help meet Turkmenistan's defense and security needs. From the start, the leadership has recognized that the forces located in Turkmenistan, inherited from the Soviet military, far exceed the country's requirements. As of April 1993, the country had sixty thousand troops, including four motorized divisions, two air force regiments, and air defense capability. The leadership has not sought to control all of them, but among the motivating factors for establishing at least some national forces were the abolition of the Turkestan Military District (when Uzbekistan decided to create its own military) and a belief that Turkmenistan's proposed share of the CIS defense budget was too high. As a result, Niyazov announced the formation of the Ministry of Defense Matters in January 1992, and Danatar Kopekov was selected as its head.[39] Kopekov's background—a former oil worker and party official, and since 1991 chairman of the KGB in Turkmenistan—and those of two of three of his senior deputies (also either former oil workers or party officials) illustrate the country's lack of ethnic officers.[40] Despite this lack of military expertise, no officials from the Central Asian Military District were selected for positions in the republic's Ministry of Defense.

Turkmenistan plans to reduce the number of forces on its territory, probably by more than half. Its military draft provides for service of eighteen months by those conscripts without higher education, twelve months for those with higher education, and two years for service in the navy.[41] Only those who volunteer are to be sent outside the republic's borders, to serve in the strategic forces. There are provisions for two-year alternative service, but only for health or family (not religious) reasons. While better than 90 percent of the soldiers stationed in the country were Turkmen even in mid-1992, 95 percent of the officers were Slavic.[42] Officers may be citizens of (and swear loyalty to) either Turkmenistan or Russia.

The most significant development in Turkmenistan's defense affairs was the signing in July 1992 of a bilateral agreement with Russia that established a joint command between the two countries. Of the sixty thousand troops in Turkmenistan, fifteen thousand are under direct Russian command (air force and air defense units), and the remainder are under joint bilateral command. Turkmenistan has pledged to provide basic living necessities (such as housing and utilities), and Russia is to provide logistical support and general financing. The agreement also stipulates that the forces in Turkmenistan cannot be involved in military action without the consent of both countries. This original agreement called for the two countries to share the financing of all military forces in Turkmenistan for a five-year transition period. An agreement signed in September 1993, however, stipulates that beginning in January 1994, Turkmenistan will pay all costs of maintaining military forces on its soil. This accord also effectively grants Russia basing rights in Turkmenistan and allows Russian citizens to perform their military service in Turkmenistan. Another accord, reached in August 1992, provided for the presence of Russian border troops for the five-year transition stage (and the option for automatic extension of another five years), during which time they would also assist in the creation of Turkmenistan's own border guards. For the training of its future officer corps, Turkmenistan places the greatest emphasis on cooperation with Russia,[43] but it also plans to turn to other CIS states and Turkey (where three hundred men are already being trained), as well as to develop some of its own training capability. In this, and all military-security issues, Turkmenistan's leadership stresses the development of bilateral rather than multilateral (such as CIS) arrangements.

The level of perceived external threat at least for the near term appears to be quite low in Turkmenistan. President Niyazov has stated that he cannot foresee a threat to his country for at least ten years, and that the war in Tajikistan poses no threat because Turkmenistan is immune to Muslim fundamentalism.[44] He has also ruled out the possibility of Turkmenistan's participation in any joint military actions in Tajikistan, calling for political solutions instead. Within the country, the combination of Niyazov's strong authoritarian leadership, a relatively ethnically homogeneous population, and good economic prospects portend a more stable situation than that faced in other Central Asian states. If the government continues to offer subsidies to keep prices on consumer goods and services cheap (or even free, as in the case of utilities), the likelihood of domestic unrest—particularly in light of the tight control over any opposition political forces—appears quite limited for the time being.

Above all, to continue to provide for its security and stability, Turkmenistan seeks avenues for developing its economy, notably its sizable natural gas reserves. Iran, with which Turkmenistan has established the closest relations outside the former Soviet Union, is likely to be an important player. Both Iran and Turkey have been competing for gas pipeline and railway deals with Turkmenistan, although only Turkey appears to have reached any agreement about military-security cooperation (including the training of officers, noted above). More generally, Turkmenistan desires defense accords with its neighbors to rule out the prospect of territorial disputes. Turkmenistan has pursued most of its security arrangements in order to be able to adhere to a fairly isolationist approach: it does not wish to be involved in others' disputes (including peace-keeping) and does not want any other state involved in its affairs. The development of its own, small force is largely meant to ensure that these principles can be maintained.

UZBEKISTAN

Of the Central Asian states, Uzbekistan moved the most quickly in taking the first steps to establish its own military forces. In January 1992 it created a national guard, based on its own Ministry of Internal Affairs troops, and later that month the Supreme Soviet placed military units and schools located in the country under Uzbekistan's jurisdiction. These units included a motorized rifle division, two air force regiments, and one air defense regiment. Still in early 1992, President Karimov signed a decree to establish border guard units under the authority of the Uzbek National Security Service and subordinated CIS border guards to this new authority. Men serving in Uzbekistan who had already sworn an oath of loyalty to the USSR were not required to swear another one to Uzbekistan; new personnel are to swear loyalty to the people and president of Uzbekistan, not to the state. The country's leadership also acted quite quickly to recall its personnel serving in other former Soviet states, although many of the reported "several thousand" ethnic Uzbek officers have apparently failed to return, creating a dearth of officers, especially among the junior ranks.[45]

Plans call for the creation of a force of twenty-five thousand to thirty-five thousand men, in the form of ground forces (the main component), air force, air defense, spetsnaz, and a national guard. As in many other states of the former Soviet Union, the length of service for conscripts is twelve months for those with higher education and eighteen months for those without such education. There are provisions for contract service personnel (including women) as well, with an initial contract period of three years. The law on alternative service, adopted in October 1992, permits this service only for family reasons, not because a draftee refuses to participate in military service. The majority of conscripts are to serve within Uzbekistan, although those who wish to serve in another republic may do so with parental permission and under the supervision of Uzbekistan's armed forces. In fact, a report in *Izvestiya* in early July 1993 noted that Uzbekistan had agreed to send ten thousand of its soldiers to serve in Germany.[46] In addition, there are provisions for some draftees to be sent to other CIS states for special training, not to exceed six months, because Uzbekistan does not have the capability to train personnel in all specialties.[47]

Recognizing that even in mid-1992, 90 percent of its enlisted personnel were of the indigenous nationality, while more than 70 percent of the officer corps serving in Uzbekistan were Russian-speaking, the government has adopted several measures to address the inevitable problems arising from this situation.[48] It is offering Uzbek language classes for officers and Russian language classes for conscripts, and it plans a very gradual transition to using the Uzbek (rather than Russian) language—over five to six years. Furthermore, the first person appointed a general in Uzbekistan's army was an ethnic Russian, and the government intends for the forces to continue to be multiethnic.[49]

While many in Central Asia see Uzbekistan as a potential threat to their security (and Kazakhstan as a counterweight to this threat) in light of Uzbekistan's desire to play an assertive role in the region, there have been some attempts apparently to assuage these concerns through the signing of security-related bilateral agreements—for instance, with Kyrgyzstan in August 1992 and Kazakhstan in January 1993.[50] The absolutely critical level of Uzbekistan's support for Tajikistan's government has already been noted as well. Indeed, Uzbekistan's willingness to send forces be-

yond its borders could imply an interest in pursuing interventionist policies and capabilities to reinforce its assertive role in the region and perhaps even outside Central Asia.

From President Karimov's viewpoint, the growth of pro-
Islamic forces and the threat that Tajikistan's conflict will spread to
his country are the greatest concerns for Uzbekistan's security. It is
quite legitimate to question, nevertheless, whether Karimov is simply using Islamic fundamentalism as an excuse for his repression of
all opposition in Uzbekistan and as a means of diverting attention
from other problems within the country. Indeed, for this second-
poorest of the Central Asian states, of at least equal importance to
Uzbekistan's security is the need for it to cope with its socioeconomic problems in order to avoid internal unrest, particularly
among its ethnic groups.

The rise of ethnic nationalism, partly connected with the
Uzbek leadership's emphasis on blaming previous leaders (that is,
Russians) for the country's economic and ecological devastation,[51]
has already precipitated the departure of a significant portion of the
republic's Slavic population. Furthermore, Russian analyst Maxim
Shashenkov has explicitly highlighted the link between economic
development and domestic order: "If living standards are further
impaired . . . growing popular dissatisfaction over economic and
social problems may trigger widespread unrest in Uzbekistan."[52]
Should this occur, the potential for its effect on neighboring regions
is enormous, and the most likely tinderbox is the densely populated
Fergana Valley. Shashenkov further notes: "Were Uzbekistan to explode, the conflagration would embrace much of the region: the republic lies in the heart of ex-Soviet Central Asia and Uzbek
minorities live in Tajikistan, Kyrgyzstan, and Turkmenistan";[53] to
that list can also be added Afghanistan and Kazakhstan. In addition
to socioeconomic difficulties furnishing a spark for such flames, it
is possible that Karimov's heavy-handed quashing of any form of
political opposition may backfire, giving greater appeal to more
radical opposition elements. As for the military's role in these scenarios, the current political leadership would clearly hope that national forces could prevent or contain domestic unrest.

Within the realm of security agreements with other states,
Uzbekistan has established accords with its Central Asian neigh-

bors (probably partly to assure these neighbors of its peaceful intentions, as noted above, and partly to ensure a central role for itself in the region) and has moved toward a closer alliance with Russia. The latter development is largely due to the ongoing conflict in Tajikistan and Karimov's belief (not necessarily shared by all) that no one besides the Russians can guarantee security and stability in the region. Moreover, the two countries have discussed such possibilities as military-technical cooperation, the joint use of military facilities, and Russia's training of Uzbekistan's personnel.

Uzbekistan has also had some security-related contacts with Turkey, and in the broader context of its foreign relations priorities, the republic has placed great emphasis on Turkey's role. For example, it is the only Central Asian state to have Turkey, not Russia, represent its interests abroad. From an economic perspective, the Chinese model seems to be more appealing to the Karimov leadership than Turkey's, however. In short, Uzbekistan's government has attempted to pick and choose what is most appealing and useful from a variety of states, a pragmatic approach that will probably continue to apply to the country's emerging defense relationships as well.

CONCLUSIONS

From these brief country overviews, it is apparent that the Central Asian states have neither adopted a uniform approach in addressing their security efforts nor perceived possible security threats in the same way. Nevertheless, it is possible to identify certain commonalities in both their military development and their security concerns. As these states proceed along the path of creating independent armed forces, all are focusing on the desirability of more mobile forces, with modern equipment. Most face problems (either technical or financial) in being able to maintain these forces and equipment. In contrast to the Slavic states, the Central Asian republics do not face a shrinking pool of eligible conscripts; rather, the problem (which virtually all the former Soviet states share) is the unwillingness of young men to serve in the armed forces in the face of a continuing decline in military morale and prestige. Thus, even though draftees are no longer sent outside their native states' borders involuntarily, incidents of draft evasion and desertion remain high. In addition, the poor health of people living in Central Asia means more conscripts are likely to have legitimate medical problems.

The fact that a majority of Central Asian conscripts who served in the Soviet armed forces did so in the construction troops deprives these states of the ability to draw on previously developed military expertise among the population. This lack of expertise is, of course, especially apparent in the ethnic officer corps; all these states face the problem of having to rely on Slavic (particularly Russian) officers to lead their forces. For now, Russia and the Central Asian states have a mutual interest in having Russian officers serve in these new militaries: Russia does not have the housing or positions for them to fill back home, and the Central Asian states need their expertise. But parliamentary regulations have stipulated that officers serving outside Russia will retain their benefits and rights as members of the Russian armed forces only until the end of December 1994. Subsequent bilateral agreements with Kazakhstan and Turkmenistan have extended this deadline until the end of 1999. Still, these constraints raise serious questions about the leadership of the other Central Asian militaries as of 1995, assuming no bilateral arrangements are made.

Certain common features related to security threats in the region have been noted throughout this chapter. It is necessary to underscore just two points. First, the large youth populations in the Central Asian states can offer fertile ground for instability and uprisings, particularly as economic difficulties are combined with the need for more jobs for these young people and as anger over environmental devastation (and consequent health disasters) grows. Second, most potential future disputes seem likely to develop out of socioeconomic problems in the region. As they are manifested, they can assume a variety of forms, including conflicts arising as a result of economic differentiation among the Central Asian states, as some are better able to exploit their natural resources than others; disputes over access to arable land, water, and housing; interethnic and clan rivalries; power politics within a given country or between countries; and the inability to control border traffic—of both people and goods, such as drugs.

Given the quite modest current plans for military force development in the Central Asian states, the militaries themselves will not necessarily pose a significant threat to each other. But neither will they truly be able to provide for their countries' security without external assistance. Should new forms of instability and conflict emerge in this region, it is not clear what capabilities from which countries will be brought to bear. At a minimum, it is necessary to examine in greater detail the range of potential threats and their implications for U.S. interests. The hope must be that any violence will be contained at a low level, although the inability to deal with the situation in Tajikistan today does not offer much reason for such hope.

NOTES

1. For additional information about Nurmagambetov and other key military leaders, see Richard Woff, *Commonwealth High Command and National Defense Forces* (Camberley, Surrey: Royal Military Academy Sandhurst, 1992), pp. A33–A34.

2. One of the major concerns is that strictly Russian control leaves these countries dependent solely on Russia for their security. For a more detailed discussion of Kazakhstan's perspectives on the nuclear weapons issue (including problems associated with signing the Non-Proliferation Treaty), see Oumirseric Kasenov and Kairat Abuseitov, *The Future of Nuclear Weapons in the Kazakh Republic's National Security* (McLean, Va.: Potomac Foundation, 1993); and Kairat Abuseitov and Murat Laumulin, "Farewell to Arms?" *Aziya International Weekly*, no. 10 (March), 1993, p. 3, translated in Joint Publications Research Service, *Arms Control* (JPRS-TAC)-93-012, pp. 9–11. For a Western perspective, see John Lepingwell, "Kazakhstan and Nuclear Weapons," *RFE/RL Research Report*, February 19, 1993, pp. 59–61.

3. In fact, Nazarbaev has even raised the possibility of Kazakhstan signing the Non-Proliferation Treaty as a nonnuclear state, but allowing Russia to station some of its nuclear forces in Kazakhstan, an arrangement parallel to the relationship between the United States and West Germany. For the ethnic composition of the various states, see Table 1 in the introduction to this volume.

4. Iain Elliot, "East-West Debate in Almaty," *RFE/RL Research Report*, May 22, 1992, p. 51.

5. As reported in Stephen Foye, "Russian Strategic Weapons to Stay in Kazakhstan," *RFE/RL Research Report*, September 4, 1992, pp. 41–42. It should also be noted that Kazakhstan ratified the Non-Proliferation Treaty, in December 1993, despite previously expressed concerns that the treaty may collapse in 1995, with Kazakhstan having committed itself to being a

nonnuclear state, and that the near-nuclear states do not really believe that the nuclear powers are committed to guaranteeing their security.

6. For example, within the Fortieth Combined Arms Army, only 3 percent of the officers are ethnic Kazakhs, according to its commander, Lt. Gen. Anatoliy Ryabtsev. Cited in Anatoliy Ladin, "National Armies: A View Inside," *Krasnaya zvezda,* July 2, 1992, p. 2, translated in Joint Publications Research Service, *Central Eurasia: Military Affairs* (JPRS-UMA)-92-026, p. 38. Information on the number of Kazakh officers overall is discussed in both Kazakh and Russian sources. See, for example, Baqtiyar Yerimbet, "How Many Officers Do the Kazakhs Have?" *Yegemendi Qazaqstan,* February 14, 1992, p. 3, translated in JPRS-UMA-92-018, p. 36; and Sergei Skorokhodov and Vladimir Tyurkin, "Foreign Mailbag: From All Around the Globe," *Rossiyskaya gazeta,* May 20, 1993, p. 7, translated in Foreign Broadcast Information Service, *Daily Report: Central Eurasia* (FBIS-SOV)-93-099, p. 13. The figure of Russians making up 70 percent of all officers in Kazakhstan is cited in a report by Moscow's Mayak Radio, July 1, 1993, translated in FBIS-SOV-93-126, p. 16. The proportion may actually be higher: following a meeting between the ministers of defense of Kazakhstan and Germany in August 1993, a German report indicated that 90 percent of the commanders (probably meaning higher-ranking officers) in Kazakhstan's military were Russian officers. See *Sueddeutsche Zeitung,* August 20, 1993, p. 2, translated in FBIS-SOV-93-160, p. 47.

7. On the movement of officers, see, for example, the interview with Kazakhstan's Minister of Defense Gen. Nurmagambetov in "Russia Is Our Strategic Ally," *Krasnaya zvezda,* June 15, 1993, p. 2, translated in FBIS-SOV-93-116, p. 48; Col. Anatoliy Ladin, "Six Laws for the Military," *Krasnaya zvezda,* January 28, 1993, p. 1, translated in FBIS-SOV-93-021, p. 44; and statement by Lt. Gen. Aleksei Khlestovich of Kazakhstan, reported by Interfax, December 8, 1992, published in FBIS-SOV-92-236, p. 36.

8. The Ministry of Defense has estimated that the size of the force could range from 0.5 percent to 0.9 percent of the overall population of some 16.5 million, depending on economic circumstances and the extent of military danger. This would put a future force roughly between 82,000 and 150,000.

9. The plants have produced artillery, infantry and tank equipment, rifles, ballistic missile components, and naval equipment. Kazakhstan also produces nuclear power reactor fuel, beryllium products, and uranium ore. It has the former Soviet Union's only known plants outside Russia designed to produce materials for chemical and biological warfare.

10. This facility is particularly important to the future of Russia's space program because it is the only geostationary earth orbit launch facility in the CIS.

11. Russian military officers have complained about the inadequacies of Kazakhstan's command over the construction troops in Baikonur, saying that the number of troops has fallen from thirty thousand to five thousand and that even basic infrastructure needs are not being met.

12. Russian sources indicate that more than 90 percent of Baikonur's funding comes from Russia.

13. For a discussion of the Almaty unrest in December 1986, when the Moscow leadership deviated from the traditional policy of maintaining a political bal-

ance between Russia and Kazakhstan, see Susan L. Clark, "Ethnic Tensions and the Soviet Military," in *Soviet Military Power in a Changing World* (Boulder, Colo.: Westview Press, 1991), pp. 218–219.

14. Nazarbaev himself has noted that the Islamic fundamentalist threat should not be overestimated (as has generally been done in the West), but neither, he cautions, should it be completely ignored. See Nursultan A. Nazarbaev, "Strategy of the Formation and Development of Kazakhstan as a Sovereign State," *Kazakhstanskaya pravda,* May 16, 1992, pp. 3–6, translated in FBIS-SOV-92-108, p. 84.

15. Interestingly, despite official statements that no national army will be established, an opinion poll conducted in February 1993 showed that 78 percent of those surveyed believed Kyrgyzstan should have its own army. See Bess Brown, "Central Asian States Seek Russian Help," *RFE/RL Research Report,* June 18, 1993, p. 85.

16. The reason for the creation of the general staff has not been explicitly stated. It is possible that Kyrgyzstan felt a need to create an institution that would give it greater say over what happens to defense forces and facilities located on its soil. The worsening situation in Tajikistan may also have been a factor. The selection of Kulov as its head is also notable, given the controversy that has frequently surrounded him, including his efforts to send peacekeeping forces to Tajikistan in the fall of 1992 (which were subsequently rejected by Kyrgyzstan's parliament).

17. The committee was chaired until July 1993 by Maj. Gen. Dzhanibek Umetaliev, who was then replaced for unknown reasons by his subordinate, Subanov.

18. Maxim Shashenkov, *Security Issues of the Ex-Soviet Central Asian Republics,* London Defence Studies, no. 14 (London: Brassey's, 1992), p. 44.

19. The dispute broke out in 1988 and led to several deaths in 1989. It was one of the reasons for a delay in the establishment of diplomatic relations between the two states, which did finally happen in mid-January 1993. See Bess Brown, "No Solution to Tajik-Kyrgyz Border Dispute," *RFE/RL News Briefs,* vol. 2, no. 4 (1993), p. 9. This conflict was also noted among disputes in Central Asia in Boris Z. Rumer, "The Gathering Storm in Central Asia," *Orbis,* Vol. 37, no. 1 (Winter 1993), p. 96.

20. It is not clear why these forces were withdrawn so quickly. A report from Kyrgyzstan indicated it was because the country had no law on the status of its citizens on active duty in hot spots, while a Russian officer stationed in Tajikistan suggested it was because the troops lacked training for operating in mountainous terrain. See Bess Brown, "Kyrgyz Troops Withdrawn from Tajikistan," *RFE/RL News Briefs,* vol. 2, no. 16 (1993), p. 9.

21. By implication, all military equipment in the country is supplied by Russia, partly because Kyrgyzstan does not have the money to purchase arms elsewhere. These bilateral agreements are discussed in more detail in an interview with Col. Gen. Stanislav Petrov, "Russia-Kyrgyzstan," *Krasnaya zvezda,* April 14, 1993, p. 3, translated in JPRS-UMA-93-014, p. 19; and in Sergei Knyazkov, "Russian Military Facilities to Remain in Kyrgyzstan," *Krasnaya zvezda,* July 7, 1993, p. 1, translated in FBIS-SOV-93-130, p. 40. The emphasis on the general importance of relations with Russia is also underscored,

for example, by Subanov and President Akaev. See Subanov statement, reported by *ITAR-TASS*, July 29, 1993, published in FBIS-SOV-93-145, p. 50; and Interfax interview with Akaev, transmitted February 24, 1993, published in FBIS-SOV-93-036, p. 69.

22. For more detail, see Brown, "Central Asian States," p. 86. One particular concern this has raised is whether Uzbekistan would use this agreement as a way of massing troops and equipment in Kyrgyzstan, including for use in Tajikistan.

23. For a fuller discussion of the conflict, see Bess Brown, "Tajikistan: The Conservatives Triumph," *RFE/RL Research Report,* February 12, 1993, pp. 9–12; and Leon Aron, "Yeltsin's Vietnam," *Washington Post,* August 22, 1993, pp. C1 and C4.

24. For such an examination, see Barnett R. Rubin's chapter in this volume.

25. See Brown, "Tajikistan: The Conservatives Triumph"; and Arkady Dubnov, "Despite Armistice, Feuding Continues," *New Times,* no. 2 (1993), pp. 10–13.

26. Bess Brown, "Tajikistan: The Fall of Nabiev," *RFE/RL Research Report,* September 25, 1992, vol. 1, no. 38, pp. 14 and 17.

27. Brown, "Tajikistan: The Conservatives Triumph," p. 10.

28. See, for example, Keith Martin, "Russian Soldiers Witness Tajik Atrocities," *RFE/RL Daily Report,* July 1, 1993.

29. Aleksandr Karpov, "Tajikistan Has Started Forming Its Own Armed Forces," *Izvestiya,* January 20, 1993, p. 1, translated in FBIS-SOV-93-013, p. 73. See also Bess Brown, "Tajik Opposition to Be Banned," *RFE/RL Research Report,* April 2, 1993, vol. 2, no. 14, pp. 9–10. In March 1993, the People's Front militia was estimated to be some eight thousand men and the main military force behind the government. See Christopher Panico, "Uzbekistan's Southern Diplomacy," *RFE/RL Research Report,* March 26, 1993, vol. 2, no. 13, p. 40.

30. This plan was outlined by Russian Minister of Defense Pavel Grachev in January 1993, following a visit by a CIS military delegation. Reported by Interfax, February 6, 1993, published in FBIS-SOV-93-024, p. 9.

31. The *Financial Times* figure is for paramilitary organizations on both sides of the conflict. See Steve LeVine, "Private Armies Bring Instability to Tajikistan," *Financial Times,* November 2, 1992, p. 10. For Karimov's statement, see his interview in *Liberation,* September 8, 1992, p. 16, translated in FBIS-SOV-92-178, p. 36.

32. Interview with Prime Minister Abdumalik Abdulladzhanov in *Nezavisimaya gazeta,* June 22, 1993, p. 3, translated in FBIS-SOV-93-119, p. 47.

33. Kazakhstan and Kyrgyzstan have both sent small numbers of peacekeeping forces to help protect the border between Tajikistan and Afghanistan. Turkmenistan refuses to do so, and is willing to assist only in political solutions to the conflict.

34. For example, Tajikistan's Foreign Minister Rashid Alimov has stated that Russian troops will not be stationed in Tajikistan after 1999 because the country will have its own forces by then, whereas Defense Minister Aleksandr Shishlyannikov (an ethnic Russian) has argued that the Russian presence should continue, since the desirability of that presence is not determined solely by Tajikistan's absence of its own forces.

35. In Abdulladzhanov interview, FBIS-SOV-93-119, p. 46.
36. Additionally, Belarus has reportedly supplied weapons and ammunition to the government of Tajikistan.
37. Nancy Lubin, U.S. Institute of Peace, personal communication, September 1993.
38. Russia's desire to maintain a military presence in Tajikistan will be determined partly by whether there will be a civilian Russian population to protect: the 1989 census gave the number of Russians living there as almost four hundred thousand, but a significant exodus has occurred since then; estimates as of mid-1993 place this population at anywhere between seventy thousand and two hundred thousand. The other major consideration will be whether Tajikistan will continue to be viewed as a buffer state or forward basing area in Russian military-strategic plans, including for the retention of the air defense system.
39. In July 1992 it was renamed the Ministry of Defense, and Kopekov became minister of defense.
40. Woff, *Commonwealth High Command,* p. A36.
41. While the creation of a navy was certainly not a top priority, Turkmenistan believed that if the Caspian flotilla were divided up, it should receive its share, based on its contribution to the creation of the Soviet navy. Turkmenistan and Russia reached agreement in mid-March 1993 that the former would have its own navy, initially under joint command, in the Caspian Sea region.
42. Interview with Turkmenistan First Deputy Minister for Defense Affairs Maj. Gen. Bekdzhan Niyazov, in *Frunzevets,* April 16, 1992, translated in JPRS-UMA-92-021, p. 37; Lt. Gen. V. Zhurbenko, "Location of Duty Assignment—Turkmenistan," *Krasnaya zvezda,* May 6, 1993, translated in FBIS-SOV-93-089, p. 58; Shashenkov, *Security Issues of the Ex-Soviet Central Asian Republics,* p. 46; and Brown, "Central Asian States," p. 86.
43. In August 1993 the two states initialed an agreement on the training of Turkmenistan's military personnel in Russian military schools; this agreement also addressed the status of Russian citizens serving in Turkmenistan's armed forces, as noted above. Reported by ITAR-TASS on August 13, 1993, published in FBIS-SOV-93-156, p. 6.
44. Brown, "Central Asian States," p. 87.
45. On the decree recalling personnel (who can continue to serve in these other states, under contract), see Maj. V. Kovalenko, "From Tashkent: Parliament Announces a Spring Recall," *Krasnaya zvezda,* March 24, 1992, p. 3, translated in JPRS-UMA-92-011, pp. 77–78. On the development of its officer corps, see Lt. Col. Valentin Astafev, "Some Still Dream of Naval Infantry," *Krasnaya zvezda,* July 16, 1992, p. 2, translated in JPRS-UMA-92-029, p. 47.
46. Igor Andreev and Nikolai Burbyga, "The Withdrawal of Troops Proceeds Normally," *Izvestiya,* July 8, 1993, translated in JPRS-UMA-93-026, p. 3. According to John Lepingwell, "Is the Military Disintegrating from Within?" *RFE/RL Research Report,* June 18, 1993, p. 14, five thousand members of Uzbekistan's military are serving in the Western Group of Forces in Germany.
47. As outlined in U. Mirzayarov, "Army Service in the Homeland," *Pravda Vostoka,* May 7, 1992, p. 1, translated in JPRS-UMA-92-020, p. 49; and in an

interview with Col. Arslan Khalmatov in *Krasnaya zvezda,* May 20, 1993, p. 2, translated in FBIS-SOV-93-102, p. 55.

48. As discussed by Uzbekistan's Minister for Defense Matters Lt. Gen. R. Akhmedov, in Astafev, "Some Still Dream," translated in JPRS-UMA-92-029, p. 46; and "To Assist Instructors of Groups for Social-Humanitarian Studies for Officers and Warrant Officers," *Vatan Pavar,* July 7, 1992, p. 3, translated in JPRS-UMA-92-033, p. 31. Nevertheless, Uzbekistan's minister of defense reportedly indicated that he was willing to replace 80 percent of the existing officer corps with national cadres. See Igor Zhukov, "Turkmenistan Is Ready to Create a Ministry of Defense," *Nezavisimaya gazeta,* January 9, 1992, translated in JPRS-UMA-92-003, p. 34.

49. Astafev, "Some Still Dream," translated in JPRS-UMA-92-029, pp. 46-47.

50. The agreement with Kyrgyzstan provides for day-to-day defense cooperation and closer defense ties generally, while the accord with Kazakhstan covers cooperation in intelligence and combating terrorism, drug trafficking, crime, and corruption.

51. This policy is particularly evident in connection with the "cotton affair." See Cassandra Cavanaugh, "Uzbekistan Reexamines the Cotton Affair," *RFE/RL Research Report,* September 18, 1992, pp. 7–11.

52. Shashenkov, *Security Issues of the Ex-Soviet Central Asian Republics,* p. 21.

53. Ibid., p. 18.

APPENDIX A TO CHAPTER 6

MILITARY DEVELOPMENTS IN THE CENTRAL ASIAN STATES

Country	Primary Military Organization and Leader	Planned Forces*
Kazakhstan	Ministry of Defense (estab. May1992) Col. Gen. Sagadat Nurmagambetov	85,000, including: • Ground, air, air defense, naval • Internal and border troops • Presidential guard
Kyrgyzstan	General Staff (estab. August 1993) Vice President Feliks Kulov State Committee on Defense Maj. Gen. Myrzakan Subanov	8,000–10,000, including: • Those serving outside Kyrgyzstan • National forces (5,000) in border troops and national guard
Tajikistan	Ministry of Defense (estab. December 1992) Maj. Gen. Aleksandr Shishlyannikov	30,000–40,000, including: • Ground (3–4 brigades), air, air defense, spetsnaz • Border troops under Russian jurisdiction, staffed with Tajik conscripts
Turkmenistan	Ministry of Defense (estab. July 1992) Lt. Gen. Danatar Kopekov	25,000, including: • Air and air defense forces under Russian control • Ground, naval forces under joint command with Russia • Border troops under Russian command for 5-year transition, while national border troops being established
Uzbekistan	Ministry of Defense (estab. early 1992) Lt. Gen. Rustam Akhmedov	25,000–35,000 including: • Ground, air, air defense, spetsnaz • National guard, internal and border troops, national security service

*Most of these states have yet to clearly define the future size of their force; these numbers are therefore only best-guess estimates.

Chapter 7

Tajikistan: From Soviet Republic to Russian-Uzbek Protectorate

Barnett R. Rubin

THE SWIFT AND SEEMINGLY INEXORABLE DESCENT OF TAJIKISTAN into a brutal civil war within months after independence exemplified the worst disaster that might befall Central Asia. What is really at stake is whether Tajikistan and the other Central Asian former Soviet republics can become genuinely sovereign states.

Like many postcolonial states, Tajikistan gained independence without a clear national identity, a viable economic and fiscal base for state power, or genuine national security forces. The attempt by political forces excluded from the communist system of power to democratize this weak state soon degenerated into civil war. An insecure population fell back on whatever resources it could find for self-defense, namely, armed struggle based on ethnic and clan affiliations and aid from external sources. The resulting disorder resembled that in Afghanistan, Somalia, Bosnia, or Liberia, and the human disaster it produced can rival any of these.

Part of this research was carried out under a grant from the United States Institute of Peace. I collected some of the information as a participant in a Helsinki Watch mission to Tajikistan in May–June 1993. I also benefited from helpful comments from Shahrbanou Tadjbakhsh, Michael Mandelbaum, and an anonymous reviewer. I would like to express my gratitude to all of the above, while noting that all conclusions and errors are my own.

Only international intervention, a far from disinterested action by Uzbekistan and Russia, enabled one faction to reconsolidate power, which it shows every sign of monopolizing. The conflict gave added impetus to a tendency for Central Asia to return to closer relations with Russia, which is emerging as the area's hegemon. Persecution in Tajikistan and exile in Afghanistan, however, are turning part of the opposition into a militant Islamic guerrilla movement, which continues to launch attacks into Tajikistan and threatens to reembroil Russia in Afghanistan.

BACKGROUND

In the Soviet period Tajikistan resembled other Central Asian republics in its poverty, external dependence, and ethnic fragmentation, but it had extreme rather than regionally typical scores on most of these measures.[1] It also had the closest ethnic links and the longest border with Afghanistan, which has vast arms stockpiles and an expanding drug trade.

Four major factors shaped the conflict in Tajikistan. The republic's degree of poverty and economic dependence meant that independence created a greater shock than elsewhere. The nature of ethnic identity in the republic meant that Tajik nationalism was a weak and ineffective alternative to communist ideology, a situation that distinguishes Tajikistan from the Turkic states. The presence in Tajikistan of mainly Slavic security forces answering to command centers in Tashkent, the capital of Uzbekistan, and Moscow provided a source of arms and support for one side. The proximity of Afghanistan provided a source of arms and money (from the drug trade) for the other side, as well as for some independent warlords.

Economic Factors

The Central Asian republics constituted the poorest area of the USSR, and Tajikistan was the poorest of them all (see Table 1). All Central Asian republics depended heavily on external subsidies to their budget, but Tajikistan was the most dependent, with Union transfers amounting to 47 percent of revenues in 1991. All republics except energy-rich Russia, Azerbaijan, and Turkmenistan

TABLE 7.1—INDICES OF POVERTY AND EXTERNAL DEPENDENCE,
SOVIET REPUBLICS

Republic	Per Capita Gross Domestic Product (current rubles, 1990)	Transfers from Union Budget as % of Total Government Revenue (1991)	Interrepublic (IR) Trade Deficit (or Surplus) as % of IR Trade at World Prices (1990)
Baltics			
Estonia	5,039	0.0	22.7
Latvia	4,542	0.0	10.6
Lithuania	3,561	0.0	26.6
Slavic/Other Europe			
Belarus	3,902	16.3	3.6
Moldova	2,920	0.0	29.3
Russia	4,224	n.a.	(20.9)
Ukraine	3,177	5.9	2.7
Trans-Caucasus			
Armenia	2,915	17.1	22.7
Azerbaijan	2,056	0.0	(2.9)
Georgia	2,731	0.0	22.1
Central Asia			
Kazakhstan	2,706	23.1	26.5
Kyrgyzstan	1,893	35.6	19.7
Tajikistan	1,341	46.6	30.5
Turkmenistan	2,002	21.7	(5.4)
Uzbekistan	1,579	42.9	22.9

Source: World Bank, *Statistical Handbook: States of the Former USSR, 1992* (Washington, D.C., 1992).

ran deficits on interrepublic trade, but Tajikistan's deficit was proportionately the largest of all. Thus the independence of Tajikistan created the greatest shock to the republic that could least afford it.

Economic grievances, however severe, do not inevitably lead to clan-based civil war. The relations that Soviet rule had created among various groups and between those groups and political power shaped the lines of competition; the weakness of political institutions, combined with the availability of arms, turned competition into armed conflict.

Ethnicity and Regionalism

The Central Asian republics had more heterogeneous populations than other regions of the Soviet Union, and Tajikistan's degree of fragmentation among official categories was average for the region.[2] At the time of the 1989 census, the population of Tajikistan was 62 percent Tajik. Thus, according to official Soviet ethnic categories, the titular nationality constituted less of the population than in Turkmenistan (72 percent) or Uzbekistan (71 percent), but more than in Kyrgyzstan (52 percent) or Kazakhstan (40 percent). Uzbeks accounted for 24 percent of Tajikistan's population. They make up a smaller share of the population than do Russians in Kazakhstan or Kyrgyzstan, but are the largest indigenous ethnic minority in the area. And like the Russians in Kazakhstan, most of the Uzbeks live in areas contiguous to their titular republic, which is also a regional power claiming an interest in the welfare of all members of its titular group.

Russians totaled 7 percent of Tajikistan's population, but the total European population came to 10 percent. As elsewhere in Central Asia, the Russian speakers were concentrated in the administrative centers, in professional and working-class positions. They slightly outnumbered the titular nationality in the capital (Dushanbe), as was typical of republic capitals in the area.[3]

Tajik nationalism, however, did not appeal equally even to the 62 percent of population who were officially Tajik. The Tajik identity, applied by the Soviets to Central Asian speakers of Iranian languages, had little historic resonance. The region's centers of Persian culture, Bukhara and Samarkand, which might have served as centers for the formation of this identity, had been the capitals of Turkic dynasties and were surrounded by rural areas dominated by Uzbeks.[4] In 1924, when the Soviets first delimited national republics in Turkestan, some areas with mainly Persian-speaking populations were joined into the Autonomous Republic of Tajikistan as part of Uzbekistan. In 1929 Tajikistan became a Union republic in its own right, but Bukhara and Samarkand remained in Uzbekistan.

Various groups of Tajiks have distinctive cultural features and political loyalties. The Pamiris of the autonomous region (oblast) of Gorno Badakhshan (covered by the Pamir Mountains) speak eastern Iranian languages distinct from Tajik, and unlike other Tajiks, who are Sunni Muslims, they follow the Ismaili sect, a dissident form of Shi'ism. Many of those classified as Tajiks in the southern province of Kurgan Tiube consider themselves to be Arabs by descent.[5]

Tajiks have no tribes, but like other settled Central Asians, they have strongly identified with their region, which formed the basis for clanlike ties based on patron-client relations. In lowland areas of Central Asia, the Persian-speaking populations have long undergone a process of acculturation to the dominant Turkic invaders and settlers. In such areas a regional identity including both Tajiks and Uzbeks may outweigh the fluid lines between the juridically distinguished nationalities.[6] Mountainous areas tend to have remained more purely "Tajik."

Such divisions are not unique to Tajikistan. Subethnic divisions based on region, tribe, or clan permeate politics throughout Central Asia. They can be mitigated through redistributive policies (as in Turkmenistan and, more precariously, Uzbekistan) or through political inclusion in representative institutions (as in Kyrgyzstan).[7] Tajikistan shows what can happen when these integrative mechanisms break down.

Of the principal regions in Tajikistan, three are heavily Uzbek with Tajik populations who often intermarry with Uzbeks and speak some Uzbek. These are Khujand, the former Leninabad (31 percent Uzbek);[8] Hissar, the area west of Dushanbe (estimated at 45 percent Uzbek);[9] and Kurgan Tiube, southwest of Dushanbe (32 percent Uzbek). All of these areas are contiguous to Uzbekistan, and Khujand was at one time actually part of that republic. The other major areas are Kulab, southeast of Dushanbe (13 percent Uzbek), Garm, east of Dushanbe (data not available), and Gorno Badakhshan (no Uzbeks reported).

The Turkicized areas received disproportionate shares of economic benefits and political power. Most of the republic's industrial investment went to Khujand and Hissar.[10] Massive irrigation projects transformed Kurgan Tiube into part of the Central Asian cotton bowl. To provide the additional farm labor needed, Stalin and his successors forcibly transferred mountain Tajiks there. These settlers became a separate subethnic group, called Garmis by their neighbors.[11]

Leninabadis came to dominate the party and state leadership. Besides their links to Uzbeks, they were allied to the Russian speakers, who played powerful roles in all the republics and linked them to Moscow. In the 1970s the Kulabis became clients of the Leninabadis, with whom they formed a single faction.[12] Garmis, Pamiris, and people from other "pure Tajik" areas formed much of the Tajik cultural intelligentsia, which, unlike the party and administration, by definition excluded Uzbeks and Russian speakers. Hence these subethnic groups played disproportionate roles in the nationalist and religious opposition.

Breakup of Soviet Security Forces

The breakup of the USSR left different fragments of the former Soviet security forces in different parts of the territory. These forces, which were usually ethnically Slavic, lacked a clear mission or political direction once the state that had commanded them dissolved, but they exhibited ethnic ties to local Russian-speaking populations allied with the old order. The most important components of the all-Soviet forces in Tajikistan were the 201st Motorized Rifle Division of the Red Army in Dushanbe, which reported to the Turkestan Military District in Tashkent, and the Border Security Forces along the Amu Darya, the river that separates Tajikistan from Afghanistan. These forces had belonged to the KGB but had subsequently been transferred to a special command in the president's office in Moscow. The local security forces were ethnically divided and weak.

Afghanistan

Across the Amu Darya, the replacement of the formerly Soviet-supported government in Kabul by a precarious coalition of *mujahedeen* (Islamic resistance fighters) strengthened forces in Afghanistan sympathetic to the opposition in Tajikistan. The *mujahedeen* forces led by Ahmed Shah Masud that played the leading role in the capture of Kabul had made the largely Tajik areas of north Afghanistan into strongholds of the Islamic resistance.

Masud's rival, Gulbuddin Hekmatyar, also had a base in the border region, as did several other Islamist parties.

The collapse of the Kabul government facilitated the flow of arms throughout the region. The drug trade already thriving in much of Afghanistan expanded both within that country and in its neighbors, providing an independent economic base for warlords.

FROM PROTEST TO CIVIL WAR: 1990–1993

Perestroika hardly came to Tajikistan. A local communist elite dependent on subsidies from Moscow was hardly likely to articulate liberal or nationalist aspirations. Beginning in 1990, however, an opposition began to surface. It included several ideological currents typical of post-Soviet politics: cultural nationalist (Rastakhez, or Rebirth); religious (the Islamic Renaissance Party, or IRP); democratic (the Democratic Party, or DP); and regional or subethnic autonomist (*La'l-i Badakhshan* or Ruby of Badakhshan, which advocated autonomy for Gorno- Badakhshan and defended the rights of Pamiris). The most prominent opposition demands were for upgrading the role of the Tajik language and Islamic religion in the country's society and politics. These movements expressed the protest of Tajik intellectuals outside of the Khujand-Kulab clientelist networks.

Tajikistan declared independence on September 9, 1991, after the failure of the August 19 coup attempt in Moscow. Opposition demonstrators forced parliament to organize a direct presidential election on November 27. The renamed Communist Party's candidate, Leninabadi conservative Rakhmon Nabiev, won 57 percent of the vote in an election of dubious fairness.

Protest erupted again in March 1992 after Nabiev arrested the pro-opposition mayor of Dushanbe on corruption charges. Pro-government groups responded with demonstrations of their own. Several days of hostage taking and intermittent fighting by both sides in Dushanbe forced Nabiev to agree to a coalition government with the opposition on May 11.

Leninabad and Kulab oblasts, however, refused to recognize the new government, and civil war began to erupt. As the conflict spread from the Dushanbe intelligentsia to the countryside, ideo-logical motives receded. The only links the protagonists in the cap-ital had with the rest of the population were regional ties, which increasingly defined the contours of the war.

On the opposition side were the Pamiris, in both Dushanbe and Badakhshan, where the local government voted for sover-eignty, and the Garmis in (besides the capital) both their native re-gions and their settlements in Kurgan Tiube. These forces obtained weapons from various sources in Afghanistan, as well as some in the government. The Kulabis formed the main armed force of the ex-communist side. Some of the latter seized or received weapons from Russian garrisons, with at least local Russian complicity. The Kulabi and ex-communist forces were led by the People's Front of Tajikistan (PF). Sangak Safarov, a Kulabi Tajik who had spent twenty-three years in prison for a variety of offenses, notably mur-der, emerged as its powerful and charismatic leader.

The war came to Dushanbe when demonstrations (reinforced by hostage taking) by armed opposition supporters forced Nabiev to sign a letter of resignation on September 7 as he fled to Khujand. Akbarshah Iskandarov, the Pamiri chairman of the Supreme So-viet, became acting president of an "opposition"-led government.

By this time, the turmoil in Tajikistan had begun to set off alarms in Tashkent, in Moscow, and elsewhere in Central Asia. President Islam Karimov of Uzbekistan was concerned not only by the spread of armed conflict in the region, but by attacks on Uzbeks in Tajikistan and irredentist claims to Bukhara and Samarkand raised by nationalist elements in Dushanbe. The con-tinuing flight from Dushanbe of Russian speakers who felt threat-ened by local nationalism and Islamic "fundamentalism" also aroused concerns in Russia.

On September 3 the presidents of Uzbekistan, Russia, Ka-zakhstan, and Kyrgyzstan issued a warning that the conflict en-dangered the security of the Commonwealth of Independent States (CIS). Since May, when supporters of the opposition had begun to enter Afghanistan in search of weapons and military training, Rus-sia had also reinforced its border guards along the Amu Darya. Russia and Uzbekistan sent additional troops and border guards in September; Kazakhstan followed later, while Kyrgyzstan's parliament refused to authorize such deployment.

Russia and Uzbekistan decided that their security interests required the imposition of order on Tajikistan, and that the only force capable of establishing such order was the ex-communists and their supporters. Mainly Uzbek fighters from Hissar and Kurgan Tiube, as well as Kulabis, received arms and training in Uzbekistan. Troops from Uzbekistan also prepared for deployment in support of an offensive.[13]

On November 16 the communist-dominated parliament invalidated Nabiev's resignation at a special session in Khujand. It abolished the office of president and elected Imomali Rakhmonov, chairman of the Kulab oblast executive committee, as parliamentary chairman, now the highest executive post. This election signified parliament's support for the Leninabadi-Kulabi alliance, but with the Kulabis now on top.

The hard-pressed Iskandarov government agreed to abide by the parliament's decisions and accepted a cease-fire, but the latter soon broke down. On December 6 forces from Hissar, with backing from Uzbekistan, attacked opposition forces in Dushanbe. After several days of bloody street fighting, by December 11 the Hissaris controlled the city. Rakhmonov took up his post in Dushanbe on December 14. The government, aided by aircraft belonging to either the CIS or Uzbekistan, captured opposition-controlled strongholds after heavy fighting.

Garmis and Pamiris, singled out for reprisal killings or executions on the basis of the place of birth indicated in their passports, fled to safer areas of Tajikistan or into Afghanistan.[14] Some who tried to cross the Amu Darya were shot by Russian border guards, and hundreds reportedly drowned while crossing. Tens of thousands camped out in freezing weather with no shelter, food, or water supplies. One kolkhoz director in Kurgan Tiube claimed on December 13 that one hundred children a day were dying.[15]

The government banned all opposition publications and initiated criminal proceedings against opposition leaders. On February 10 the procurator general asked the supreme court to outlaw the four principal opposition groups on the grounds that they had violated their charters and engaged in unlawful actions. On June 24 the court agreed.

In addition to the military aid from Russia and Uzbekistan, the new government again began to receive subsidies from Moscow. A few months after its victory, the government felt itself in sufficient control to initiate certain conciliatory policies. In March it signed an agreement with the government of Gorno-Badakhshan oblast, under which the latter would rescind its claim of sovereignty, and Dushanbe would refrain from sending armed forces to the area. The government decided in principle to disband and disarm the irregular armed groupings, such as the PF. It also decided to return displaced people to their homes and invite refugees to return.

PF leader Sangak Safarov supported these moves, but his deputy, Faizali Saidov, who represented non-Kulabi factions of the PF, opposed them. The two men killed each other at a meeting on March 29. This conflict was symptomatic of strains within the governing coalition. The Kulabis, represented by Safarov, had also made off with most of the power and spoils of victory, leading to tensions with other elements of the victorious coalition.

The new government set about establishing new security forces with the aid of Uzbekistan and Russia. The defense minister and commander of the planned national army of Tajikistan, Maj.-Gen. Aleksandr Shishlyannikov, is a Russian from Tashkent whose appointment was personally approved by President Karimov. Officers in the Turkestan Military District in Tashkent (mostly Russian speakers) have been offered three years' credit toward their pensions for each year they volunteer to serve in the Tajikistan army. The Uzbekistan KNB (former KGB) and MVD (Interior Ministry) are providing assistance to their counterparts in Tajikistan, and the Uzbekistan MVD itself patrols Khujand.[16] Russia and Tajikistan signed a wide-ranging pact of mutual assistance and cooperation.

THE OPPOSITION IN EXILE AND THE START OF CROSS-BORDER RAIDS

About sixty thousand Tajik refugees, mainly Garmis from Kurgan Tiube, remained in northern Afghanistan by the spring of 1993. Despite Kabul's denials, some Afghan *mujahedeen* commanders, supported by Arab and Pakistani Islamists, have helped more radical segments of the opposition (mainly the IRP) to arm and train some of the refugees as guerrillas. Common Tajik ethnicity and the widespread use of Persian by all groups in Northern Afghanistan facilitate collaboration and communication, but Tajik nationalist solidarity or aspirations for a "Greater Tajikistan" appear to play little if any role in the complex political game being played out along both banks of the Amu Darya. Tajik, Uzbek, and Pashtun commanders are all involved in aiding the IRP guerrillas, and their actions seem to be dictated by Islamist ideology and support, shifting political alignments in Kabul, and local rivalries.

Northern Afghanistan, like the rest of the country, is effectively controlled by a variety of commanders and warlords, not by the central government. The refugees lived in two areas under different authorities. Until May 1993, when the United Nations High Commissioner for Refugees (UNHCR) began a voluntary repatriation of some refugees, about thirty thousand lived in and around the city of Mazar-i Sharif, in areas controlled by Gen. Abdu Rashid Dostum. Dostum is an Afghan Uzbek whose mutiny against President Najibullah (for whom he had long fought) was key to toppling the ex-communist regime in April 1992. He permits access to the refugees by UNHCR, which already had an office in Mazar-i Sharif. Dostum, who has emerged as a regional ally of President Karimov, does not permit any Tajikistan opposition military training in his area, despite pressure from former *mujahedeen* in the area, with whom he maintained a precarious cooperation until January 1994.

East of the area controlled by Dostum and his allies are the provinces of Kunduz and Takhar. Kunduz borders directly on Kurgan Tiube, and UNHCR estimates that thirty thousand Tajiks found refuge in different parts of that province. Takhar is largely under the control of commanders of the Jamiat-i Islami (Islamic Society) who have united in the Supervisory Council of the North (SCN), led by former Defense Minister (and *mujahedeen* commander) Masud. SCN's headquarters are in Taliqan, the administrative center of Takhar.

The administrative center of the Kunduz province is controlled by Amir Chughai, a Pashtun commander of the Ittihad-i Islami Bara-yi Azadi-yi Afghanistan (Islamic Union for the Freedom of Afghanistan). This party owes its existence to the generous financial support it has received from radical Islamist Arabs, especially Wahhabi groups in Saudi Arabia and Kuwait.

The town of Imam Sahib, on the Amu Darya in north Kunduz, is largely controlled by Uzbek commanders of the Hizb-i Islami (Islamic Party), a radical organization headed by Gulbuddin Hekmatyar, a Pashtun born in Imam Sahib. Alliances among these various power centers shift frequently.

Most refugees in Kunduz and Takhar receive aid only from Arab and Pakistani Islamists, as UNHCR was forced to withdraw its staff following a series of disputes with the local authorities culminating in the killing of two UNHCR staff members in February 1993. UNHCR refused to provide aid that indirectly supported military training. Perhaps three thousand to five thousand young Tajiks are undergoing military training under IRP auspices in different parts of Kunduz and Takhar. The SCN trains the guerrillas in Taliqan (where the IRP's exile headquarters is located), Amir Chughai trains them in Kunduz, and Hekmatyar's commanders train them in Imam Sahib.[17] Those who provide such training are rewarded with support from Arab and Pakistani Islamists.

Foreign training and support, however, are not the only sources of resources for fighters. Some areas of northern Afghanistan are centers of opium cultivation, and warlords have been able to use the drug trade to finance arms purchases and create independent bases of power.[18]

Since the spring of 1993, small groups of fighters have periodically launched attacks into Tajikistan from Afghan bases. During a May 3 engagement on the border, they used a US-supplied Stinger missile to down a Sukhoi-24 jet fighter transferred to Tajikistan from the Uzbekistan air force.[19] The opposition launched a major attack across the Amu Darya into Kulab on July 14, 1993, killing between one hundred and two hundred villagers and twenty-five Russian border guards. Russia responded by launching artillery attacks on Afghan villages and increasing its military commitment to the defense of the Dushanbe government. It sent ten thousand more troops, bringing the border forces to fifteen thousand.[20] At a Moscow meeting on August 7 the presidents of Russia, Tajikistan, Uzbekistan, Kyrgyzstan, and Kazakhstan underlined their "collective responsibility" to guarantee the inviolability of the frontier. Each state promised to send at least one battalion to the border.[21]

CONCLUSION

The crisis in Tajikistan illustrates some salient facts about the emerging state system in Central Asia and Russia's developing policy toward this and other regions of the former Union. It also poses a challenge to the West. Promoting genuine stability in the region will require opening a dialogue with Islamic forces that superficially resemble those that—in Algeria, Palestine, Iran, and elsewhere—are often seen as posing the kind of threat that can be answered only by political exclusion and military repression. Tajikistan, like its neighbor Afghanistan, illustrates how such attitudes may contribute to creating the enemy they assume. It may not be too late at least partially to reverse the process, but such a reversal will require international pressure on Russia and its regional partner, Uzbekistan.

The role of Russia shows that, contrary to much speculation following the juridical independence of the Central Asian republics, the area has not simply joined the Middle East. Turkey and Iran, which some prognosticators had called the protagonists of a new "great game," have been notable for their absence and impotence, while the continuing dominant position of Russia has made itself felt through military, political, economic, and social channels.

This continuing Russian influence results not solely from inherited ties, but from the Russian government's active pursuit of a security doctrine (infelicitously if memorably dubbed the "Monroeski Doctrine"), according to which the territory of the former USSR (the "near abroad") constitutes a Russian zone of influence in which Moscow has a right to intervene. President Yeltsin has gone so far as to say that the Tajikistan-Afghanistan border is "in effect, Russia's."[22] Yeltsin has claimed that many newly independent states, especially in Central Asia, "have had enough of sovereignty" and are looking for new forms of confederation with Russia, the only state capable of protecting them.[23]

What Russia is protecting them from is clear: Islamic fundamentalism, which Moscow increasingly sees as the main external threat. Guerrillas and propagandists, enjoying financial and logistic support from sources in Pakistan and the Arab world, and drawing on the profits of the drug trade and the arms stockpiles of Afghanistan, face virtually no border controls between the Amu Darya and Moscow. Not just the security of the near abroad, some Russians believe, but the territorial integrity of Russia itself is at stake, as Russia's Tatars, Bashkirs, Chechens, and others become increasingly assertive.

The fear of "fundamentalism" has caused the leaders of democratic Russia to cast their lot with some of the most repressive of the Soviet successor states. In a policy reminiscent of the use of human rights rhetoric by some American administrations during the Cold War, Moscow protests discrimination against Russians in the Baltic states, while sending troops to Central Asia to defend a government that massacred thousands of people. It has made Uzbekistan its major regional partner in this policy, leaving open the question of whether Russia might find itself the captive of Tashkent's agenda. Russia already experienced this difficulty when it protested against a joint Uzbekistan-Tajikistan offensive in Badakhshan, while simultaneously rushing forces to defend the regime from which it was trying to distance itself.

Hard-liners in the former Soviet military may simply wish to reestablish Russian imperial control through the increased presence and influence of Russian-dominated military units, whatever flag they nominally serve. Some may also want to avenge their humiliation in Afghanistan.

The political leadership, however, takes a different, if ambiguous, stance. Even while pledging to shut the border to guerrilla infiltration, gun running, and drug trafficking, Yeltsin declared that "measures of reconciliation, not repression," were needed. Even Uzbekistan's President Karimov declared that there was "no military solution" to the conflict in Tajikistan. The Russian and Central Asian presidents, at their August 7, 1993, summit, addressed an appeal to the UN secretary-general to help in the search for a "political settlement," and President Yeltsin has said that he would eventually like to see the border guards turn into a blue-helmeted peacekeeping force.[24]

While this area is distant from the major centers of Western interest, its situation at the confluence of the Islamic and post-Soviet worlds, as well as in the center of one of the world's major opium-producing regions, makes promotion of stability and disarmament a Western interest. The appeal by the Russian and Central Asian presidents to these international bodies provides Western states with the opportunity to press for a genuine political process in Tajikistan. A genuine solution, however, will require both measures that contradict Russia's emerging regional doctrine and at least a limited economic revival.

A political settlement requires that the Islamic movement be included in any dialogue aimed at setting up a broad-based government or holding new elections. At the same time, however, that Yeltsin and even Karimov called for negotiations, even Russian Foreign Minister Andrei Kozyrev, one of the most liberal officials in Yeltsin's entourage, distinguished between an opposition with which one could negotiate and another (presumably fundamentalist), with which one could speak only "through missiles."[25]

Offering negotiations leading, say, to a new election would not be sufficient. The opposition would likely fear to participate as long as the security forces remained under the control of Russians, Uzbeks, and PF commanders. Even a Cambodia-style international interim regime or at least a partly non-CIS peacekeeping force might be needed to create adequate confidence. Such a proposal would contradict Russia's security doctrine, but Moscow's declarations (and acts) of support for the current government have probably deprived it of the opportunity to act as an honest broker.

Weaning a significant section of the exiled opposition away from the international Islamist groups, however, will require more than some seats at a table or even a peacekeeping force. The international community will have to provide leaders in Afghanistan with some alternative to the international Islamists, to whom the country has been more or less abandoned. In 1992 the UN was unable to raise $100 million for the reconstruction of Afghanistan from states that had spent over $10 billion on its destruction. Any Afghan commander who hopes for foreign aid today must either join the drug trade or cater to the wishes of the Arab and Pakistani funders who wish to spread the *jihad* into Central Asia. A modestly increased level of Western funding for Afghan reconstruction (especially in the north), combined with a political opening to the exiled Tajik opposition, would provide a package that might succeed in deescalating the war. The renewed fighting in Afghanistan since January 1994, however, makes such a program even less likely than previously.

At the same time, the West can and should emphasize to the authorities in Dushanbe that a predictable, law-bound state is necessary to encourage foreign investment. Elements of the Russian government, notably the president and foreign minister, have also tried to communicate such a message, but these may not be the Russian institutions with the most influence in Tajikistan.

The economy remains perhaps the hardest obstacle to surmount. Even more than in other post-Soviet states, the standard of living in Tajikistan, the poorest of them all, has plummeted since independence. Khujand, relatively untouched by the war and the site of the lion's share of industrial investment, has also attracted most of the foreign investment (such as an Israeli joint venture with the former prime minister's family, a denim factory). The rest of the country, locked into the cotton economy and subsistence farming, continues to suffer from vast underemployment and chronic shortages. In the fall of 1993 Tajikistan became the first non-Russian former Soviet republic to adopt the new Russian ruble as its official currency, and only a 120 billion ruble credit from Russia kept the monetary system functioning. Enterprises are increasingly dominated by "mafias," largely Kulabis. The drug trade provides not just money, but dollars, the one medium of exchange with which goods can nearly always be bought. Here again, physical proximity and existing trade patterns dictate that any plan for reconstruction of Tajikistan's economy involve northern Afghanistan as well as the neighboring former Soviet republics.

In early 1994, the UN secretary-general's special envoy, Ambassador Ramiro Piriz-Ballon of Uruguay, obtained agreement from both the government and opposition to meet without preconditions. The Commission on Security and Cooperation in Europe (CSCE) appointed French scholar Olivier Roy as head of a mission to Dushanbe with the task of complementing the UN's work through support for building institutions of governance in Tajikistan. Russia, seeking above all a settlement between

Dushanbe and what it saw as "secular democrats," excluding "fundamentalists," insisted on a Moscow venue and a Russian presence at any talks. The Tajik exiles in Iran opposed holding the talks in Moscow and asked for the presence of Iran, Afghanistan, and Pakistan as well as Russia.

These events showed the obstacle that Russia's security doctrine may pose to resolving the conflict. The official Russian discourse about democrats and fundamentalists also shows a risk inherent in organizing negotiations. Negotiations favor the solidification of two or three opposed parties, whereas the source of the violence in Tajikistan is fragmentation, not polarization. Rushing into paper agreements that cannot be enforced on the ground (as in neighboring Afghanistan) could set back attempts at conflict resolution for years. Hence coordinating the work of the UN on negotiations with that of the CSCE on institution building and including all groups will be key to any precarious success these efforts might enjoy.

NOTES

1. Deutsche Bank, Economics Department, *The Soviet Union at the Crossroads: Facts and Figures on the Soviet Republics* (Frankfurt, 1990), p. 11, gave Tajikistan the lowest score of all republics on ten of twelve indicators of economic potential, as well as the lowest overall rating, 25 percent below Kyrgyzstan, the next to lowest.
2. Ibid., p. 12. Deutsche Bank ranked all Central Asian republics as "heterogeneous" to "extremely heterogeneous."
3. Statisticheski Komitet Sodruzhestva Nezavisimykh Gosudarstv (SKSNG), *Itogi Vsesoiuznoi perepisi naseleniia 1989 goda.* Vol. 7: *Natsional'nyi sostav naseleniia SSSR* (Minneapolis: East View Publications, 1993), pt. 2, p. 130.
4. Olivier Roy, "Tajikistan." (Paper presented at the United States Institute of Peace, Washington, D.C., February 25, 1993.)
5. The same group exists across the Amu Darya in Afghanistan. See Thomas J. Barfield, *The Central Asian Arabs of Afghanistan: Pastoral Nomads in Transition* (Austin, Tex.: University of Texas Press, 1981).
6. Roy, "Tajikistan"; and Shahrbanou Tadjbakhsh, "Causes and Consequences of the Civil War," *Central Asian Monitor,* vol. 2 no. 1 (1993), pp. 10–14.
7. Kazakhstan combines these two strategies.
8. SKSNG, *Itogi Vsesoiuznoi,* vol. 7, pt. 2, pp. 130 and 132.
9. This estimate comes from a Western diplomat in Dushanbe. Census data are not available, as the *raions* (districts) comprising the Hissar and Garm regions are administered directly by the republic's government rather than by an oblast, and the published nationality data are disaggregated only to the oblast level.

10. Teresa Rakowska-Harmstone, *Russia and Nationalism in Central Asia: The Case of Tadzhikistan* (Baltimore and London: Johns Hopkins Press, 1970), p. 55, estimates that 40 percent went to Leninabad and 30 percent to Dushanbe.
11. Ibid., p. 57.
12. Tadjbakhsh, "Causes and Consequences," p. 10; and Roy, "Tajikistan."
13. Interview with Uzbekistan Militia officers, Khujand, May 29, 1993; and interview with former commander of the PF, Shartuz, Tajikistan, June 2, 1993.
14. Amnesty International, *Tadzhikistan Hidden Terror: Political Killings, "Disappearances" and Torture since December 1992,* (London, 1993).
15. "Tajikistan: End of Civil War," *Central Asian Monitor,* vol. 2, no. 1 (1993), p. 6, citing an Interfax report.
16. Interview with official of the Ministry of Defense of Uzbekistan, Tashkent, May 13, 1993; and interview with officials of Uzbekistan KNB, Tashkent, May 14, 1993.
17. Steve LeVine, "Afghan, Arab Militants Back Rebels in Ex-Soviet State," *Washington Post,* April 27, 1993, p. A10; interview with personnel of humanitarian organizations, Dusti, Tajikistan, June 4, 1993; and interview with *Washington Post* and *Newsweek* correspondent Steve LeVine, Dushanbe, Tajikistan, June 6, 1993.
18. Sophie Shihab, "Le Pamir entre deux feux," *Le Monde,* August 12, 1993, p. 3.
19. TASS, May 4, 1993. The pilots were ethnic Russians.
20. "The Empire Strikes Back," *Economist,* August 7, 1993, p. 36.
21. Jan Krauze, "La Russie va accroître son engagement militaire au Tadjikistan," *Le Monde,* August 10, 1993, p. 4; and Jan Krauze, "Les 'casque bleus' de Boris Eltsine au Tadjikistan," *Le Monde,* August 12, 1993, p. 3.
22. "The Empire Strikes Back," *Economist,* August 7, 1993, p. 36.
23. Krauze, "Les 'casque bleus' de Boris Eltsine," p. 3.
24. Ibid.; and Krauze, "La Russie va accroître son engagement militaire," p. 4.
25. Ibid.

Chapter 8

Central Asia and China

Ross H. Munro

Two GREAT HISTORIC EVENTS ARE UNDER WAY IN EURASIA. ONE IS the continuing collapse of the Russian Empire and the Soviet communist system. The other is the rapid growth of China's economy and its military power, a trend that seems destined to continue and make China a full-fledged superpower early in the next century. While the implications of the first event for Central Asia are being widely discussed and intensively examined, the implications for the region of the second event have only recently been noticed. Indeed, the first wave of analyses of the international implications of the emergence of the five newly independent Central Asian republics dealt cursorily, if at all, with China. But today it is clear that an economically dynamic and militarily ascendant China must be considered a major player in the region, clearly outranked in importance only by Russia.

Since the Soviet Union began to unravel, China's interests in Central Asia have repeatedly been characterized, as one observer put it, as "primarily defensive—to stop instability from spilling over into Chinese Turkestan,"[1] the Xinjiang Uighur Autonomous Region, which, despite its name, is a region of China tightly controlled by Beijing. In a narrow sense, the characterization of China's concern over Central Asia is accurate. Although all nation-states try to guard their sovereignty and territorial integrity, few put quite as much emphasis on it as the People's Republic of China. While Hong Kong, Taiwan, and Tibet are most often cited in this connection, the Chinese often have Xinjiang in mind as well. Indeed, Chinese rulers have considered Xinjiang a territorial integrity issue for centuries. This century alone has witnessed at least two serious attempts by Xinjiang's Turkic Muslims to win effective independence from China. More recently, from 1989 until 1991, unrest intermittently reached serious—and, in one or two pockets, insurrectional—proportions[2] among elements of the Turkic Muslim population, who officially constitute 60 percent of the population.[3] Nevertheless, it seems in retrospect that both the Chinese authorities and foreign analysts may have overestimated the significance of these disturbances.

That the Chinese overreacted, there is little doubt. But given the other events occurring at the time of the disturbances, the Chinese response is completely understandable. The spring of 1989 was dominated by the demonstrations at Tiananmen Square that ended in violence on June 4. We know now that the Chinese leadership really did not regain its balance and self-confidence before late 1991. Simultaneously, the Soviet Union was unraveling, prompting predictions that Leninism was doomed everywhere, including China. With the formal breakup of the Soviet Union in December 1991, following the failure of the hard-liners' coup attempt in August, the five Central Asian republics were in effect set loose. This prompted analysts worldwide to opine that the situation in Central Asia was not only fluid, but volatile. China was not immune to such speculation, particularly when the unrest in Xinjiang suggested that the forces of instability in the former Soviet Union had somehow already leaped over the border.

Until the spring of 1992, the Xinjiang media regularly carried articles attacking "splittists," "separatists," and other subversives in the Xinjiang Uighur Autonomous Region. Equally intriguing were articles exhorting local militias in Xinjiang to do their jobs vigilantly and well, particularly in securing the border areas. Xinjiang officials openly acknowledged that they were concerned about the impact of the breakup of the Soviet Union[4] and that Chinese troops were reinforcing Xinjiang's border with what was then still Soviet Central Asia.[5]

It must be assumed that their words and actions reflected genuine and widespread alarm among Chinese authorities. But another, political element was also at work. The demands for tighter controls clearly reflected, at least in part, the China-wide effort by conservatives to reassert their influence in the wake of the Tiananmen incident. It should be noted, for instance, that previous calls for tightening up militia work in China could often be explained only as part of a more general political clampdown. Significantly, as the political climate in China changed in the first half of 1992, to the obvious detriment of conservative forces, reports in the Xinjiang media about unrest and militia building declined dramatically, along with references to "splittists" and separatists. Instead, news of economic reform and development, including many reports of Xinjiang's burgeoning trade ties with its Central Asian neighbors, dominated official media reports from the region.

Several other factors, some probably more important than the workings of domestic Chinese politics, also explain why the alarm of Chinese authorities over the situation in Xinjiang and Central Asia did not last. One was that the wave of Muslim unrest itself evidently subsided. This in turn probably can be largely attributed to China's long-term approach to minority issues. Since 1949, except during the Great Leap Forward and the Cultural Revolution, China's minority policies have arguably been among the world's most sophisticated, although not the most benign. Beijing, on the one hand, deliberately leaves no doubt about its willingness to use force to quell anything smacking of ethnic separatism. On the other hand, Beijing assiduously recruits, co-opts, and rewards members of non-Han Chinese groups who are able or ambitious. It has set minority quotas for higher education and for government employment, as well as a network of minority institutions that recruit and reward co-optees with lifetime sinecures.[6] Meanwhile, Beijing continues to promote the movement of Han Chinese into Xinjiang and other minority regions in order to tilt the population ratio against the non-Han. As recently as December 1991, China was reportedly moving Han Chinese farmers and forestry workers to areas along Xinjiang's border with Kazakhstan and Kyrgyzstan, presumably to stabilize the frontier.[7] This adroit mix of policies has been largely successful in Xinjiang and the rest of China—with the partial exception of Tibet—in limiting restiveness and maintaining control in areas where large numbers of non-Han minorities live.

In addition, relieved Chinese leaders seem to have concluded by early 1992 that neither pan-Turkic nationalism nor militant Islam was about to sweep the Central Asian republics. That in turn meant that neither force posed a serious and immediate threat to Xinjiang itself. The ruling secular elites of all five new republics had made their hostility to militant Islam very clear. Iran, apparently wanting for now to work with those elites and to avoid confrontation, was being notably cautious in promoting its brand of Islam. Moreover, China remained on good terms with Iran, as well as with Pakistan, where a political movement, Jamiat-i Islami (Islamic Party), was also circumspectly promoting militant Islam in Central Asia. China has long appeared to be more concerned about pan-Turkic nationalism. China views Turkey with suspicion, not only because organizations promoting a separate Turkic state in China have long been based in Istanbul, but also because of the pan-Turkic element inherent in Turkey's primarily cultural approach to the five republics. But here also, the foreign message was not falling on fertile soil in the five republics, where attitudes toward Turkey often seemed wary.

Even before the 1989–1991 period, when Chinese anxiety about Central Asia was still high, the authorities in Xinjiang were slowly but steadily developing border trade and other ties with the Central Asian republics, which were then an integral part of the Soviet Union. But by the end of 1991, once these republics achieved de jure independence and sovereignty, the stage was set for Beijing to establish state-to-state relations and formulate a more ambitious and far-reaching Central Asia policy. Confident by then that it was not facing any serious and immediate danger from Central Asia, China recognized that it nevertheless has a strong national interest in promoting the long-term stability and economic development of the Central Asian republics. Here China and the five new republics had strong mutual interests. By the beginning of the 1990s, with more than a decade of rapid economic growth already behind it, China could offer major trade opportunities as well as modest amounts of capital and technology to the economically weak Central Asian republics. By doing this, Chinese leaders could justifiably assure themselves that they were strengthening the republics' economies and responding to what Central Asian leaders consider their most basic need. It is not cultural, linguistic, or religious "aid" that Central Asia's elites crave; it is economic development. The Chinese clearly agree that economic development offers the region the only possibility of limiting future ethnic and religious conflict.[8]

Of course, China intends to do well by doing good. Almost by definition, increased Chinese trade and investment in Central Asia means increased Chinese influence. Furthermore, given the mutual benefit inherent in market transactions, Chinese trade and investment in Central Asia also help China's domestic economy, particularly the neighboring Xinjiang economy. Indeed, the Chinese authorities view Xinjiang as an important growth center because of its strategic location. In September 1992 Premier Li Peng officiated at the opening of a major trade fair in Urumqi, Xinjiang's capital. Although the fair attracted ten thousand businessmen from thirty-eight countries, its focus was on developing trade and other economic ties between Xinjiang and its Central Asian neighbors.

Xinjiang is attracting the interest of even Hong Kong and Taiwan investors. At the Xinjiang border town of Horgos, a Hong Kong businessman invested U.S.$55 million in an international trade center.[9] That investment exemplified yet another advantage that China enjoys vis-à-vis Central Asia: it not only can draw on the resources of the burgeoning mainland economy, it also has access to the capital, technology, and entrepreneurial resources of Hong Kong and Taiwan. The advantage does not end there. The business communities in Hong Kong and Taiwan can also act as a bridge to world capital markets and multinational corporations.

China's emerging, economics-based approach to Central Asia can be best understood by first examining the dramatic developments in its relations with Kazakhstan and Kyrgyzstan since 1991. We will look briefly at China's economic ties with the other three republics. But China's relations with Kazakhstan and Kyrgyzstan deserve close attention, not only because they are the most advanced and extensive, but also because these relationships provide us with ample illustrations of China's overall approach to Central Asia.

Although available statistics are far from satisfactory, they leave no doubt that China's bilateral trade with Kazakhstan has been soaring since early 1992. Reports from the Chinese news agency, Xinhua, indicated that Xinjiang's total foreign trade in 1992 increased to more than $500 million. Exports and imports that went through regular channels jumped by 130 percent to about $300 million.[10] Meanwhile, during the first eleven months of 1992, what China classifies as local or border trade, much of it barter, almost quadrupled to $220 million.[11] Those statistics apparently cover all neighboring countries, including Pakistan and Mongolia, as well as the three adjoining Central Asian republics. But other reports left no doubt that Xinjiang's trade with Kazakhstan was responsible for much, possibly most, of the growth in 1992. Xinhua reported that by late 1992, 50 percent of Kazakhstan's imports of consumer goods—a broad category that includes food, clothing, and household goods—were from China.[12] (In the spring of 1993, peeved acknowledgments of this fact surfaced in the Russian media.) The most basic Chinese products—such as soap, matches, and cooking pots—are prized among Asia's poor for their quality and value. A small proportion of Kazakhstan's imports were financed by 30 million yuan in commodity credits from China,[13] a form of aid that several countries are extending to the republics. The strong complementarity of the two economies was highlighted when China turned to Kazakhstan for industrial commodities it badly needs, such as fertilizer, steel, and ores. To put this in perspective, we estimate, admittedly with only fragmentary data, that China's two-way trade with Kazakhstan alone in 1992 quite possibly exceeded Turkey's trade with all five republics combined.

Further evidence of China's burgeoning trade relationship with Kazakhstan came in a May 1992 report that "a network of Chinese shops" had opened in the republic.[14] By April 1993, Xinhua reported, China had established 150 small joint ventures in Kazakhstan as well.[15] June 1992 witnessed the first train to travel the full length of a rail line linking Xinjiang's capital of Urumqi to Kazakhstan's capital, Almaty.[16] Construction of that rail line had begun in 1956! Daily air service was also instituted between the two capitals,[17] and additional cross-border roads were opened.

The increase in transportation links between Xinjiang and Kazakhstan was apparently largely responsible for almost a doubling of the number of "foreign tourists and businesspeople" visiting Xinjiang in 1992. Their numbers increased that year to 230,000 (90 percent of whom were from neighboring countries), from 100,000 in 1991.[18] Most of the new arrivals appeared to be "shoppers" from Kazakhstan and the two other Central Asian republics bordering on Xinjiang, Tajikistan and Kyrgyzstan.

Going in the opposite direction to work in Kazakhstan were hundreds of Chinese experts and technicians. Some may well have replaced departing Russians. The Chinese experts are yet another nice "fit" between China and the Central Asian republics. China is potentially an ideal provider of low-cost, low-technology approaches that the republics can use in agriculture, industry, and infrastructure development. Similarly, the Chinese may prove to be the most experienced and empathetic advisors for Central Asian republics so poorly prepared for the privatization of land and the transition to a market economy. China rightly represents to the impoverished republics an excellent example of successful economic transition from socialism and a command economy. Indeed, in mid-1993 references to "the Chinese model" appeared in both Kazakhstan's and Uzbekistan's media.

Clearly, strong constituencies in both China and Kazakhstan favor closer relations between the two countries in almost every field. Evidence of this emerged after talks between China's Premier Li Peng and Kazakhstan's Premier Tereshchenko in Beijing in February 1992. A joint communiqué noted that agreements had been signed on trade, scientific and technological cooperation, communications and transport, personnel exchanges, and the establishment of a joint committee for the development of further ties.[19] By late 1992, Almaty Radio was reporting that a "treaty on cooperation and military assistance between Kazakhstan and China is expected to be signed in the near future."[20] While little more has been heard of this proposed treaty, such an announcement by a government radio station is yet another indication that ties between China and Kazakhstan will continue to grow.

Another, largely unnoticed exchange between Xinjiang and Kazakhstan is the exodus of tens of thousands of ethnic Kazakhs from Xinjiang. While it was reported in December 1992 that sixty thousand Kazakhs had moved to Kazakhstan from Mongolia and from other parts of the Commonwealth of Independent States (CIS),[21] the movement of another thirty thousand from Xinjiang remained unpublicized outside Kazakhstan itself.[22] Both the Chinese authorities and ethnic Kazakh authorities in Kazakhstan appear to be facilitating this movement, which simultaneously increases the ratio of Hans to non-Hans in Xinjiang while increasing the proportion of Kazakhs in Kazakhstan. Thus the arrangement serves both the presumed interest of the Chinese government and the interest of ethnic Kazakhs in reducing ethnic Russian influence in Kazakhstan.

China has an even greater economic presence in Kyrgyzstan, which also shares a long border with Xinjiang. Kyrgyzstan is making greater efforts than the four other Central Asian republics to establish its de facto as well as its de jure independence. It is the only one, for instance, that has successfully introduced its own currency. Kyrgyzstan has also been eagerly reaching out for recognition, assistance, and economic ties to several foreign countries, including the United States, Japan, South Korea, India, Iran, Israel, and Turkey. But it is with China that Kyrgyzstan's ties are the most extensive. Four months after the two countries established diplomatic relations in January 1992, Kyrgyzstan's President Askar Akaev visited Beijing. Today, China has a full-fledged embassy in Bishkek, the capital of Kyrgyzstan. In the summer of 1993 high-ranking officials from the two countries visited each other's capital.

It is on the economic plane, however, that ties have developed most dramatically. Indeed, it is conceivable that Kyrgyzstan's economy will be dominated by China before the end of the decade. China has established a free trade zone in the city of Naryn. In Bishkek, Chinese are buying considerable amounts of real estate. And Beijing has posted agricultural and other experts in the country.

Trade between the two countries is burgeoning. Basic Chinese consumer goods—such as food, clothing, and simple electronic products—have been flooding into Kyrgyzstan. China has encouraged the trend by extending credits equivalent to $5.7 million.[23] China has been importing such industrial commodities as rolled metal, sheet steel, mineral fertilizer, and copper. Many of these items, the Russian-language media in Moscow have charged, were actually reexports of commodities purchased elsewhere in the CIS at fixed low prices and then sold to China at world market prices. China is also purchasing electricity from the republic.[24]

In August 1992 China proposed exploring the possibility of exploiting four rivers whose waters Xinjiang and Kyrgyzstan share.[25] By January 1993, the two countries had reached agreement to "jointly build a water conservancy works over the Horgos River along the border."[26] The article implied that all the potential uses of the river—irrigation, hydroelectric power, flood control, and navigation—would be pursued. All such proposals should be carefully watched for their political implications. Water is a vital and scarce resource in Central Asia, and conflict between upstream and downstream users is already a serious one. In fact, this appears to be the only immediate issue where China could find itself in conflict with one or more of the five republics. One possible source of conflict, analysts believe, is that a river development agreement between China and Kazakhstan or Kyrgyzstan could harm the interests of a downstream user, such as Uzbekistan.

Although parts of Tajikistan are still in turmoil, its trade with China is rising rapidly in percentage terms from a tiny starting point. Total bilateral trade in 1992 was a mere $2.7 million, but the first four months of 1993 saw total trade rise to $4.4 million.[27] Understandably, when Tajikistan's senior leader, Imomali Rakhmonov, paid an official visit to China in March 1993, nearly all official references to economic ties between the two countries were in the future tense. China granted Tajikistan the equivalent of about $5 million worth of yuan credits to buy Chinese food products and consumer goods. China also gave Tajikistan humanitarian food and medical aid worth approximately $500,000. In 1992 and 1993 the two countries signed ten cooperation agreements.[28] Among other things, those agreements call for the establishment of joint Tajik-Chinese ventures to process cotton. Agreement has been reached on setting up a Chinese dye-works in a Tajik textile mill.[29]

A leading democrat from Uzbekistan has complained that his country's leaders were adopting the "Chinese model," evidently because China enjoys rapid economic growth while retaining an authoritarian political structure.[30] President Islam Karimov of

Uzbekistan has indeed made no secret of his desire for stronger economic ties with China since state-to-state ties were inaugurated. At the January 1992 ceremony establishing diplomatic relations, Karimov urged China to open both an embassy and trade office. Since then, he has frequently called for closer ties and declared that Uzbekistan has much to learn from China. In March 1992 he visited Beijing where he signed fourteen bilateral agreements,[31] including umbrella agreements to facilitate scientific and technical cooperation, as well as to provide credits to Uzbekistan to import Chinese goods.[32] China opened its Tashkent embassy in October 1992, when it was announced that joint Uzbek-Chinese enterprises were already in operation in Uzbekistan.[33] In March 1993 the Tashkent oblast reached a "twinning" agreement with China's Hunan Province. Under the agreement, it was announced, a wide variety of joint enterprises would be established in Uzbekistan—bottling plants, a fruit processor, a brewery, a garment factory, and Chinese restaurants.[34]

By the end of 1992, China already ranked as Uzbekistan's leading trade partner outside the CIS.[35] Both countries are apparently eager to develop better land links so that their bilateral trade can continue to grow. Although the two countries have already established an Urumqi-Tashkent air link, a large portion of their trade is routed through the Trans-Siberian Railway and the border crossing at Khabarovsk, three thousand miles east of Tashkent.

China's relations with Turkmenistan are obviously at an early stage. It was not until November 1992 that President Supramurad Niyazov visited Beijing, where he signed eight cooperation agreements and a joint communiqué. And only in July 1993 did China send what it described as its "first . . . high-ranking delegation" to Turkmenistan. China has agreed to set up textile and food-processing factories in Turkmenistan and to construct a hotel in the capital, Ashgebat.[36] The most intriguing aspect of China-Turkmenistan relations are continuing discussions of an ambitious proposal, being promoted by Japanese corporations, for a gas pipeline between the two countries.[37] According to a December 1992 report, President Niyazov, the Mitsubishi group, and China's national petroleum company had reached an agreement in principle to build the pipeline.[38] Talks were reportedly continuing in the spring of 1993. Although it is far from certain that the proposed pipeline will become reality, it may well prove a harbinger of future China–Central Asia ties.

Proposals such as this mesh with repeated calls in China during the past two years for a modern-day version of the ancient Silk Road, which linked China with Central Asia and the West.[39] Although it may initially strike many as romantic boilerplate, such Chinese rhetoric is highly significant. China sees a new Silk Road of modern railways and highways as a transmission belt that could project Chinese wealth and influence far westward, not only through Central Asia, but to Iran and the Middle East. While most discussions of Central Asia's future physical links with the outside world focus on north-south links, the logic of east-west links are often overlooked. These could well include establishing a modern railway that would directly link Central Asia to the huge and growing China market and ultimately to deep-sea ports on China's east coast. A new Silk Road of modern railroads and highways that would effectively give China a land route far to the west, ultimately to Europe and to an Iranian opening on the Persian Gulf, would have enormous strategic consequences, conceivably comparable to the impact that the advent of the Suez and Panama canals once had.

Speculation is also increasing about future pipelines that would bring petroleum not only from Central Asia but conceivably from the Middle East to China and other destinations in industrialized East Asia. Meanwhile, China is aggressively trying to locate and develop its own oil resources in Xinjiang. With China projected to become a net oil importer as early as 1994,[40] the prospect of a multibillion-dollar pipeline that would bring petroleum to eastern China from Xinjiang and ultimately Central Asia and even the Middle East seems increasingly likely. Of all the players in Central Asia, possibly only China—or, rather, Greater China, perhaps working with South Korea or Japan—will prove to have the access to world financial markets and multinationals' technology that is needed to transform such ambitious ideas into reality.

By helping create even modest versions of a modern Silk Road—linking, for example, Xinjiang with Uzbekistan and Turkmenistan—China would be helping to break down the walls constructed by the Soviet Union to isolate the Central Asian republics from each other. As we have already indicated, China's growing role in Central Asia will tend to reduce both the absolute and the relative influence that Russia wields in the five republics. Clearly, China and the non-Russian ethnic groups in the republics have a mutual interest in building economic ties that achieve this. One of the great uncertainties of this region is whether Russia and the ethnic Russians resident in Central Asia will eventually make a major attempt to confront and resist China's growing economic power. It is not inevitable; both sides have strong interests in avoiding conflict that could easily expand and escalate. Despite deep antipathy in some Russian circles for China, and persistent suspicion in China regarding Russia's motives, the two countries are almost compelled to continue pursuing rapprochement and to avoid military competition. As Leszek Buszynski, of the Strategic and Defence Studies Centre at the Australian National University, observes, "a troubling discrepancy between obvious geopolitical need and political preferences will continue to plague the Moscow leadership's relationship with China."[41] One manifestation of this is Russia's almost reckless abandon in selling advanced weapons systems to its erstwhile archfoe.

While Russia is preoccupied by internal priorities and its resources are already stretched beyond the limit, China wants to continue shifting the focus of its military resources away from Russia. China is focused more on the south—Taiwan, the South China Sea, and Southeast Asia. While tensions may grow, China as well as Russia will try to avoid any serious clash over Central Asia.

But there is no uncertainty about China's intention, and ability, to play a major role in Central Asia for the foreseeable future. Even if China's vision of a modern Silk Road is never realized, an economically dynamic and militarily ascendant China seems destined to exert tremendous influence over neighboring Kazakhstan and Kyrgyzstan. This is still not widely appreciated. A survey of Central Asia's prospects by an acknowledged U.S. authority on the region listed the United States, Turkey, Iran, and Saudi Arabia as potential investors in the five republics. But if the petroleum sector is excluded, China's investments in Central Asia will probably soon outrank any of the four, and one day all four combined.

Clearly all future assessments of the role of outside players in Central Asia must treat China seriously indeed.

NOTES

1. *Economist,* December 26, 1992.
2. "Tomur Dawamat's Speech at Party Meeting," Xinjiang Ribao, Urumqi, July 29, 1990, cited in Foreign Broadcast Information Service (FBIS)-CHI-90-201, October 17, 1990. The head of the Xinjiang regional government described the outbreak of violence in Baren Township in 1989 as a "counterrevolutionary armed rebellion."
3. This figure is inflated. Indeed, some Sinologists suspect that Han Chinese now form a majority in Xinjiang if one counts technically "temporary" residents, including military personnel and some Han Chinese in civilian jobs who retain an official residence elsewhere in China.
4. "Xinjiang Chairman Tomur Dawamat Says the Situation in the Region Is Very Stable Despite Separatist Attempt," Ta Kung Pao, Hong Kong, March 25, 1990, cited in FBIS-CHI-90-058, March 26, 1990.
5. "Xinjiang Prepares for Crackdown on Separatists," Agence France Presse, Hong Kong, March 13, 1990, cited in FBIS-CHI-90-049, March 13, 1990.
6. For detailed data on the results of Xinjiang's efforts to recruit minority groups into the regional government and to facilitate their entrance into institutions of higher education, see "Tomur Dawamat's Speech."
7. *South China Morning Post,* December 12, 1991.
8. For a typical Chinese view of Central Asia, see "Central Asia on the Rise," *Beijing Review,* August 3–9, 1992, p. 12.
9. "Faster Economic Development Seen in Xinjiang," Beijing Xinhua, November 4, 1992, cited in FBIS-CHI-92-214, November 4, 1992, p. 53.
10. "Xinjiang Gives 1992 Import, Export Statistics," Beijing Xinhua, January 19, 1993, cited in FBIS-CHI-93-017, January 28, 1993, p. 45.
11. "Xinjiang's Border Trade Volume Up 359 Percent," Xinhua Domestic Service, December 21, 1992, cited in FBIS-CHI-92-252, December 31, 1992, p. 7.
12. "China Provides Half of Kazakhstan's Imports," Beijing Xinhua, October 27, 1992, cited in FBIS-CHI-92-210, October 29, 1992.
13. "Package of Joint Documents Signed with PRC," Moscow TASS International Service, February 26, 1992, cited in FBIS-SOV-92-039, February 27, 1992, p. 67.
14. "Trade Talks Held with Xinjiang-Uighur Delegation," Almaty Kazakh Radio Network, May 9, 1992, cited in FBIS-SOV-92-092, May 12, 1992, p. 55.
15. "Kazakh Minister Seeks Economic Ties with China," Beijiang Xinhua, April 30, 1992, cited in FBIS-CHI-93-082, April 30, 1993, p. 7.
16. "Rail Link with PRC City Inaugurated," Moscow Teleradiokompaniya Ostankino Television First Program Network, June 23, 1992, cited in FBIS-SOV-92-124, June 26, 1992, p. 81.
17. "Air Route Opens between Beijing, Almaty," Beijing Xinhua, December 17, 1992, cited in FBIS-CHI-92-246, December 22, 1992, p. 6.

18. "Xinjiang Reports Tourism Boom," Beijing Xinhua, January 4, 1993, cited in FBIS-CHI-93-001, January 4, 1993, p. 74.
19. "Kazakh Prime Minister, Delegation Continues Visit," Beijing Xinhua, February 28, 1992, cited in FBIS-CHI-92-041, March 2, 1992, p. 10.
20. "Military Treaty with China in 'Near Future,'" Almaty Radio Almaty World Service, December 15, 1992, cited in FBIS-SOV-92-242, December 16, 1992, p. 43.
21. "Authorities Agree to Take Refugees from Tajikistan," Moscow ITAR-TASS December 22, 1992, cited in FBIS-SOV-92-247, December 23, 1992, p. 69.
22. Travelers' reports, based on conversations with officials in Kazakhstan.
23. "Akayev on 'Realistic, fruitful' Talks," Beijing Xinhua, May 14, 1992, cited in FBIS-CHI-92-095, May 15, 1992, p. 7.
24. "Electric Power Line Begins Supplies to China," Moscow ITAR-TASS, October 1, 1992, cited in FBIS-SOV-92-193, October 5, 1992, p. 51.
25. "Premier Leaves for PRC for Border Issue Talks," Moscow Radio Rossii Network, August 3, 1992, cited in FBIS-SOV-92-153, August 7, 1992, p. 74.
26. "Xinjiang, Kazakhstan Plan Border Water Project," Beijing Xinhua, January 23, 1993, cited in FBIS-CHI-93-015, January 26, 1993. p. 9.
27. "Wu Yi Meets Tajik Counterpart; Accords Signed," Beijing Xinhua, June 18, 1993, cited in FBIS-CHI-93-116, June 18, 1993, p. 8.
28. "More on Talks between Wu Yi, Tajik Counterpart," *Beijing China Daily*, June 19, 1993, p. 2, cited in FBIS-CHI-93-117, June 21, 1993, p. 12.
29. "Rakhmonov Reviews PRC Visit," Interfax, Moscow, March 12, 1993, cited in FBIS-SOV-93-048, March 15, 1993, p. 89.
30. Muhammad Salih, "As Uzbekistan Shifts from the Turkish to the Chinese Model," *Turkish Times* (Washington), August 15, 1993. Salih is leader of the Erk Democratic Party of Uzbekistan.
31. "Signs Cooperation Agreements," *Beijing China Daily*, March 14, 1992, p. 1, cited in FBIS-CHI-92-051, March 16, 1992, p. 5.
32. "More Economic Agreements Signed with China," Pravda Vostoka, March 21, 1992, cited in FBIS-USR-92-043, April 17, 1992, pp. 100–5.
33. "People's Republic of China Embassy Opens," Ozbekiston Ovozi, October 16, 1992, cited in FBIS-USR-92-160, December 16, 1992, p. 107.
34. "Tashkent Oblast 'Twinned' with China's Hunan Province," Uzbekistan APN, March 29, 1993, cited in FBIS-SOV-93-059, March 30, 1993, p. 73.
35. Ibid.
36. "Trade, Economic Agreements Signed with PRC," Radio Ashgebat, January 7, 1992, cited in FBIS-SOV-92-005, January 8, 1992, p. 70.
37. "Project Signed with Japan, PRC for Gas Pipeline," Moscow InterTass, December 13, 1992, cited in FBIS-SOV-92-242, December 16, 1992, p. 49.
38. "Agreement Reached with China, Japan on Gas Supply," ITAR-TASS, December 10, 1992, cited in FBIS-SOV-92-239, December 11, 1992, p. 33.
39. See, for example, "Northwest to Revive the Silk Road," *Beijing Review*, September 14–20, 1992.
40. Carl Goldstein, "Final Frontier," *Far Eastern Economic Review*, June 10, 1993, p. 54
41. Leszek Buszynski, "Russia and the Asia-Pacific Region," *Pacific Affairs*, vol. 65, no. 4 (Winter 1992–93).

Appendix

Symposium on
The International Relations
of Central Asia

June 17–18, 1993

Chairman: Michael Mandelbaum—Council on Foreign
        Relations
Authors: Martha Brill Olcott—Foreign Policy Research
        Institute
        Graham Fuller—Rand Corporation
        Daniel Pipes—Foreign Policy Research Institute
        Robert Cullen
Coordinator: Audrey McInerney—Council on Foreign Relations
Rapporteurs: Audrey McInerney—Council on Foreign Relations
        Scott Monje—Columbia University

Aurel Braun—University of Toronto
Donald Carlisle—Boston College
Susan Clark—Institute for Defense Analyses
Patrick Clawson—National Defense University
Edward Chow—Chevron
Nadia Diuk—National Endowment for
    Democracy
Paul Henze—Rand Corporation
Shafiqul Islam—Council of Foreign Relations
Stephen Kaplan—Central Intelligence Agency
Nancy Lubin–United States Institute of Peace
Mark Medish—Covington & Burling
Rajan Menon—Lehigh University
Roza Otunbayeva—Embassy of Kyrgyz Republic
    to the United States and Canada
Barnett Rubin—Columbia University
Seth Singelton—Pacific University
Marat Tazhin—Kazakhstan Department of
    International Affairs
Theresa Weber—International Executive Service
    Corps

Index

About the Authors

Susan Clark is an analyst on the research staff in the Strategy, Forces and Resources Division at the Institute for Defense Analyses in Alexandria, Virginia, where she specializes in the security and foreign policies of the former Soviet states. She is currently writing a book on the development of the new militaries in these states (tentatively entitled *The New Militaries of the Old Soviet States*), to be published later this year. She is also the editor of and contributor to *Soviet Military Power in a Changing World* (1991) and *Gorbachev's Agenda: Changes in Soviet Domestic and Foreign Policy* (1989). Among her other recent publications are "Security Issues and the Slavic States," *The World Today* (October 1993) and "Russia in a Peacekeeping Role," in Leon Aron and Kenneth Jenkins, eds., *Emerging National Security Doctrine of the New Russia* (Washington, D.C.: U.S. Institute of Peace, 1993).

Robert Cullen is a journalist and author who has been writing about the former Soviet Union for more than a decade. He was Moscow bureau chief for *Newsweek* from 1982 to 1985, and since 1988 has contributed frequent articles on Russia and the former Soviet republics to *The New Yorker, The Atlantic Monthly*, and *Foreign Affairs*. In 1991, he published *Twilight of Empire: Inside the Crumbling Soviet Bloc*, an account of the disintegration of the Warsaw Pact and the Soviet Union. He was educated at the University of Virginia and at Stanford University, where he was a Professional Journalism Fellow.

Shafiqul Islam is Senior Fellow for International Economics and Finance at the Council on Foreign Relations. He has an undergraduate degree in mathematics and economics from the University of Missouri and a Ph.D. in economics from Harvard University. Before joining the Council, he was a Visiting Fellow at the Institute for International Economics (1986–1987) and Chief of the Industrial Economies Division at the Federal Reserve Bank of New York (1984–1986). He has published widely on international monetary and financial issues. Most recently he co-edited *Making Markets: Economic Transformation in Eastern Europe and the Post-Soviet States* (1993).

Graham E. Fuller is a Senior Political Scientist at RAND. He is author of *Central Asia: The New Geopolitics* (RAND, 1992) as well as *The Center of the Universe: The Geopolitics of Iran* (Westview, 1991), and *Turkey's New Geopolitics: From the Balkans to Western Chin* (Westview, 1993). He is also author of *The Democracy Trap: Perils of the Post-Cold War World* (Dutton, 1992). He has produced many other studies for RAND on Islamic Fundamentalism, Iraq, and broader topics on the Middle East. He is the former Vice-Chairman of the National Intelligence Council at CIA where he was responsible for long-range strategic forecasting.

Michael Mandelbaum is Director of the Project on East-West Relations at the Council on Foreign Relations and the Christian A. Herter Professor of American Foreign Policy at the Paul H. Nitze School of Advanced International Studies of the Johns Hopkins University in Washington, D.C. He is also the Associate Director of the Aspen Institute's Project on American Relations with Central and Eastern Europe and a regular columnist on foreign affairs for *Newsday*. Professor Mandelbaum received an M.A. from King's College, Cambridge, and a Ph.D. from Harvard University where he taught in the Government department. He has also taught at Columbia University and the United States Naval Academy. He is the author or editor of twelve books, including *The Rise of Nations in the Soviet Union: American Foreign Policy and the Disintegration of the USSR* (1991); *The Fate of Nations: The Search for National Security in the 19th and 20th Centuries* (1988); with Seweryn Bialer, *The Global Rivals* (1988); and with Strobe Talbott, *Reagan and Gorbachev* (1987).

Ross H. Munro is Coordinator of the Asia Program at the Foreign Policy Research Institute in Philadelphia. Before joining FPRI in 1990, he was a correspondent for *Time* Magazine, serving as its bureau chief in Hong Kong, New Delhi, and Bangkok. Earlier he was Beijing correspondent for *The Globe and Mail*, Toronto. Since joining FPRI, his research has focused primarily on China and India. He is the author of several articles on U.S.–China relations, India's military and foreign policy, and Hong Kong's and Taiwan's relations with the People's Republic.

Martha Brill Olcott is a Professor in the Department of Political Science at Colgate University and Senior Fellow at the Foreign Policy Research Institute in Philadelphia. She is the author of *The Kazakhs* (Hoover Institution, Stanford University Press, 1987), as well as the recently completed monograph, *Islam and Statebuilding in Central Asia*. She has published some thirty articles, including several which have appeared in *Foreign Affairs, Foreign Policy, Current History*, and *Orbis*. Dr. Olcott has also edited two books, and is currently finishing a history of contemporary Central Asia for Cambridge University Press. Dr. Olcott has also served as a consultant for business firms and for various U.S. and international government agencies, and she held a formal appointment as Consultant on Central Asian Affairs for former Acting Secretary of State Lawrence Eagleburger.

Daniel Pipes is director of the Middle East Forum and editor of the *Middle East Quarterly*. He received his A.B. (1971) and Ph.D. (1978) from Harvard University, both in history. He has taught at the University of Chicago, Harvard University, and the U.S. Naval War College. Presently he is Senior Lecturer at the University of Pennsylvania. Mr. Pipes has served in three positions in the Department of State and is currently a member of the presidentially-appointed J. William Fulbright Board of Foreign Scholarships, where he oversees U.S. government international exchange programs. For seven years, 1986–1993, he served as director of the Foreign Policy Research Institute. He has written seven books and edited two; most recently, he edited *Sandstorm: Middle East Conflicts and America* (1993).

Barnett R. Rubin is Associate Professor of Political Science and Director of the Center for the Study of Central Asia at Columbia University. He has a Ph.D. in Political Science from the University of Chicago. He was previously assistant professor of political science at Yale University and a fellow at the U.S. Institute of Peace in Washington, D.C. He is currently serving as Director of Columbia University's Project on Conflict Prevention and Resolution in the Former Soviet Union and is a member of the board of Asia Watch, a division of Human Rights Watch. He is the author of *Mirror of the World: Afghanistan's State and Society in the International System* and *From Regional Conflict to State Disintegration: The Failure of International Conflict Resolution in Afghanistan* (both forthcoming). He has written widely on human rights, state formation, and conflict resolution in Central and South Asia.